Civil Procedure

MBE Practice Questions

AmeriBar
Phone (800) 529-2651 • Fax (800) 529-2652

Civil Procedure MBE Practice Questions

Copyright 2015 AmeriBar

ISBN: 1505550939

TOPICS INDEX

QUESTION 1

An inventor from State A holds a patent for a device that increases fuel economy in gasoline-fueled combustion engines. An opportunist from State B learns of the inventor's device and begins manufacturing and selling an identical device, marketing it as the opportunist's own invention.

The inventor sues the opportunist in federal court in State B. The inventor's complaint sought $500,000 in damages and alleged patent infringement under federal law. The opportunist denied the allegations by filing an answer to the complaint. The day after filing the answer, the opportunist moved to dismiss the action for lack of subject-matter jurisdiction.

Should the court grant the motion to dismiss?

(A) No, because the inventor's claim satisfies the amount in controversy requirement.

(B) No, because the inventor's claim arises under federal law.

(C) Yes, because the inventor's claim does not arise under federal law.

(D) Yes, because although the inventor's claim arises under federal law, the opportunist denied the allegations by filing an answer to the complaint.

QUESTION 2

A trucker is traveling at a high rate of speed, loses control of the truck, and crashes into a driver. The driver files a claim based on negligence in federal court against the trucker. The trucker asks his lawyer, "Is there a way to get information from the driver regarding the case?" The lawyer responds, "Yes, we will have an initial conference with the driver where we will plan the discovery process. The conference has to take place as soon as possible, or at least 14 days before the scheduling conference."

Did the lawyer correctly respond to the trucker's question?

(A) No, because the initial conference must take place at least 21 days before a scheduling conference.

(B) No, because the parties to a lawsuit do not hold an initial conference to plan discovery unless the court directs the parties to do so.

(C) Yes, because the initial conference must take place at least 14 days before the scheduling conference.

(D) Yes, except the initial conference must take place at least seven days before the scheduling conference.

QUESTION 3

A homeowner from State B traveled to State A to enter into a contract with an electrician from State A. The contract covered the installation of new wiring in the homeowner's garage in State B. The contract was silent as to which state's laws would govern. The homeowner was dissatisfied with the work provided and refused to pay the electrician. The electrician filed a federal diversity action in State A alleging breach of contract and seeking $150,000 in damages. The highest court in State A has held that in contract cases, the law of the state in which the work was performed will govern. State B's highest court applies the law of the state where the contract was made.

In deciding the case, the federal court would apply:

(A) the law of State A because the court sits in State A

(B) the law of State A because the electrician is domiciled in State A

(C) the law of State B because the work was performed in State B

(D) the law of State B because the contract was made in State A

QUESTION 4

A resident files a verified complaint that meets all the requirements for seeking a temporary restraining order ("TRO"). The resident alleges that the TRO is necessary to prevent a construction company from causing immediate irreparable injury to the resident's house due to a construction project that has been ongoing near the resident's property.

After reviewing the complaint and the allegations contained in it, the court issues a TRO against the construction company for it to cease, for three days, the conduct that will allegedly cause irreparable harm. However, the court does so without holding a hearing and without the construction company's presence.

Was it proper for the court to issue the TRO?

(A) No, because the court did not hold a hearing.

(B) No, because the court did not first give the construction company an opportunity to respond to the complaint in writing.

(C) Yes, because the court found the TRO was necessary to prevent immediate irreparable injury.

(D) Yes, because a TRO is temporary in nature, and therefore it is not an extraordinary remedy.

QUESTION 5

A plaintiff in a civil case filed in federal court seeks $15.00 in damages from the defendant. The defendant desires that a jury decide the matter. The defendant asks his lawyer if a jury trial is possible, and the lawyer says, "Oh yes, based on your claim and damages sought, you have a right to a jury trial."

Did the lawyer correctly advise the defendant?

(A) No, because a party possesses a right to a jury trial in all actions at law for claims exceeding a claim amount of $20.

(B) No, because there is no right to a jury trial in actions at law in federal court.

(C) Yes, because a party possesses a right to a jury trial in all actions at law for claims exceeding a claim amount of $10.

(D) Yes, because there is a right to a jury trial in all actions at law in federal court

QUESTION 6

A trucker is traveling at a high rate of speed over icy roads. The trucker loses control of the truck and is involved in an accident with a driver. The driver files a claim based on negligence in federal court in the jurisdiction where the accident occurred. The complaint alleges that the trucker negligently operated the truck and caused $100,000 in damages. The trucker files a timely answer denying all of the allegations in the driver's complaint. A day before trial, the trucker files a motion to dismiss based on a challenge to personal jurisdiction.

Should the court grant the trucker's motion?

(A) No, because the trucker filed an answer.

(B) No, because the accident occurred in the same state in which the claim is filed.

(C) Yes, because the trucker had not yet raised the defense.

(D) Yes, because the trucker filed the motion prior to trial.

QUESTION 7

A trucker is traveling at a high rate of speed, loses control of the truck, and crashes into a driver. The driver files a claim based on negligence in federal court against the trucker. The parties hold an initial conference to plan discovery. Twenty days after the initial conference, the parties submit a written report to the court outlining the discovery plan.

Was the report properly submitted to the court?

(A) No, because it is improper for the court to receive a report outlining the parties' discovery plan.

(B) No, because the report should have been filed within 14 days after the initial conference.

(C) Yes, because the report was filed within 21 days after the initial conference.

(D) Yes, because the report was filed within 30 days after the initial conference.

QUESTION 8

A trucker is traveling at a high rate of speed during a rainstorm. The trucker loses control of the truck and is involved in an accident with a driver. The driver files a claim based on negligence in federal court. The trucker does not respond to the complaint, and the driver makes an application to the clerk to file an entry of default. The driver includes in the application an affidavit and other proof relevant to show the trucker's failure to respond to the suit. The clerk examines the docket and the driver's filing and determines that the trucker has not filed an answer. The clerk then enters a default. The driver's lawyer calls the driver and says, "I've got some great news. You've won! The clerk entered the default." The driver says, "Is there anything else we have to do?" The lawyer responds: "No. That's it. It's over; the clerk's entry of default constitutes a default judgment."

Were the lawyer's statements to the driver correct?

(A) No, because the clerk's entry of default is not a judgment.

(B) No, because a clerk may not enter a default.

(C) Yes, because the clerk's entry of default is a judgment.

(D) Yes, because only the clerk may enter a default judgment.

QUESTION 9

A resident seeks an injunction against a neighboring construction company. The resident has filed a lawsuit against the construction company alleging that the company's negligence has caused and is causing damage to the resident's property. The court enters an interlocutory order granting the injunction. The company is unsatisfied with the court's order and seeks to appeal the injunction order.

May the company appeal the court's order?

(A) No, because the order is an interlocutory order.

(B) No, because orders concerning injunctions are not appealable.

(C) Yes, because a party may appeal, as a matter of right, an interlocutory order or decree that grants an injunction.

(D) Yes, because all court orders or decrees are appealable.

QUESTION 10

A driver from State A was operating a 1963

Corvette Stingray sports car on a highway in State B and was involved in a crash with a motorcyclist from State B. The motorcyclist was miraculously unhurt in the crash. The driver believed that the accident was caused by the motorcyclist's recklessness, and the driver filed a negligence claim in federal court in State B, seeking $75,000 from the motorcyclist for the damage sustained to the driver's car.

Does the federal court have original jurisdiction over the case?

(A) No, because although the opposing parties are citizens of different states, the amount in controversy is $75,000.

(B) No, because negligence is not a case or controversy arising under federal law.

(C) Yes, because the Commerce Clause gives federal courts original jurisdiction over negligence claims that arise from accidents occurring on highways within the United States.

(D) Yes, because the opposing parties are citizens of different states, and the amount in controversy is $75,000.

QUESTION 11

A motorcyclist is traveling at a high rate of speed on a highway when a deer runs into the road. The motorcyclist swerves to avoid the deer and loses control of the motorcycle. The motorcyclist crashes into a bicyclist, who is injured in the crash. The bicyclist files a claim based on negligence in federal court against the motorcyclist. Before the parties hold an initial conference to plan discovery, the bicyclist serves the motorcyclist with a set of interrogatories.

Was it proper for the bicyclist to serve the motorcyclist with a set of interrogatories?

(A) No, because the parties had not yet held an initial conference.

(B) No, because interrogatories may not be served until depositions are taken.

(C) Yes, because no initial conference is necessary before engaging in discovery.

(D) Yes, because the bicyclist is the plaintiff in the case.

QUESTION 12

A State A corporation decided to acquire an apartment complex in State B from a businessperson. The corporation's bylaws require its president to sign all real estate contracts. The contract's signature block, which the businessperson drafted, misspelled the president's last name. Despite this fact, the president signed correctly. State B's statutes require contract signatories to use their exact legal names. For years, courts in state B have held that a contract will not be invalid if the signatory's identity can be determined from context. After signing the contract, the businessperson developed seller's remorse and tried to back out of the contract.

The corporation sued the businessperson in federal court in State B. There was complete diversity between the parties, and the corporation sought two million dollars in damages.

The court will find for:

(A) the corporation, because the president signed her name correctly.

(B) the corporation, because the president is authorized to sign real estate contracts.

(C) the businessperson, because the president's legal name was not typed into the contract.

(D) the businessperson, because federal common law construes the contract against the drafter.

QUESTION 13

An inventor from State A holds a patent for a device that increases fuel economy in gasoline-fueled combustion engines. An opportunist from State B learns of the inventor's device and begins manufacturing and selling an identical device, marketing it as the opportunist's own invention. The opportunist's sales of the device are strong, and the opportunist travels to China to develop manufacturing contracts to increase output of the device. While the opportunist is in China, the inventor learns of the opportunist's manufacturing and selling of the device. The inventor files a verified complaint seeking a temporary restraining order ("TRO") from the court in State B to order the opportunist to temporarily cease manufacturing and selling the device. The inventor had made numerous attempts to give notice to the opportunist of the pending action, but he was unsuccessful due to the opportunist's trip to China. In the complaint, the inventor explains the efforts made to give notice and the reasons why notice should not be required. The verified complaint also states: "Immediate and irreparable injury will result to the inventor before the opportunist can be heard in opposition." The inventor also provides a bond to the court in order to compensate the opportunist in the event the TRO is wrongfully entered. Without holding a hearing, the court considers issuing the TRO.

Which of the following is the best argument for why the court should not issue the TRO?

(A) A court may not accept a bond to compensate a party in the event the court's decision to issue a TRO is wrongful.

(B) The court must first schedule a hearing to permit both parties to present evidence and argument.

(C) The inventor did not first obtain a judgment on the merits regarding patent infringement by the opportunist.

(D) The inventor did not set out specific facts in his complaint showing that immediate and irreparable injury will result to the inventor before the opportunist can be heard.

QUESTION 14

A plaintiff files one claim against a defendant in federal court. The plaintiff's claim is based solely in equity. The plaintiff desires to have a jury decide the claim, and the plaintiff consults her lawyer who advises the plaintiff as follows: "Sorry, but because you are asserting a claim based solely in equity, you do not have a right to a jury trial."

Did the lawyer properly advise the plaintiff?

(A) No, because a party asserting solely equitable claims or remedies has a right to a jury trial.

(B) No, because the plaintiff is master of the complaint and always has a right to a jury trial.

(C) Yes, because a party asserting solely equitable claims or remedies does not have a right to a jury trial.

(D) Yes, because a plaintiff asserting solely equitable claims must request a hearing before filing the complaint, if the party desires to assert the right to a trial by jury.

QUESTION 15

A trucker is traveling at a high rate of speed over wet roads. The trucker is involved in an accident with a driver. The driver files a claim based on negligence against the trucker. The driver seeks $100,000 in damages from the accident. The trucker files a motion to dismiss based on insufficient service of process. The court denies the motion. The trucker then files an answer denying the allegations in the complaint. A day before trial, the trucker files a motion to dismiss based on improper venue.

Has the trucker waived the defense of improper venue?

(A) No, because the defense of improper venue can be raised in a motion or an answer.

(B) No, because the defense of improper venue can be raised at any time prior to the rendering of a judgment.

(C) Yes, because the defense was not raised in the trucker's initial motion.

(D) Yes, because the defense was not

raised in the trucker's answer.

QUESTION 16

A patient sues a doctor in federal court on a claim of medical malpractice. During the initial disclosures, the doctor provides various pieces of information, including the names and contact information of all persons likely to have discoverable information. The doctor's attorney signs the disclosure and includes the attorney's e-mail address and telephone number.

Did the attorney properly sign the disclosure?

(A) No, because the doctor, not the attorney, should have signed it.

(B) No, because the attorney did not provide the attorney's address.

(C) Yes, because at least one attorney must always sign an initial disclosure.

(D) Yes, because the attorney signed the disclosure and included the attorney's e-mail address and telephone number.

QUESTION 17

A developer enters into a contract with a construction company to build an apartment complex. The contract states that when the project is completed, the developer will pay the construction company two million dollars. The construction company completes the project, but the developer fails to pay the construction company. The construction company files a lawsuit against the developer in federal court on a breach of contract claim. The developer fails to answer the complaint, and the construction company properly makes an application for

an entry of default. The clerk enters a default. The construction company then presents an affidavit detailing the exact sum of damages to the clerk, and the clerk enters a default judgment.

Did the construction company properly obtain the default judgment?

(A) No, because a clerk may not enter a default judgment.

(B) No, because the developer did not respond to the complaint.

(C) Yes, because the claim was for a definite identifiable amount of money damages.

(D) Yes, because a clerk may enter a default judgment in any case.

QUESTION 18

During a products liability case proceeding in federal court, the court denies the defendant's motion, which was based on a claim regarding a controlling issue of law. The defendant seeks to appeal the order denying relief. The judge believes that an immediate appeal may materially advance the ultimate termination of the litigation, but the judge is not sure whether the defendant can take an appeal of the issue while the case is still pending. The judge asks the judge's law clerk for advice as to whether the judge can certify for appellate review the issue raised in the defendant's motion.

What should the law clerk tell the judge?

(A) The order denying the defendant's motion is not appealable until the case is final.

(B) The judge may certify a controlling question of law for appellate review if an immediate appeal may materially advance the ultimate termination of the litigation.

(C) The judge must certify a controlling question of law for appellate review if an immediate appeal may materially advance the ultimate termination of the litigation.

(D) The judge may permit at any time an interlocutory appeal of any issue raised in a motion that the judge denies.

QUESTION 19

A driver from State A was operating a 1963 Corvette Stingray sports car on a highway in State B and was involved in a crash with a motorcyclist from State B. The motorcyclist was killed in the crash. The executor of motorcyclist's estate is domiciled in State A. The driver believed that the accident was caused by the motorcyclist's stunt-riding, and the driver filed a negligence claim in federal court in State B, seeking $100,000 from the motorcyclist's estate for the damage sustained to the driver's car.

Does the federal court have original jurisdiction over the case?

(A) No, because the opposing parties are not citizens of different states.

(B) No, because negligence is not a case or controversy arising under federal law.

(C) Yes, because the Commerce Clause gives federal courts original jurisdiction over negligence claims that arise from transportation over highways within the United States.

(D) Yes, because the opposing parties are citizens of different states, and the amount in controversy is $100,000.

QUESTION 20

A patient sues a doctor in federal court on a claim of medical malpractice. The patient's attorney serves the doctor with a request that the doctor admit or deny the truth of a particular statement. The patient's attorney does not sign the request, but the request includes the attorney's address, e-mail address, and phone number. The doctor does not respond to the request for admission, and the court strikes the request for admission after no signature is provided promptly.

Was it proper for the court to strike the request for admission?

(A) No, because the request included the attorney's address, e-mail address, and phone number.

(B) No, because the doctor had not yet responded to the request.

(C) Yes, because the attorney did not sign it.

(D) Yes, because it is improper for one party to request that the opposing party admit the truth of a statement.

QUESTION 21

A student from State A took a spring break trip to State B. While in State B, the student was injured at a hotel owned by a State C corporation. In State C, the student filed a negligence action against the corporation, and claimed $76,000 in injuries and lost income. The corporation moved to transfer the case to a federal court in State B. The corporation argued that State B was more convenient for the witnesses. The student consented to the transfer.

If the court grants the motion, what negligence law should it apply to decide the case?

(A) The court should apply federal common law.

(B) The court should apply State C negligence law.

(C) The court should apply State B negligence law.

(D) The court should examine State A's and State B's negligence law and apply the law the court believes is fairest to both parties.

QUESTION 22

An inventor from State A holds a patent for a device that increases fuel economy in gasoline-fueled combustion engines. An opportunist from State B learns of the inventor's device and begins manufacturing and selling an identical device, marketing it as the opportunist's own invention. The opportunist's sales of the device are strong, and the opportunist travels to China to develop manufacturing contracts to increase output of the device. While the opportunist is in China, the inventor learns of the opportunist's manufacturing and selling of the device. Furious at the opportunist, the inventor immediately files a verified complaint seeking a temporary restraining order ("TRO") from the court in State B to order the opportunist to temporarily cease manufacturing and selling the device. The

verified complaint pleads specific facts showing that immediate and irreparable injury will result to the inventor before the opportunist can be heard in opposition. The inventor also provides a bond to the court in order to compensate the opportunist in the event the TRO is wrongfully entered. Without holding a hearing, the court considers issuing the TRO.

Should the court issue the TRO?

(A) No, because the inventor did not certify to the court the efforts made to give notice to the opportunist and why such notice should not be required.

(B) No, because the court must first schedule a hearing.

(C) Yes, because the opportunist is in China, and therefore requiring notice and an opportunity to be heard might present a substantial and unjust burden on the inventor.

(D) Yes, because the opportunist's continued manufacturing and selling of the inventor's patented device will cause immediate and irreparable financial harm to the inventor.

QUESTION 23

A trucker is traveling at a high rate of speed over icy roads. The trucker loses control of the truck and is involved in an accident with a driver. The driver files a claim based on negligence in federal court. The complaint alleges that the trucker negligently operated the truck and caused $100,000 in damages. Three weeks after the filing of the last pleading directed to the issue of whether the trucker's negligence caused the damages, the trucker files a jury trial demand.

Did the trucker waive the right to a trial by jury?

(A) No, because the trucker filed a demand for a jury trial.

(B) No, because the jury trial demand was filed within 30 days of the filing of the last pleading directed to the issue for which the basis of the right to a jury trial exists.

(C) Yes, because the trucker did not file the demand for a trial by jury before answering the complaint.

(D) Yes, because the jury trial demand was not filed within 14 days of the filing of the last pleading directed to the issue for which the basis of the right to a jury trial exists.

QUESTION 24

While traveling for the first time in a mountainous state, a vacationer is involved in a car accident with a driver. The vacationer files a negligence claim in federal court, seeking $80,000 in damages. While shopping for a new car, the driver is personally served with process. The driver files a timely answer and denies the allegations in the complaint. The parties complete depositions. The day before the trial, the driver's attorney files a motion to dismiss based on insufficient process.
Will the driver's motion be successful?

(A) No, because the driver waived the defense of insufficient process.

(B) No, because the defense of insufficient process may only be raised by answer.

(C) Yes, because the driver raised the

defense in the first responsive motion.

(D) Yes, because the driver's attorney filed the motion in good faith.

QUESTION 25

A trucker is traveling at a high rate of speed, loses control of the truck, and crashes into a driver. The driver hires an attorney and files a claim based on negligence in federal court against the trucker. During initial disclosures, the driver makes all required disclosures except for one: the driver intentionally does not disclose the name and address of one person who likely has discoverable information. The driver asks the attorney, "What significance does your signature have on the disclosure? I'm a little concerned because we didn't disclose the information about that person." The attorney responds, "My signature only means that I am certifying that the information contained in the disclosure is correct, which it is. The signature doesn't certify that the information is complete. Don't worry about it."

Is the attorney correct about what the signature certifies?

(A) No, because the signature also certifies that, among other things, the disclosure is complete.

(B) No, because the signature merely certifies that the signer is the person who filed the document with the clerk of court.

(C) Yes, because the signature certifies that the information is correct.

(D) Yes, because the signature certifies that the information is correct and that the signer is the person who filed the document with the clerk of court.

QUESTION 26

A computer geek invents and patents an unbreakable screen for smartphones. Without the geek's knowledge, an unscrupulous corporation begins manufacturing smartphones that use the geek's design for smartphone screens. The geek sues the corporation in federal court on a claim of patent infringement. The corporation fails to answer the complaint, and the geek properly makes an application for an entry of default. The clerk enters a default. The geek applies to the clerk for a default judgment with an affidavit asking the clerk to determine the amount of damages, and after considering the geek's application, the clerk finds that the geek suffered $100,000 in damages. The clerk enters a default judgment.

Did the geek properly obtain a default judgment?

(A) No, because the clerk did not hold a hearing to hear evidence regarding damages.

(B) No, because the geek did not apply to the court for a default judgment.

(C) Yes, because the geek submitted an affidavit requesting the clerk to determine the damages.

(D) Yes, because the corporation failed to answer the complaint.

QUESTION 27

A painter, who is driving a van, is involved in an accident with a driver. The painter files a lawsuit based on negligence against the driver in federal court. During the proceedings, the court enters a ruling that does not permit the admission of a piece of evidence offered by the painter. While the case is pending, the painter desires to appeal the court's ruling, and the painter asks his attorney to do so.

May the attorney appeal the court's ruling?

(A) No, because the court has not yet entered a final judgment in the case.

(B) No, because the attorney must not permit the painter to make the legal decisions in the case.

(C) Yes, because the court's ruling is adverse to the painter's interests.

(D) Yes, because any order entered by a court is appealable once the order is rendered.

QUESTION 28

A driver was operating a 1963 Corvette Stingray sports car on a highway in State A and was involved in a crash with a motorcyclist. Both the driver and the motorcyclist lived in State A at the time of the accident. The motorcyclist was miraculously unhurt in the crash. One week after the accident, believing that the roads were safer in State B, the motorcyclist moved to State B with the intent to reside there permanently. The driver believed that the accident was caused by the motorcyclist's recklessness, and the driver filed a negligence claim in federal court in State B, seeking $100,000 from the motorcyclist for the damage sustained to the driver's car.

Does the federal court have original jurisdiction over the case?

(A) No, because the parties were both citizens of State A at the time of the accident.

(B) No, because original jurisdiction requires that the claim must arise under federal law and the amount in controversy requirement must be satisfied.

(C) Yes, because the parties were citizens of different states at the time the claim was filed.

(D) Yes, because original jurisdiction requires that the claim must arise under federal law and the amount in controversy requirement must be satisfied.

QUESTION 29

A trucker is traveling at a high rate of speed, loses control of the truck, and crashes into a driver. The driver hires an attorney and files a claim based on negligence in federal court against the trucker. The trucker hires an attorney who serves a series of interrogatories on the driver intended to be unreasonably burdensome and slow the process of the litigation. The trucker is concerned about the attorney's tactics and mentions the concern to the attorney, who responds, "Don't worry about it. My signature is on the interrogatories, so you have nothing to worry about."

Is the attorney correct?

(A) No, because the court may impose

sanctions on the signer, the party on whose behalf the signer is acting, or both.

(B) No, because although the signer cannot receive sanctions, the court may impose sanctions on the party whom the signer represents.

(C) Yes, because only the signer may be sanctioned.

(D) Yes, because the court may not impose sanctions for conduct occurring during the discovery process.

QUESTION 30

A doctor entered into an employment contract with a hospital. The doctor was a citizen of State A. The hospital was incorporated in State B, but its principal place of business was State C. Under the contract terms, the doctor was entitled to $100,000 if the hospital terminated the contract before the fifth year. When the hospital terminated the contract in year four, it refused to pay the termination fee. The doctor appropriately filed a diversity action in federal court in State B seeking the fee and other damages. After further consideration, the doctor moved to transfer the case to State C. State C case law is more favorable to plaintiffs in similar contract disputes. The hospital consented to the transfer.

In deciding the case, the court in State C should apply:

(A) The contract law of State A, the doctor's state of citizenship.

(B) The contract law of State B, because the case was originally filed in State B federal court.

(C)   The contract law of State C, because the doctor initiated the transfer.

(D)   The contract law of State C, because the deciding federal court sits in State C.

QUESTION 31

An inventor from State A holds a patent for a device that increases fuel economy in gasoline-fueled combustion engines. An opportunist from State B learns of the inventor's device and begins manufacturing and selling an identical device, marketing it as the opportunist's own invention. The opportunist's sales of the device are strong, and the opportunist travels to China to develop manufacturing contracts to increase output of the device. While the opportunist is in China, the inventor learns of the opportunist's manufacturing and selling of the device. The inventor files a verified complaint seeking a temporary restraining order ("TRO") from the court in State B to order the opportunist to temporarily cease manufacturing and selling the device. The verified complaint pleads specific facts showing that immediate and irreparable injury will result to the inventor before the opportunist can be heard in opposition, and it includes a certification of the efforts made to give notice to the opportunist and the reasons for why notice is not required.

Should the court issue the TRO?

(A)   No, because the opportunist is overseas.

(B)   No, because the inventor did not provide a bond to the court.

(C)   Yes, because the opportunist is overseas.

(D)   Yes, because the verified complaint pleads specific facts showing that immediate and irreparable injury will result.

QUESTION 32

A trucker is traveling at a high rate of speed over icy roads. The trucker loses control of the truck and is involved in an accident with a driver. The driver files a claim based on negligence in federal court. The complaint alleges that the trucker negligently operated the truck and caused $100,000 in damages. Ten days after the filing of the last pleading directed to the issue of whether the trucker's negligence caused the damages, the trucker files a jury trial demand.

Was the demand for a jury trial timely?

(A)   No, because the trucker did not file the demand before answering the complaint.

(B)   No, because the jury trial demand was not filed within 7 days of the filing of the last pleading directed to the issue for which the basis of the right to a jury trial exists.

(C)   Yes, because the jury trial demand was filed within 14 days of the filing of the last pleading directed to the issue for which the basis of the right to a jury trial exists.

(D)   Yes, because the jury trial demand was filed within 30 days of the filing of the last pleading directed to the issue for which the basis of the right to a jury trial exists.

QUESTION 33

A motorcyclist is traveling at a high rate of speed on a highway when a deer runs into the road. The motorcyclist swerves to avoid the deer and loses control of the motorcycle. The motorcyclist crashes into a bicyclist, who is injured in the crash. The bicyclist files a claim based on negligence in federal court against the motorcyclist. The court directs the parties to appear before it for a pre-trial conference for the purpose of discouraging wasteful pre-trial activities.

Was it proper for the court to direct the parties to appear before it for the pre-trial conference?

(A) No, because a court may not direct parties to have a pre-trial conference for the purpose of discouraging wasteful pre-trial activities.

(B) No, because the court must not interfere in the manner in which the parties control the case and its management.

(C) Yes, because a court must always direct the parties to have a pre-trial conference for the purpose of discouraging wasteful pre-trial activities.

(D) Yes, because a court may direct parties to appear before the court for a pre-trial conference for the purpose of discouraging wasteful pre-trial activities.

QUESTION 34

A defendant is sued by a plaintiff on a breach of contract claim. The plaintiff personally serves the defendant the summons and complaint by handing them to the defendant at a coffee shop. Before filing an answer, the defendant files a motion to dismiss based on lack of personal jurisdiction and improper venue. The court denies the motion. The day before trial, the defendant files a motion to dismiss based on a defense of insufficient service of process.

Should the court grant the motion?

(A) No, because the plaintiff personally served the defendant with the summons and complaint.

(B) No, because the defense was waived.

(C) Yes, because the defense was preserved.

(D) Yes, because the plaintiff personally served the defendant with the summons and complaint.

QUESTION 35
Verdicts and Judgments

A defendant in a lawsuit makes an appearance in the case but later fails to defend the lawsuit. The plaintiff properly obtains an entry of default and applies to the court for a default judgment. The defendant is given 10 days' notice of a hearing to be held regarding the amount of damages.

Did the defendant receive proper notice?

(A) No, because if the party against whom the default judgment is sought has appeared, the party must be given at least thirty days' notice for the hearing.

(B) No, because if the party against whom the default judgment is sought has appeared, the party must be given at least fourteen days' notice for the hearing.

(C) Yes, because if the party against whom the default judgment is sought has appeared, the party must be given at least five days' notice for the hearing.

(D) Yes, because if the party against whom the default judgment is sought has appeared, the party must be given at least seven days' notice for the hearing.

QUESTION 36

A contractor agrees to remodel a homeowner's house. During the remodeling, one of the contractor's employees drops a hammer, which strikes and injures the homeowner's child. The homeowner sues the contractor, the contractor's employee, and the manufacturer of the hammer in federal court. During the proceedings, after finding no just reason for delay, the court directs entry of a final judgment as to the contractor and employee, though the proceedings against the manufacturer are still pending.

Is the court's entry of final judgment as to the contractor and employee appealable?

(A) No, because a final judgment as to the manufacturer has not yet been entered.

(B) No, because a court may not direct entry of a final judgment as to specific claims or parties, making a final judgment on the severed claim appealable.

(C) Yes, because a court may direct entry of a final judgment as to specific claims or parties, making a final

judgment on the severed claim appealable.

(D) Yes, because all orders of a court are appealable once entered.

QUESTION 37

A customer from State A files a products liability suit in federal court in State C against a corporation that is incorporated in State A. The corporation directs, controls, and coordinates its activities from State A. The customer seeks $100,000 in damages. The corporation does not have any contacts with State C, but believing that it would be in the interests of fair play and justice to defend the lawsuit in State C, the corporation consents to the federal court having subject-matter jurisdiction over the case.

Does the federal court have original jurisdiction over the case?

(A) No, because subject-matter jurisdiction cannot be consented to or waived by the parties.

(B) No, because subject-matter jurisdiction is not proper in a products liability case.

(C) Yes, because subject-matter jurisdiction can be consented to when the consent given is based on interests of fair play and justice.

(D) Yes, because diversity of citizenship exists between the federal court and the parties, and the amount in controversy is satisfied.

QUESTION 38

A trucker is traveling at a high rate of speed, loses control of the truck, and crashes into a driver. The driver hires an attorney and files a claim based on negligence in federal court against the trucker. The parties are scheduled to appear before the court for a pre-trial conference. Two attorneys, Bill and Patty, represent the trucker; however, only Patty is authorized to enter into stipulations and make admissions regarding matters that the parties might discuss at the conference.

Which of the following choices best states who must be present at the pre-trial conference?

(A) Bill and Patty, because they both represent the trucker.

(B) Patty, because she is authorized to enter into stipulations and make admissions.

(C) The trucker without the attorneys.

(D) No one, because the court may not order the parties or attorneys to appear at a pre-trial conference.

QUESTION 39

State A and State B share a water reservoir beneath their common border. A city in State B has used the reservoir for 50 years as its primary source of water. State A began a farming initiative to increase farming in previously undeveloped properties served by the reservoir. State B brought suit in federal court seeking to enjoin State A's program. State B alleged that the program resulted in State A taking an unfair amount of water from the reservoir. The statutes of State A hold that surface owner has first right to groundwater. On the contrary, State B's courts have held that the first party to put groundwater to use has priority rights. In disputes between states over federal water rights statutes, federal courts have developed a body of case law holding that groundwater should be equitably divided.

How should the court rule?

(A) For State A, because the surface owners are using the water.

(B) For State B, because the city had used the property prior to the farmers' activities.

(C) For State B, because State A was using more water than State B.

(D) For State A, because the initiative is a compelling state interest.

QUESTION 40

A resident files a verified complaint seeking a temporary restraining order ("TRO"). The resident alleges that the TRO is necessary to prevent a construction company from causing immediate irreparable injury to the resident's house due to a construction project that has been ongoing near the resident's property. The complaint includes specific facts showing that immediate and irreparable injury will result before a hearing can be held, and the complaint otherwise meets the pleading requirements for a TRO. After reviewing the complaint and the allegations contained in it, the court issues a TRO against the construction company for it to cease, for 21 days, the conduct that will allegedly cause irreparable harm.

Was the court's TRO proper?

(A) No, because the duration of the TRO is 21 days.

(B) No, because the construction company was denied due process when it was not given an opportunity to be heard before the TRO was entered.

(C) Yes, because the duration of the TRO is 21 days.

(D) Yes, because it likely prevented immediate and irreparable injury.

QUESTION 41

Three persons are being considered to serve on a jury: Juan, Mary, and Bill. Juan is a citizen of Mexico, and he is 18 years of age, fluent in English, and does not have a criminal record. Mary is a citizen of the United States, and she is 17 years of age, fluent in English, and she does not have a criminal record. Bill is a United States citizen, and he is 57 years of age, fluent in English, and he has a criminal record.

Which of the following is a correct statement regarding who may serve on a jury?

(A) Juan, Mary, and Bill are all disqualified from serving on a jury.

(B) Juan, Mary, and Bill may all serve on a jury.

(C) Juan is disqualified from serving on a jury, but both Mary and Bill may serve on a jury.

(D) Juan and Mary are disqualified from serving on a jury, but Bill may serve on a jury.

QUESTION 42

A driver is traveling at a high rate of speed over wet roads. The driver loses control of the vehicle, and is involved in an accident with a motorcyclist. The motorcyclist files a claim based on negligence against the driver in federal court. The motorcyclist seeks $175,000 in damages for harm resulting from the accident. Before filing an answer, the driver files a motion to dismiss based on insufficient service of process, insufficient venue, and lack of personal jurisdiction. The court denies the motion. The motorcyclist then files an answer denying the allegations in the complaint. After the commencement of trial, the driver raises the defense of lack of subject-matter jurisdiction in a motion to dismiss.

Is the driver's motion timely?

(A) No, because the driver failed to raise the defense in his initial motion.

(B) No, because the driver failed to raise the defense in his answer.

(C) Yes, because the driver raised the defense before the court rendered a final judgment.

(D) Yes, because the driver raised the defense.

QUESTION 43

A driver is involved in an accident with a motorcyclist. The motorcyclist files a claim against the driver in federal court alleging that the driver's negligence caused the accident. However, before the driver serves the answer to the complaint, the motorcyclist files a notice of dismissal.

Was it permissible for the motorcyclist to file the notice?

(A) No, because the driver did not file a motion for summary judgment.

(B) No, because a dismissal may only be obtained by court order.

(C) Yes, because the notice of dismissal was filed before the driver served an answer.

(D) Yes, because the plaintiff is master of the complaint and may at any time voluntarily dismiss the case.

QUESTION 44

A trucker is traveling at a high rate of speed during a rainstorm. The trucker loses control of the truck and is involved in an accident with a driver. The driver files a claim based on negligence in federal court. The trucker does not respond to the complaint, and the driver obtains an entry of default from the clerk. Subsequently, the trucker files a motion to set aside the default. The grounds for relief in the trucker's motion are that ultimate facts exist in support of a meritorious defense to the default, and the motion states those facts. The court considers the motion and finds that the facts stated in the motion would support a meritorious defense. Consequently, the court sets aside the default.

Did the court properly set aside the default?

(A) No, because once a default is entered it may not be set aside.

(B) No, because the trucker did not

demonstrate good cause or a reasonable excuse for failure to answer the complaint.

(C) Yes, because the trucker alleged ultimate facts in support of a meritorious defense to the default.

(D) Yes, because the trucker alleged ultimate facts in support of a meritorious defense to the default, and the court found that the facts stated in the motion would support a meritorious defense.

QUESTION 45

During a case that is pending in federal court, the court enters an interlocutory order that finally disposes of a disputed question that was completely collateral to the cause of action. The court's ruling on the collateral issue is adverse to the plaintiff. The court's order involves an important right that would probably be lost irreparably if the plaintiff waits to appeal the order until after a final judgment is entered in the case.

May the plaintiff appeal the court's order before a final judgment occurs in the case?

(A) No, because the final judgment rule prevents appeal until a final judgment occurs.

(B) No, because the court's order pertains to an issue that was completely collateral to the cause of action.

(C) Yes, because the collateral order exception to the final judgment rule applies.

(D) Yes, because the ruling was adverse to the plaintiff.

QUESTION 46

A contractor from State A completed the remodeling of a corporation's main office, located in State A. The corporation's principal place of business is in State A, and the corporation is incorporated in State C. The corporation failed to pay the contractor for the completed work. The contractor filed a breach of contract claim in federal court in State C against the corporation. The contractor seeks $100,000 in damages.

Does the federal court have original jurisdiction over the case?

(A) No, because the suit was filed in State C, when it should have been filed in State A, the State in which the contractor is domiciled.

(B) No, because diversity of citizenship does not exist.

(C) Yes, because diversity of citizenship exists and the amount in controversy requirement is satisfied.

(D) Yes, because the contractor's claim arises under federal law.

QUESTION 47

A driver is involved in an accident with a motorcyclist. The motorcyclist files a claim against the driver in federal court alleging that the driver's negligence caused the accident. The driver serves the answer to the complaint. Subsequently, the motorcyclist seeks dismissal of the case. The court enters an order dismissing the case. The order does not indicate whether the dismissal is with or without prejudice. The case has not previously been dismissed.

Is the court's dismissal without prejudice?

(A) No, because the court may not dismiss a case without prejudice absent consent of the party seeking dismissal.

(B) No, because unless otherwise stated, the first dismissal by court order is with prejudice.

(C) Yes, because the court may not dismiss a case with prejudice absent consent of the party seeking dismissal.

(D) Yes, because unless otherwise stated, the first dismissal by court order is without prejudice.

QUESTION 48

An investor purchased a parcel of land at a tax sale. Six months after the sale, the investor brought a quiet title action in state court to clear title. The federal government had a lien on the property for unpaid federal taxes. Federal courts had long held that the federal statutory one-year redemption period for the federal government could be shortened to three months in certain situations. The federal government invoked state law, which gave lien holders a one-year redemption period, and asked to redeem.

How should the court rule?

(A) The court should transfer the case to the district court because it involves a federal issue.

(B) The court should quiet title in favor of the investor.

(C) The court should allow the federal government to redeem the property.

(D) The court should consider both the state and federal laws and apply the one it believes most appropriately governs.

QUESTION 49

A resident files a complaint under oath to prevent a construction company from causing immediate irreparable injury to the resident's property due to a construction project that has been ongoing near the resident's property. Liquid waste material from the construction project has been overflowing onto the resident's property. Due to the exigency of the situation, the resident seeks a preliminary injunction without notice to the construction company.

Should the court grant the motion?

(A) No, because the construction company has not filed a timely objection.

(B) No, because the construction company was not provided with notice.

(C) Yes, because no notice to the construction company was necessary.

(D) Yes, because the exigency of the situation requires a preliminary injunction.

QUESTION 50

A trucker is traveling at a high rate of speed during a rainstorm. The trucker loses control of the truck and is involved in an accident with a driver. The driver files a claim based on negligence in federal court. The complaint alleges that the trucker negligently operated the truck and caused $175,000 in damages. The driver properly files a demand for a jury trial. During voir dire, the judge questions the potential jurors to determine their qualifications and suitability, and the court permits the parties' lawyers to ask supplemental questions.

Did the court properly conduct the questioning of the potential jurors during voir dire?

(A) No, because only the parties or the parties' lawyers may ask potential jurors questions during voir dire.

(B) No, because the court permitted the lawyers to ask supplemental questions.

(C) Yes, because the court may ask questions of the prospective jurors and then permit the lawyers for the parties to ask supplemental questions.

(D) Yes, because the court must always ask questions of the prospective jurors.

QUESTION 51

An inventor has developed a new type of plastic device that he believes may have great potential in the automotive industry. The inventor patents the invention and begins soliciting for sales of the device to various automakers. Meanwhile, an entrepreneur begins manufacturing a similar device and enters into a contractual relationship with several automakers, including ones the inventor solicited in regard to his invention. The inventor believes the entrepreneur has wrongfully infringed on his patent rights, and he sues the entrepreneur in federal court. The entrepreneur answers the complaint, and the parties eventually proceed to trial. At trial, the entrepreneur moves to dismiss the case, raising the defense that the inventor has failed to state a claim on which relief can be granted.

Did the entrepreneur waive the defense?

(A) No, because the entrepreneur raised the defense in a motion, rather than in the answer.

(B) No, because the defense may be raised at trial.

(C) Yes, because the defense must be raised prior to trial.

(D) Yes, because the defense must be raised in the first responsive motion or pleading.

QUESTION 52

A driver is involved in an accident with a motorcyclist. The motorcyclist files a claim against the driver in federal court alleging that the driver's negligence caused the accident. After extensive negotiations, the parties agree to settle the case out of court. The parties set forth their signed settlement agreement. The court signs the parties' consent judgment and enters it on the record.

May the court enforce the judgment?

(A) No, because the parties did not proceed to either a bench trial or jury trial.

(B) No, because settlement is not an adjudication.

(C) Yes, because settlement is an adjudication.

(D) Yes, although settlement is not technically an adjudication, settlement has the same effect when the parties

enter into a consent judgment.

QUESTION 53

A driver was operating a 1963 Corvette Stingray sports car on a highway and was involved in a crash with a motorcyclist. The driver believed that the accident was caused by the motorcyclist's recklessness, and the driver filed a negligence claim in federal court. The motorcyclist believes that the driver was at fault, but fails to file a counterclaim. The motorcyclist also fails to defend the lawsuit. The driver obtains a default judgment.

May the motorcyclist file a claim against the driver alleging that the driver's negligence caused the accident?

(A) No, because the default judgment precluded the motorcyclist from making claims that were subject to a compulsory counterclaim requirement.

(B) No, because the motorcyclist was at fault.

(C) Yes, because the motorcyclist's claim is a compulsory counterclaim.

(D) Yes, because a default judgment does not preclude the losing party from raising defenses or claims that could have been raised during the litigation.

QUESTION 54

A motorcyclist is involved in an accident with a driver. The motorcyclist files a lawsuit based on negligence against the driver in federal court. The case proceeds to a jury trial. During the trial, the driver offers into evidence a particular piece of evidence. The motorcyclist remains silent when the evidence is offered, though the motorcyclist has a genuine concern that the evidence might not be admissible under the Rules. The evidence is admitted. Eventually, the jury returns a verdict in favor of the driver.

May the motorcyclist raise on appeal the issue of the admission of the particular piece of evidence?

(A) No, because the driver offered the evidence for admission during trial.

(B) No, because the motorcyclist did not preserve the matter for appeal.

(C) Yes, because the motorcyclist did not prevail during trial.

(D) Yes, because the motorcyclist has a genuine concern that the evidence was not admissible under the Rules.

QUESTION 55

A taxi driver from State B entered into a written agreement with a painter from State A in which the painter agreed to paint the taxi driver's home. The painter completed the work, but the taxi driver failed to pay the painter as required by the contract. Two months after the taxi driver's failure to pay the painter for his work, the painter and the taxi driver were involved in an accident on a highway in State B. The accident was unrelated to the taxi driver's failure to pay the painter. The painter sued the taxi driver in federal court on a claim of negligence regarding the accident and a claim of breach of contract regarding the painting of the taxi driver's home. The painter sought $60,000 in damages for the negligence claim and $25,000 in damages for the breach of

contract claim. The taxi driver moved to dismiss the case for lack of subject-matter jurisdiction.

Should the federal court grant the taxi driver's motion?

(A) No, because the parties are diverse and the amount in controversy is satisfied.

(B) No, because the accident occurred in the taxi driver's state of residence, and therefore the federal court has subject-matter jurisdiction over the claim.

(C) Yes, because the breach of contract claim is unrelated to the negligence claim.

(D) Yes, because at least one claim must independently satisfy the amount in controversy requirement.

QUESTION 56

A trucker is traveling at a high rate of speed, loses control of the truck, and crashes into a driver. The driver hires an attorney and files a claim based on negligence in federal court against the trucker. The driver's complaint seeks $120,000 in damages. Three weeks prior to the trial date, the trucker serves the driver with an offer of judgment against the trucker for $80,000. The driver refuses the offer and proceeds to trial. The driver obtains a judgment for $76,000.

Is the driver responsible for the costs of the trial from the date when the trucker made the offer?

(A) No, because each party is responsible for its own costs.

(B) No, because the driver prevailed in the

lawsuit.

(C) Yes, because the driver did not obtain a judgment that was more favorable than the trucker's offer.

(D) Yes, because the driver did not obtain a judgment for the amount sought in the complaint.

QUESTION 57

Company A threatened to publish reports that Company B's product was defective and dangerous if Company B did not pay one million dollars and cease production. Company A has its principal place of business in State X, while Company B maintains its headquarters in State Y. Company B, knowing the reports to be fraudulent, files a civil, federal racketeering suit against Company A. The suit is filed in a federal district court sitting in State X. Company B claims two million dollars in actual damages. Under State X common law, the maximum damages available in a racketeering case are three times the actual damage amount. State Y common law permits recovery of only actual damages. The federal statute permits recovery of actual damages and attorney's fees.

If the court finds for Company B, it should award:

(A) Actual damages only.

(B) Actual damages and attorney's fees.

(C) One and one-half times the actual damages.

(D) Treble damages.

QUESTION 58

A resident files a complaint under oath to prevent a construction company from causing immediate irreparable injury to the resident's property due to a construction project that has been ongoing near the resident's property. Liquid waste material from the construction project has been overflowing onto the resident's property whenever the construction company is working on the project. The resident properly moves for a preliminary injunction. At a hearing on the resident's motion, with the construction company present, the resident presents evidence that the waste material is toxic and has been killing the lawn and getting into the water supply. The resident presents information showing that the waste material is also flowing onto other residential property. The construction company will not be substantially harmed if the court grants the preliminary injunction.

Should the court grant the preliminary injunction?

(A) No, because the resident has not shown that the construction company was negligent in maintaining the construction site.

(B) No, because the resident has not shown that the construction company has willfully caused irreparable harm.

(C) Yes, because the resident made a showing that it has a reasonable claim and that the resident could suffer significant injury if the injunction is not granted.

(D) Yes, because the resident made a strong showing that it would prevail on the merits, that the resident will suffer irreparable injury if the injunction is not granted, that the construction company will not be substantially harmed by the injunction, and public interest would favor preventing contamination of the water supply.

QUESTION 59

A black construction worker is injured while working on a construction project. The worker sues the construction company in federal court, alleging that the company's negligence caused his injuries. The case proceeds to trial, and during selection of the jury, the company uses all of its peremptory challenges against black jurors, which leaves a panel of all white jurors except for one. The worker's attorney is concerned about the racial makeup of the jury.

What, if anything, may the attorney do about the makeup of the jury panel?

(A) The attorney should file a notice of appeal.

(B) The attorney may not challenge the makeup of the jury panel.

(C) The attorney may challenge the jury panel on the basis that it does not represent a fair cross section of the community.

(D) The attorney may challenge the jury panel on the basis that it was not empanelled in favor of the plaintiff.

QUESTION 60

An inventor has developed a new type of plastic device that he believes may have great potential in the automotive industry. The inventor patents the invention and begins soliciting for sales of the device to various automakers. Meanwhile, an entrepreneur begins manufacturing a similar device and enters into a contractual relationship with several automakers, including ones the inventor solicited in regard to his invention. The inventor believes the entrepreneur has wrongfully infringed on his patent rights, and he sues the entrepreneur in federal court. The entrepreneur files a timely motion to dismiss, alleging that the inventor has failed to state a claim on which relief can be granted.

When considering the motion, the court:

(A) may accept the well-pleaded factual allegations as true.

(B) may use common sense and judicial experience to decide whether the claim for relief is plausible.

(C) must accept the well-pleaded legal conclusions as true.

(D) must have the jury decide whether the well-pleaded factual allegations are true.

QUESTION 61

A trucker is traveling at a high rate of speed, loses control of the truck, and crashes into a driver. The driver hires an attorney and files a claim based on negligence in federal court against the trucker. The judge presiding over the case has a passion for the adversarial process of trials and never requires litigants to consider the use of alternative dispute resolution (ADR) processes. Nevertheless, the trucker and driver enter into ADR, and the court provides for the confidentiality of the parties' confidential communications.

Did the court follow proper procedure?

(A) No, because the court did not require that the trucker and driver consider the use of alternative dispute resolution processes.

(B) No, because the court improperly intertwined itself in the litigation by providing for confidentiality of the parties' confidential communications.

(C) Yes, because the court is not required to require that litigants consider the use of alternative dispute resolution processes in civil litigation.

(D) Yes, because the court permitted the parties to consider the use of alternative dispute resolution processes.

QUESTION 62

A driver was operating a 1963 Corvette Stingray sports car on a highway and was involved in a crash with a motorcyclist. The driver believed that the accident was caused by the motorcyclist's recklessness, and the driver filed a negligence claim in federal court. The motorcyclist failed to defend the lawsuit, and the driver obtained a default judgment. When the driver attempts to enforce the judgment, the motorcyclist challenges the jurisdiction of the court that entered the default judgment.

Is the motorcyclist's challenge to the court's jurisdiction permitted?

(A) No, because a default judgment precludes the losing party from raising defenses that could have been asserted

in the lawsuit.

(B) No, because the motorcyclist's negligence caused the accident.

(C) Yes, because a defaulting party may challenge the jurisdiction of the court entering the default in the court where the judgment creditor attempts to enforce the judgment.

(D) Yes, because a default judgment does not preclude the losing party from raising defenses or claims that could have been raised during the litigation.

QUESTION 63

A motorcyclist is involved in an accident with a driver. The motorcyclist files a lawsuit based on negligence against the driver in federal court. The case proceeds to a jury trial. During the trial, the driver attempts to offer particular testimony from a witness. The motorcyclist objects to the admissibility of the testimony, and the judge sustains the objection, which prevents the testimony from being offered. In response, the driver makes an offer of proof that demonstrates what the testimony was intended to prove. The jury enters a verdict in favor of the motorcyclist.

May the driver raise on appeal the issue concerning the court's ruling regarding the testimony?

(A) No, because the driver did not properly preserve the issue.

(B) No, because the judge sustained the objection.

(C) Yes, because the driver made an offer of proof that demonstrated what the purported evidence was intended to prove.

(D) Yes, because the driver thought the evidence would be admissible.

QUESTION 64

A driver from State A was operating a 1963 Corvette Stingray sports car on a highway in State B and was involved in a crash with a motorcyclist from State B. The driver believed that the accident was caused by the motorcyclist's recklessness, and the driver filed a negligence claim in federal court in State B, seeking $85,000 from the motorcyclist for the damage sustained to the driver's car. The motorcyclist filed a counterclaim against the driver, alleging that the driver was negligent. The motorcyclist sought $50,000 for damages sustained in the accident.

Does the court have original jurisdiction over the counterclaim?

(A) No, because the counterclaim does not satisfy the amount in controversy requirement.

(B) No, because the motorcyclist's claim is not a compulsory counterclaim.

(C) Yes, because the motorcyclist's claim is a permissive counterclaim.

(D) Yes, because the motorcyclist's claim is a compulsory counterclaim.

QUESTION 65

A patient sues a doctor in federal court on a claim of medical malpractice. Both parties are represented by attorneys. The parties engage in discovery, and the case is on track to proceed to trial. As close to the trial date as possible, the court holds a final pre-trial conference. The patient, the patient's attorney, and the doctor attend the conference.

Did all of the required parties attend the conference?

(A) No, because the patient's attorney attended, and the purpose of the final pre-trial conference is for the parties— without their attorneys present—to have one final opportunity to settle the matter without the cost and expense of a trial.

(B) No, because the doctor's attorney was absent.

(C) Yes, because at least one representative from each side attended the conference.

(D) Yes, because attendance and participation in a final pre-trial conference is optional.

QUESTION 66

A homeowner was injured by a lawnmower he purchased from a nationwide retailer. The homeowner lived in State M. A State N company manufactured the lawnmower at its factory in State O. The homeowner sued the company in federal court in State M alleging that the lawnmower was defectively manufactured and sought $250,000 in damages. After hearing all arguments, the court ruled that both the company and the homeowner were negligent. State M has adopted a comparative negligence approach, but the statute is unclear on whether a plaintiff will recover if the plaintiff is 51%

responsible. In fact, State M courts have been inconsistent in their application of the law, and the state's highest court has not ruled on the issue. State N, in contrast, has a very well-established common law interpretation of its comparative negligence statute.

In determine damages, the court should:

(A) apply the federal common law of comparative negligence.

(B) apply the rule established by the last State M court case.

(C) look at all relevant State M case law and determine how State M's highest court is likely to rule.

(D) apply State N's common law.

QUESTION 67

A painter enters into a contract with a homeowner to paint the homeowner's house. After the painter has completed painting the house, the homeowner says, "I don't think I like this color anymore, and I want to hire a different painter. I'm not paying you." The painter sues the homeowner, and the complaint seeks relief for breach of contract, and in the alternative, unjust enrichment.

Is the painter's pleading proper?

(A) No, because the pleading violates the Election of Remedies Doctrine.

(B) No, because the pleading is inconsistent.

(C) Yes, because a pleading may be inconsistent or alternative.

(D) Yes, because the homeowner refused to provide timely payment.

QUESTION 68

A motorcyclist is involved in an accident with a driver. The motorcyclist sues the driver in federal court, alleging that the driver's negligence caused the accident and $80,000 in damages. After making three challenges for cause regarding potential jurors, without seeking the court's permission, the motorcyclist's lawyer challenges a fourth potential juror for cause on the ground that the juror is the driver's brother-in-law. The driver objects to the challenge on the ground that the motorcyclist has already used the total number of challenges for cause permitted by the Rules.

Will the driver's objection be successful?

(A) No, because a party may make up to five challenges for cause without permission from the court.

(B) No, because a party may make an unlimited number of challenges for cause on grounds that a juror has a bias or relationship to a party.

(C) Yes, because a party may only make three challenges for cause on grounds that a juror has a bias or relationship to a party.

(D) Yes, because a party may only make one challenge for cause without permission from the court.

QUESTION 69

An inventor has developed a new type of

plastic device that he believes may have great potential in the automotive industry. The inventor patents the invention and begins soliciting for sales of the device to various automakers. Meanwhile, an entrepreneur begins manufacturing a similar device and enters into a contractual relationship with several automakers, including ones the inventor solicited in regard to his invention. The inventor believes the entrepreneur has wrongfully infringed on his patent rights, and he sues the entrepreneur in federal court. The inventor's complaint alleges just enough facts of the entrepreneur's misconduct to support a possible claim for relief. The entrepreneur files a timely motion to dismiss, alleging that the inventor has failed to state a claim on which relief can be granted. The court grants the motion to dismiss.

Should the court have granted the motion to dismiss?

(A) No, because the inventor's complaint contained just enough facts to support a possible claim for relief.

(B) No, because the inventor held the patent on which the cause of action was based.

(C) Yes, because the inventor's complaint contained just enough facts to support a possible claim for relief.

(D) Yes, because the entrepreneur filed a timely motion to dismiss.

QUESTION 70

A patient sues a doctor in federal court on a claim of medical malpractice. Both parties are represented by attorneys. The parties

engage in discovery and the case is on track to proceed to trial. As close to the trial date as possible, the court holds a final pre-trial conference. The required parties attend the conference, including the patient's attorney. However, the attorney is substantially unprepared to participate in the conference.

May the judge sanction the attorney?

(A) No, because the conference was held very near to the trial date.

(B) No, because the attorney did not need to be prepared to participate, as the conference was optional.

(C) Yes, because the attorney was substantially unprepared to participate in the conference.

(D) Yes, because the attorney represents the plaintiff.

QUESTION 71

A trucker is traveling at a high rate of speed during a rainstorm. The trucker loses control of the truck and is involved in an accident with a driver. The driver files a claim based on negligence in federal court. The trucker answers the complaint but fails to comply with discovery orders. The trucker also fails to attend pre-trial conferences that were ordered by the court. Consequently, the court sanctions the trucker by entering a default judgment.

Was it proper for the court to enter a default judgment against the trucker?

(A) No, because the trucker answered the complaint.

(B) No, because the court may not impose

a default judgment as a sanction.

(C) Yes, because the trucker admitted negligence by failing to participate in the proceedings.

(D) Yes, because the trucker failed to comply with discovery orders and failed to attend pretrial conferences.

QUESTION 72

A driver and a trucker are involved in an accident on a state road. The driver sues the trucker in federal court, alleging that the trucker's negligence caused the accident. The driver seeks $80,000 in damages. The case proceeds to a jury trial, during which the court makes an error during voir dire that seriously affects the trucker's substantial rights and causes an unfair prejudicial impact on the jury's deliberations. However, the trucker fails to object at the time of the error, and the court and driver are unaware of the error. The jury returns a verdict for the driver. The trucker hires a new attorney who, in reviewing the proceedings, notices the error.

May the trucker raise the issue concerning the error on appeal?

(A) No, because the trucker failed to preserve the issue.

(B) No, because the trucker hired a new attorney who did not work on the case during the trial.

(C) Yes, because the losing party has a fundamental right to select one unpreserved issue to raise on appeal.

(D) Yes, because the error constituted plain error.

QUESTION 73

Frustrated with his marriage, a wealthy husband decides to seek a divorce. The husband and wife reside in State A. The husband hires an attorney, and after a painful and very expensive process, the husband and wife obtain a divorce decree in State court, in State A. Several years later, the former husband, who still resides in State A, believes that due to a substantial decrease in his income, he can no longer afford to pay the alimony he has been paying. He also believes he is entitled to a return of a portion of the alimony he has paid to his former wife over the past several years. The former wife now lives in State B, and the former husband files a suit in federal court in State B seeking $80,000 in damages stemming from the initial alimony decree.

The federal court should:

(A) Hear the case because the parties are diverse and the amount in controversy is satisfied.

(B) Hear the case because the federal court has jurisdiction over cases involving alimony.

(C) Decline jurisdiction to hear the case because the case involves an alimony decree.

(D) Decline jurisdiction to hear the case because both parties were domiciled in State A at the time of the divorce decree, which divested the federal court of diversity jurisdiction over the alimony claim.

QUESTION 74

A patient sues a doctor in federal court on a

claim of medical malpractice. Both parties are represented by attorneys. The parties engage in discovery and the case is on track to proceed to trial. The patient's attorney is routinely late for hearings and has missed several deadlines in the case without a legitimate excuse. The court imposes sanctions against the attorney, requiring the attorney to pay the reasonable expenses incurred because of the tardiness. Despite the imposition of sanctions, the attorney continues to miss deadlines and appear late for hearings. The court reschedules the most recent hearing, and the attorney again appears late for that hearing. The court reprimands the attorney in open court, at which time, the attorney says, "Your Honor, you can't fault me for my reasonable trial strategy. My tardiness is calculated to cause my opponent stress. That stress gives my client and I the upper hand in litigation, and I object to any further sanctions by the Court." Consequently, the court dismisses the lawsuit.

Was it permissible for the court to dismiss the lawsuit?

(A) No, because the court may not dismiss a lawsuit on its own motion.

(B) No, because the trial had not yet taken place and the attorney explained that the lateness was a matter of reasonable trial strategy.

(C) Yes, because the attorney missed deadlines.

(D) Yes, because the attorney repeatedly and willfully missed deadlines.

QUESTION 75

A banker from State L was injured in an automobile accident while traveling in State M. The driver who hit him was a State M citizen. Due to a strong shipping lobby, State M's negligence laws heavily favor the defendants in all automobile actions. Under State M's laws, the driver would prevail. Hoping for a more favorable outcome, the banker filed his negligence suit in State L's state court. State L applies the law of the state of the plaintiff's citizenship in negligence actions. Under State L's laws, the banker would prevail. The banker sought $100,000 in damages. The driver filed a timely removal action to federal court in State L, citing diversity jurisdiction.

How should the federal court rule?

(A) for the banker, because the State L court would have applied State L law.

(B) for the banker, because it must apply the common law of the plaintiff's residence.

(C) for the driver, because it must apply the common law of the defendant's residence.

(D) for the driver, because it must apply the law of the removing party.

QUESTION 76

A salesman makes a sales pitch to a homeowner regarding a cleaning product that the salesman says is non-toxic, biodegradable, and cleans better than anything else available. The salesman also tells the homeowner that the cleaning solution may also be used as a sugar substitute, and that hundreds of scientific studies have been done that support the salesman's claims. The homeowner is convinced that the product is a miracle, and the homeowner buys two cases of the product. The product turns out to be extremely toxic, and the homeowner requires hospitalization after using it. Further, the product cleans no better than plain water. The homeowner sues the salesman on a claim of fraud. The complaint is simple, concise, and direct, stating that the homeowner was suing "for fraud" that caused $80,000 in damages.

Is the homeowner's pleading sufficient?

(A) No, because it involved a special matter that should have been pleaded with particularity.

(B) No, because it violated the Election of Remedies doctrine.

(C) Yes, because it provided the salesman with notice.

(D) Yes, because it was simple, concise, and direct.

QUESTION 77

A motorcyclist is involved in an accident with a driver. The motorcyclist sues the driver in federal court, alleging that the driver's negligence caused the accident and $80,000 in damages. During jury selection, the driver challenges a prospective juror for cause on the ground that the prospective juror is a motorcycle enthusiast who has previously been in a motorcycle accident in which the prospective juror sustained injuries as a result of the other party's negligence. During questioning of the prospective juror, the prospective juror says, "I can fairly consider the evidence."

May the court take the prospective juror's statement into consideration?

(A) No, because the prospective juror is clearly biased.

(B) No, because the prospective juror did not submit the statement in a sworn affidavit.

(C) Yes, because neither party objected to the prospective juror's statement.

(D) Yes, the court may take the prospective juror's statement into consideration.

QUESTION 78

A landowner sues a rancher in federal court. The rancher raised the defense of improper venue before trial, but the court denied relief. The rancher answers the landowner's complaint without raising any more defenses, and the parties proceed to trial. After the commencement of trial, the rancher files a motion to dismiss based on the defense of failure to join an indispensable party.

Has the rancher waived the defense?

(A) No, because the defense may be raised at trial.

(B) No, because the defense may be raised only at trial.

(C) Yes, because the defense was not raised in the rancher's first responsive pleading.

(D) Yes, because, although it was not necessary to raise the defense in the first responsive pleading, it must be raised prior to trial.

QUESTION 79

A trucker is traveling at a high rate of speed, loses control of the truck, and crashes into a driver. The driver hires an attorney and files a claim based on negligence in federal court against the trucker. After receiving the parties' discovery reports, the court enters a scheduling order that limits the time to join other parties and to amend the pleadings, file motions, and complete discovery.

Was it proper for the court to enter the scheduling order?

(A) No, because a court may not enter a scheduling order that limits the time to join other parties and to amend the pleadings, file motions, and complete discovery.

(B) No, because the driver was represented by an attorney.

(C) Yes, because after receiving the parties' discovery reports, a federal district court must enter a scheduling order that limits the time to join other parties and to amend the pleadings, file motions, and complete discovery.

(D) Yes, because after receiving the parties' discovery reports, a federal district court may enter a scheduling order that limits the time to join other parties and to amend the pleadings, file motions, and complete discovery.

QUESTION 80

A trucker is traveling at a high rate of speed during a rainstorm. The trucker loses control of the truck and is involved in an accident with a driver. The driver files a claim based on negligence in federal court.

The judge is known for demanding punctuality. Nevertheless, the trucker and his attorney appear 15 minutes late at a pretrial conference. Consequently, the judge enters a default judgment against the trucker. The trucker appeals the default judgment.

What standard should the appellate court apply when reviewing the appeal?

(A) preponderance of the evidence

(B) beyond a reasonable doubt

(C) de novo

(D) abuse of discretion

QUESTION 81

A driver and a trucker are involved in an accident on a state road. The driver sues the trucker in federal court, alleging that the trucker's negligence caused the accident. The driver seeks $80,000 in damages. The case proceeds to a jury trial, during which the court gives an erroneous jury instruction. The jury returns a verdict in favor of the trucker. The driver appeals, and specifically, the driver raises the issue regarding the court's erroneous charge to the jury. The appellate court finds that the erroneous charge of the jury would not likely have affected the result of the trial.

What rule did the appellate court apply when deciding the issue regarding the erroneous jury instruction?

(A) Harmless error rule

(B) Minimal error rule

(C) Non-prejudicial rule

(D)   Substantive error rule

QUESTION 82

A defendant is sued in federal court. The complaint alleges two claims for relief. Claim one arises under federal law. Claim two originates from the same controversy that generated claim one, but claim two arises under state law and the relief requested is $20,000. The defendant does not file a motion to dismiss the case.

Would it be proper for the federal court to exercise jurisdiction over the state law claim?

(A)   No, because the state law claim does not satisfy the amount in controversy requirement.

(B)   No, because the state law claim arises under state law, and therefore, the court does not have federal question jurisdiction over the claim.

(C)   Yes, because the defendant failed to file a motion to dismiss, and the state law claim is part of the same case or controversy as claim one.

(D)   Yes, because claim one arises under federal law and claim two is part of the same case or controversy.

QUESTION 83

A small business owner sued a big box company in federal court for trademark infringement, seeking two million dollars in damages. The small business sought an ex parte temporary restraining order to prevent the big box company from utilizing the trademark in advertising and marketing materials.

In its request, the small business alleged, by affidavit, that allowing the big box company to continue utilizing the trademark would cause them immediate and irreparable injury because it causes confusion among customers resulting in lost consumer dollars. The affidavit set forth specific facts demonstrating the potential for irreparable injury.

The small business further alleged that notifying the big box company of its request for a temporary restraining order would give the company an opportunity to release its newest batch of advertising material utilizing the trademark, before the court rules on the temporary restraining order request. It also offered to post a $5,000 bond. The small business requested that the order stay in effect through the outcome of the litigation.

Should the court grant the ex parte temporary restraining order?

(A)   No, because a temporary restraining order cannot be issued ex parte.

(B)   No, because a temporary restraining order cannot be issued for the period of time sought by the small business.

(C)   Yes, because the small business established that it would suffer immediate and irreparable injury, and that notice to the big box company should not be required.

(D)   Yes, because the small business established that it would suffer immediate and irreparable injury, that notice to the big box company should not be required, and it offered to post a sufficient bond.

QUESTION 84

An investor from State A procured a loan from a State B bank to construct a shopping center on property in State B. The bank secured its loan with a mortgage and fixture filing, and filed in the appropriate county in State B. The bank failed to include an after-acquired property clause in its fixture filing. State A and State B have both adopted versions of the UCC. State B courts have ruled that mortgagees always intend to have an interest in after-acquired property and will imply an appropriate clause. State A courts have strictly construed the UCC to require a clause in order to create an interest. Subsequently, the investor defaulted on a later obligation to a State C creditor. The bank filed suit against the investor and the other creditor asserting its priority interest in all of the real and personal property relating to the shopping center that was acquired after its mortgage. The bank also sought payment of the $500,000 loan balance. The bank brought its action in federal court in State A.

To whom should the court award the property?

(A) the bank, because the court disagrees with State A's interpretation of the UCC.

(B) the bank, because State B would have implied the after-acquired property clause.

(C) the other creditor, because federal common law strictly construes the UCC.

(D) the other creditor, because the fixture filing did not contain an after-acquired property clause.

QUESTION 85

A driver is involved in an accident with a trucker. The driver files a verified complaint alleging that the trucker's negligence caused the accident and $78,000 worth of damages to the driver's Ferrari. The trucker is served with the complaint, and is furious at the driver for alleging that the trucker was negligent. The trucker responds to the complaint with an unsworn answer in which he denies all of the allegations.

Is the trucker's answer sufficient?

(A) No, because a responsive pleading need not be verified when it merely denies the allegations in a verified complaint.

(B) No, because once a pleading is verified, responsive pleadings must also be verified.

(C) Yes, although the complaint was verified, a responsive pleading need not be verified.

(D) Yes, because the trucker denied the allegations.

QUESTION 86

A motorcyclist is involved in an accident with a truck driver. The motorcyclist files a lawsuit based on negligence against the driver and the company the trucker works for, in federal court. The court permits both the truck driver and the company to exercise three peremptory challenges each, for a total of six peremptory challenges.

Was it permissible for the court to permit six peremptory challenges?

(A) No, because only three peremptory challenges are permitted.

(B) No, because each party may make two peremptory challenges.

(C) Yes, because a court may allow additional peremptory challenges.

(D) Yes, because a party may make unlimited peremptory challenges.

QUESTION 87

A trucker is involved in an accident with a driver. The driver files a claim based on negligence in federal court. The complaint alleges that the trucker negligently operated the truck and caused $70,000 in damages. The trucker files a motion to dismiss the case. The court grants the trucker's motion and dismisses the case with prejudice.

What is the effect of the court's dismissal of the driver's case?

(A) The driver must file an amended complaint against the trucker in that court within 20 days of the rendition of the court's dismissal order.

(B) The driver may file an amended complaint against the trucker in that court within 15 days of the rendition of the court's dismissal order.

(C) The driver may file a cross-claim against the trucker.

(D) The driver may not file a revised complaint against the trucker.

QUESTION 88

A young real estate broker sued a real estate company for breach of contract for failing to follow through with the sale of a lakefront mansion worth three million dollars. The real estate company told the young broker that several other offers on the house were higher than what the young broker and the company previously agreed upon, so they planned to sell the mansion to someone else within the next two weeks. The young broker sought a preliminary injunction to prevent the company from selling the mansion to any other buyers pending the outcome of the lawsuit.

In his request, the young broker alleged that if the preliminary injunction was not granted, he would lose the business of a rich movie star as well as a large commission from the resale of the mansion to the movie star. The young broker set the matter for a hearing in front of the presiding judge to consider and rule upon his request.

Should the court grant the request for a preliminary injunction?

(A) No, because preliminary injunctions are limited to 14 days.

(B) Yes, because the young real estate broker established that he would likely succeed on the merits of the lawsuit.

(C) No, because notice and an opportunity to be heard were not provided to the real estate company.

(D) Yes, because the young real estate broker established that he would suffer irreparable injury if the preliminary injunction is not granted.

QUESTIONS   35   AMERIBAR

QUESTION 89

A computer geek invents and patents an unbreakable screen for smartphones. Without the geek's knowledge, an unscrupulous corporation begins manufacturing smartphones that use the geek's design for smartphone screens. The geek sues the corporation in federal court on a claim of patent infringement. However, after being served with the corporation's answer, the geek does not file any documents or conduct any activity in the case. Two years pass, and the court enters an order dismissing the case.

Was it proper for the court to dismiss the case?

(A) No, because the plaintiff is master of the complaint, and the court may not interfere with the timeline established by the plaintiff in prosecuting its case.

(B) No, because inactivity by the plaintiff alone may not justify dismissal.

(C) Yes, because inactivity by the plaintiff alone may justify dismissal.

(D) Yes, because the court may dismiss a case at any time.

QUESTION 90

An inventor holds a patent for a device that increases fuel economy in gasoline-fueled combustion engines. An opportunist learns of the inventor's device and begins manufacturing and selling an identical device, marketing it as the opportunist's own invention. The inventor sues the opportunist in federal court on a claim of patent infringement. The court enters a final judgment in favor of the inventor. The opportunist appeals the judgment, arguing that the court incorrectly applied the law.

What standard will the appellate court apply when reviewing the opportunist's appellate claim?

(A) abuse of discretion

(B) clearly erroneous

(C) preponderance of error

(D) de novo

QUESTION 91

A patient from State A sues a doctor from State B in state court in State B. The patient's complaint seeks $100,000 damages for the doctor's alleged negligence. On the advice of the patient's attorney, the patient decides that the suit will have a better chance of success in federal court in State A. Twenty days after service of the initial complaint on the doctor, the patient files a notice of removal containing a short and plain statement of the grounds for removal, together with a copy of all process, pleadings, and orders served upon the defendant.

Is removal to the federal court in State A proper?

(A) No, because the notice of removal was filed more than 10 days after the doctor had been served with the initial complaint.

(B) No, because only defendants may remove cases to federal court.

(C) Yes, because the notice of removal was timely filed.

(D) Yes, because the notice of removal was timely filed, and the federal court has diversity jurisdiction over the case.

QUESTION 92

The wife of Driver A sued Driver B in federal district court for injuries Driver A sustained in a car accident. Driver A's wife sued on his behalf because Driver A was in a persistent vegetative state since the accident. Ninety days after the complaint was filed, Driver A died as a result of his injuries.

Thirty days after Driver A's death, Driver A's wife moved to supplement the complaint with the additional fact that her husband died as a result of the car accident. Driver A's wife did not explain in her motion why she waited 30 days to file her motion. Driver A's wife served Driver B with a copy of her motion.

Should the court allow Driver A's wife to file the supplemental pleading?

(A) Yes, because Driver A's wife filed a motion for supplemental pleading after her husband's death.

(B) No, because Driver A's wife did not file her motion to supplement within 15 days of Driver A's death.

(C) Yes, because Driver A's wife filed a motion seeking to supplement the complaint and provided notice to Driver B.

(D) No, because Driver A's wife did not provide good cause for her delay in seeking to supplement the complaint after her husband's death.

QUESTION 93

A trucker is traveling at a high rate of speed over icy roads. The trucker loses control of the truck and is involved in an accident with a driver. The driver files a claim based on negligence in federal court. The complaint alleges that the trucker negligently operated the truck and caused $100,000 in damages. The complaint alleges that the trucker was exceeding the speed limit at the time of the accident and was driving on the wrong side of the road. The trucker files a timely answer and denies all of the allegations in the complaint except for the allegation regarding speed.

May the court deem the allegation concerning the trucker's speed admitted?

(A) No, because the trucker did not affirmatively admit the allegation.

(B) No, because the trucker denied most of the allegations, which indicates denial of all allegations.

(C) Yes, because the trucker lost control of the truck on the icy roads.

(D) Yes, because the trucker did not address the allegation.

QUESTION 94

A motorcyclist is involved in an accident with a truck driver. The motorcyclist files a lawsuit based on negligence against the driver and the company the trucker works for, in federal court. The court treats both defendants as a single party for the purposes of making peremptory challenges.

Was the court's treatment of the defendants permissible?

(A) No, because multiple defendants may not be considered a single party for the purpose of making challenges.

(B) No, because only multiple plaintiffs may be considered a single party for the purpose of making challenges.

(C) Yes, because multiple defendants or plaintiffs may be considered a single party for the purposes of making challenges.

(D) Yes, because no party is entitled to peremptory challenges, as the matter is discretionary with the court.

QUESTION 95

A mechanic installs a new set of brakes on a driver's car. After leaving the mechanic's shop, the brakes fail to work on the driver's car, and the driver veers off the road and crashes into a tree. The driver sues the mechanic in federal court, but the driver's complaint is vague, and the mechanic cannot reasonably frame an answer.

Which of the following would be an appropriate course of action for the mechanic?

(A) File a motion to strike.

(B) Answer the complaint after considering the most reasonable interpretation of its vagueness.

(C) File a motion for a more definite statement.

(D) File a Rule 60 motion to obtain relief from judgment.

QUESTION 96

A lawyer failed to sign six pleadings, including the complaint, request for admissions, and interrogatories. The presiding judge set a hearing to discuss the lawyer's continued failure to sign the pleadings, and sent a notice of hearing to all the parties.

At the hearing, the presiding judge stated that the lawyer had failed to sign all six of his pleadings, that this had now become a habit of the lawyer in all the cases in which he appeared before the judge, and that the judge was tired of the lawyer failing in his duties. When the lawyer attempted to explain his failure to sign the pleadings, the judge stated "I don't want to hear it; I'm imposing sanctions for your flagrant violation of the requirement to sign all pleadings."

Did the court appropriately impose sanctions?

(A) No, because a court cannot impose sanctions when the opposing party did not request imposition of sanctions for rule violations.

(B) No, because the court did not allow the lawyer a reasonable opportunity to respond.

(C) Yes, because the court provided notice of the hearing to all parties.

(D) Yes, because the lawyer violated the rule requiring a lawyer to sign all pleadings.

QUESTION 97

A computer geek invents and patents an

unbreakable screen for smartphones. Without the geek's knowledge, an unscrupulous corporation begins manufacturing smartphones that use the geek's design for smartphone screens. The geek sues the corporation in federal court on a claim of patent infringement. However, the court dismisses the action for lack of prosecution. The order of dismissal does not state whether the dismissal is an adjudication on the merits.

Does the court's order of dismissal constitute an adjudication on the merits?

(A) No, because a dismissal is not an adjudication on the merits.

(B) No, because the order did not state that the dismissal was an adjudication on the merits.

(C) Yes, because the order did not state that the dismissal was an adjudication on the merits.

(D) Yes, because all dismissals constitute an adjudication on the merits.

QUESTION 98

A motorcyclist is involved in an accident with a driver. The motorcyclist files a lawsuit based on negligence against the driver in federal court. The case proceeds to a jury trial. During the trial, the driver offers a particular piece of evidence. The court permits the introduction of the evidence over the motorcyclist's objection. Eventually, the jury enters a verdict in favor of the driver. The motorcyclist appeals the judgment, and in particular, the motorcyclist alleges that the trial court erred in permitting the introduction of the evidence over the motorcyclist's objection.

What standard should the appellate court apply when viewing the motoryclist's appellate claim?

(A) de novo

(B) abuse of discretion

(C) clearly erroneous

(D) reasonable doubt

QUESTION 99

While traveling for the first time in State A, a vacationer from State B was involved in a car accident with a driver from State A. The vacationer filed a negligence claim in federal court in State B, seeking $80,000 in damages. The driver has never had any contact with State B, except when he traveled there two weeks after the accident to shop for a new car. After being in State B shopping for a car for less than an hour, he was personally served with process in the case. Disgusted and angry after being served with process, the driver immediately left State B without buying a car, vowing that he would never return to such a miserable State.

Does the federal court in State B have personal jurisdiction over the driver?

(A) No, because the driver did not have any contact with State B prior to the accident.

(B) No, because the driver did not make a purchase while in State B.

(C) Yes, because the driver was involved in an accident with the vacationer, who is domiciled in State B.

(D) Yes, because the driver was served with process within the forum state

(D) No, because the first businessman will not suffer irreparable injury.

QUESTION 100

A businessman sued a second businessman in federal court for failing to abide by the terms of a contract wherein the second businessman would sell the first businessman a five-passenger private airplane. Immediately after filing his lawsuit, the first businessman sought an ex parte temporary restraining order to prevent the second businessman from selling the airplane to someone else.

In his motion, the first businessman certified in an attached affidavit that he intended to use the airplane for personal and business trips. The first businessman certified that notice could not be provided to the second businessman because he planned on selling the airplane in less than 24 hours to a third businessman. The first businessman also posted a bond that would be sufficient to compensate the second businessman if the temporary restraining order was wrongfully entered.

Should the court issue the ex parte temporary restraining order?

(A) Yes, because the first businessman posted a sufficient bond.

(B) No, because the first businessman could have given the second businessman notice of the request for a temporary restraining order.

(C) Yes, because there was a contract for the second businessman to sell the airplane to the first businessman, and he failed to do so.

QUESTION 101

A trucker is traveling at a high rate of speed over icy roads. The trucker loses control of the truck and is involved in an accident with a driver. The driver files a claim based on negligence in federal court. The complaint alleges that the trucker negligently operated the truck and caused $100,000 in damages. The complaint alleges that the trucker was exceeding the speed limit at the time of the accident and was driving on the wrong side of the road. Thirty days after service of the complaint, the trucker serves an answer denying all of the allegations.

Did the trucker properly answer the complaint?

(A) No, because the trucker denied all of the allegations.

(B) No, because the trucker served the answer 30 days after service of the complaint.

(C) Yes, because the trucker served the answer 30 days after service of the complaint.

(D) Yes, because the trucker served the answer within 60 days after service of the complaint.

QUESTION 102

A contractor agrees to remodel a homeowner's house. During the remodeling, one of the contractor's employees drops a hammer, which strikes and injures the homeowner's child. The homeowner sues the employee and the contractor in federal court on a negligence theory. The case proceeds to trial. In the interests of what the judge believes to be justice, the judge permits a jury of 13 to decide the case. The jury returns a verdict in favor of the homeowner.

Was the court's decision regarding the jury proper?

(A) No, because a jury may only consist of 12 jurors.

(B) No, because a jury must consist of a minimum of 6 and a maximum of 12 jurors.

(C) Yes, because a jury must consist of a minimum of 4 and a maximum of 16 jurors.

(D) Yes, because a jury must consist of at least 12 jurors.

QUESTION 103

A mechanic installs a new set of brakes on a driver's BMW. After leaving the mechanic's shop, the brakes fail to work on the BMW, and the driver veers off the road and crashes into a tree. The driver sues the mechanic in federal court, claiming that the mechanic was negligent. The driver's complaint alleges $85,000 in damages. The complaint states a clear claim for relief, and it also states that the mechanic is a "buffoon" and "a fool" who "isn't qualified to tie his own shoelaces, let alone install brakes on a BMW." The mechanic is distraught over being sued, and has not yet answered the complaint.

Which of the following would be an appropriate course of action for the mechanic?

(A) Answer the complaint.

(B) File a motion to strike.

(C) File a motion for judgment on the pleadings.

(D) Move for summary judgment.

QUESTION 104

An art enthusiast sued an art dealer in federal court for failing to sell an original Van Gough painting, in violation of the explicit terms of their contract. In his verified complaint, the art enthusiast sought an ex parte temporary restraining order.

In support, he alleged that the Van Gough painting was the only original of this particular Van Gough painting, and that the art dealer stated he was not going to follow through with the contract because he got a higher offer from another buyer. The art enthusiast alleged that if the art dealer was not enjoined from selling the painting to another buyer, he would suffer irreparable injury because there was no other painting like this one. Along with his verified complaint, the art enthusiast posted a bond for the amount the other buyer offered to pay for the painting, which he alleged would be sufficient to compensate the art dealer if the temporary restraining order was later determined to be wrongfully entered.

Should the court issue an ex parte temporary restraining order?

(A) Yes, because the Van Gough painting is the only original, so the art enthusiast will suffer irreparable harm if the art dealer violates the contract.

(B) No, because the art enthusiast failed to certify the efforts made to provide notice to the art dealer, or the reasons why notice should not be provided.

(C) Yes, because the art enthusiast posted a bond that would be sufficient to compensate the art dealer if the temporary restraining order were wrongfully entered.

(D) No, because temporary restraining orders cannot be issued on an ex parte basis when the underlying cause of action is breach of contract.

QUESTION 105

A motorcyclist is involved in an accident with a driver. The motorcyclist files a lawsuit based on negligence against the driver in federal court. The case proceeds to a jury trial. The court permits the parties to stipulate that only 6 of 8 jurors must agree in order to reach a verdict.

Was it permissible for the court to permit the stipulation?

(A) No, because the parties may not stipulate to matters in cases that proceed to trial.

(B) No, because a verdict must be unanimous.

(C) Yes, but the stipulation was unnecessary because the Rules only require that three-fourths of the jury agree on the verdict.

(D) Yes, because the parties may stipulate to a non-unanimous verdict.

QUESTION 106

A contractor enters a written agreement with a company to build the company a new office building. The contract states that the company shall pay half the price of the construction project when the construction begins, and the balance will be paid within 30 days of the completion of the construction of the office building. The contractor begins the project. However, the company fails to pay the contractor the agreed-upon sum that was stated in the contract. Eventually, the contractor files a lawsuit against the company. The case proceeds to a bench trial, and the court enters a judgment in favor of the contractor. The company appeals the court's ruling. The appellate court applies an abuse-of-discretion standard when reviewing the trial court's findings of fact.

Did the appellate court apply the correct standard of review?

(A) No, because an appellate court reviewing a trial court's finding of fact in a bench trial uses the de novo standard.

(B) No, because an appellate court reviewing a trial court's finding of fact in a bench trial uses the clearly erroneous standard.

(C) Yes, because an appellate court reviewing a trial court's finding of fact in a bench trial uses the abuse-of-discretion standard.

(D) Yes, because an appellate court reviewing a trial court's finding of fact in a bench trial may use the clear and convincing standard or abuse-of-discretion standard.

QUESTION 107

While traveling for the first time in State A, a vacationer from State B was involved in a car accident with a driver from State A. The vacationer filed a negligence claim in federal court in State B, seeking $80,000 in damages. The driver is served with process in State A. The driver has never had any contact with State B, except when he traveled there two weeks after the accident to shop for a new car. After being in State B shopping for a car for less than an hour, he decided there weren't any cars that suited him in State B, and he went home to State A and bought a car there. The driver objects to the court's personal jurisdiction over him regarding vacationer's claim, and on the same day, the driver files a counterclaim against the vacationer seeking $50,000 in damages sustained in the accident.

Will the driver's challenge to the court's personal jurisdiction be successful?

(A)   No, because the driver traveled to State B to purchase a car.

(B)   No, because the driver waived his objection.

(C)   Yes, because the driver's contacts with State B are not sufficient to reasonably require the driver to defend the lawsuit in State B.

(D)   Yes, because the accident occurred in State A.

QUESTION 108

A car collector sued a car dealer in federal court after the car dealer failed to sell the car collector a rare, vintage 1962 Ferrari convertible, in violation of the terms of a contract. The car collector sought an ex parte temporary restraining order to prevent the car dealer from selling the car to another buyer.

In an affidavit in support of his request, the car collector alleged that the car is worth $250,000, that there is only 1 other known make and model but the owner of that car will not sell it, and that it has been his life-long pursuit to purchase this particular car. The car collector further alleged that he attempted to provide notice to the car dealer, but the car dealer plans to sell the car to a higher bidder in less than 24 hours, so notice should not be required. The car collector also posted a $1,000 bond.

Should the court issue the ex parte temporary restraining order?

(A)   Yes, because the car collector provided specific facts under oath establishing that he would suffer irreparable injury if the temporary restraining order was not issued.

(B)   Yes, because the car collector met all the conditions necessary for the court to issue an ex parte temporary restraining order, including establishing irreparable injury, giving notice or reasons why notice should not be required, and posting a bond.

(C)   No, because the car collector did not provide notice to the car dealer.

(D)   No, because the car collector did not post a bond that would properly compensate the car dealer if the temporary restraining order were later determined to be wrongfully entered.

QUESTION 109

An inventor holds a patent for a device that increases fuel economy in gasoline-fueled combustion engines. An opportunist learns of the inventor's device and begins manufacturing and selling an identical device, marketing it as the opportunist's own invention. The inventor sues the opportunist in federal court on a claim of patent infringement. The opportunist serves a timely answer. Fourteen days after serving the answer, the opportunist amends the answer.

Is the opportunist's amendment of the answer proper?

(A) No, because an answer may not be amended without leave of court.

(B) No, because the opportunist amended the answer more than 10 days after serving the initial answer.

(C) Yes, because the opportunist amended the answer within 21 days after serving the initial answer.

(D) Yes, because the opportunist amended the answer within 30 days after serving the initial answer.

QUESTION 110

A motorcyclist is involved in an accident with a driver. The motorcyclist files a lawsuit based on negligence against the driver in federal court. The case proceeds to trial. The driver's lawyer properly requests that the court give a jury instruction on a particular matter. The court does not reject the request. However, when the court instructs the jury, the court fails to give the instruction requested by the driver's lawyer.

The driver's lawyer objects by saying, "I'd like to state for the record that I object."

Has the lawyer preserved the issue of the court's failure to give the requested instruction?

(A) No, because the lawyer did not object with particularity regarding the court's failure to provide the requested instruction.

(B) No, because the lawyer did not wait to object until after the jury began deliberations.

(C) Yes, because the lawyer objected.

(D) Yes, because the lawyer requested the instructions, and the request is on the record.

QUESTION 111

A driver is involved in a collision on a highway with a bicyclist, who miraculously survives, despite having sustained serious physical injuries. The bicyclist files a lawsuit based on a claim of negligence against the driver in federal court. The driver answers the complaint. After the pleadings are closed, the bicyclist files a motion for judgment on the pleadings.

When considering the bicyclist's motion, the court should:

(A) hold a hearing to permit the parties to present testimony, evidence, and argument.

(B) deny the motion because it was filed after the close of pleadings.

(C) grant the driver 30 days' leave to

amend the complaint.

(D)   determine whether, on the face of all pleadings, the bicyclist is entitled to judgment.

QUESTION 112

A jewelry dealer sued a diamond owner in federal court for breach of contract after the diamond owner failed to follow through with the sale of the rarest diamond in the world. In his verified complaint, the jewelry dealer sought an ex parte temporary restraining order to prevent the diamond owner from selling the diamond to someone who offered more than the previously agreed upon contract price.

In support of his request for a temporary restraining order, the jewelry dealer alleged that he would suffer irreparable injury if the temporary restraining order was not issued. The jewelry dealer also alleged that he attempted to give notice of his request to the diamond owner, and that notice should not be required because this was the rarest diamond in the world and he feared that once the diamond owner knew about his lawsuit, he would sell the diamond and the jewelry dealer would never see it again. The jewelry dealer also posted a one million dollar bond, which was the amount the other buyer offered to pay for the diamond.

Should the court issue the ex parte temporary restraining order?

(A)   No, because the jewelry dealer failed to allege specific facts showing he would suffer irreparable injury if the temporary restraining order was not issued.

(B)   No, because someone else offered a

higher price for the diamond, so the diamond owner should not be prevented from making more money.

(C)   Yes, because the jewelry dealer established that the diamond owner might sell the diamond if he found out about the request for a temporary restraining order.

(D)   Yes, because the jewelry dealer posted a bond sufficient to compensate the diamond owner if the temporary restraining order is wrongfully issued.

QUESTION 113

A driver and a trucker are involved in an accident on a state road. The driver sues the trucker in federal court, alleging that the trucker's negligence caused the accident. The case proceeds to trial, and the jury returns a verdict, finding that the trucker was liable for the damage resulting from the accident.

What type of verdict did the jury return?

(A)   general verdict

(B)   basic verdict

(C)   special verdict

(D)   inconsistent verdict

QUESTION 114

A federal statute required that any individual or entity owning more than 100 acres of land had to provide an alternative energy source, located on the land, to produce at least 15% of the electricity consumed on the property.

A factory owned a 220-acre parcel of land. The factory filed suit in federal district court against the federal official who enforced this statute. The factory sought a preliminary injunction prohibiting enforcement of the statute. The factory argued that the statute was unconstitutional. The court denied the injunction. The factory appeals the order denying the injunction.

Is the order appealable?

(A) Yes. The factory may appeal the order because all court orders may be appealed.

(B) Yes. The factory may appeal the order because the order denies an injunction.

(C) No. The factory may not appeal the order because it is an interlocutory order.

(D) No. The factory may not appeal the order because it is a final judgment.

QUESTION 115

A college sued the city in federal court for entering into an agreement to sell a piece of property to a private land developer who plans to build a mall on the property. The college claims that the sale would violate a decades-old land use agreement that requires the property to revert to the college if it is no longer used for educational purposes.

Immediately after filing its lawsuit, the college filed a motion for a preliminary injunction to prevent the city from selling the property, pending the outcome of the litigation. At the hearing on their motion, the college established that they would likely succeed on the merits of their lawsuit because the provisions of the land use

agreement are very clear. Before the college could continue, the judge stated "No need to say anything further. I am granting your request for a preliminary injunction because you have established a high likelihood of success on the merits of your lawsuit, and that is the only factor I need to consider. The city shall not sell the subject property until resolution of the lawsuit."

Did the court properly grant the request for a preliminary injunction?

(A) Yes, because preliminary injunctions should always be entered where property might be sold before resolution of the lawsuit.

(B) Yes, because the college established the likelihood of their success on the merits of the lawsuit.

(C) No, because the judge failed to consider whether the college would suffer irreparable injury without the preliminary injunction, whether the preliminary injunction would substantially harm any other parties, and whether it was in the best public interest.

(D) No, because the judge failed to state how many days the injunction was in effect.

QUESTION 116

A citizen of State A purchased a car from a dealer in State A. While driving the car in State B, the citizen was involved in a 15-car pileup on State B's highway system. The citizen filed a tort action in state court in State B and sought $90,000 in damages from the dealer. The dealer has never specifically directed any advertising or activity toward

State B. The dealer does not consent to the court's jurisdiction and makes no appearance in the court other than to assert a challenge to personal jurisdiction.

Will the dealer's challenge to personal jurisdiction be successful?

(A) No, because the dealer placed the car into the stream of commerce and materially benefitted from the sale of the car.

(B) No, because it was foreseeable that the car could be driven in State B and become involved in an accident.

(C) Yes, because the dealer did not consent to the court's jurisdiction.

(D) Yes, because the dealer merely placed the car into the stream of commerce.

QUESTION 117

A motorcyclist is driving carefully on a highway. A vacationer, who is driving a large recreational vehicle ("RV"), is texting on a cellphone and looking at a map while driving. The vacationer does not notice that the RV has crossed over into oncoming traffic. The motorcyclist sees the RV in the oncoming lane and swerves to avoid the RV. If the motorcyclist hadn't swerved, the motorcyclist and RV would have had a head-on collision. However, by swerving, the motorcyclist loses control of the motorcycle and crashes into a bicyclist, who is injured in the crash. The bicyclist files a complaint in federal court, suing the vacationer on a claim of negligence. The vacationer serves a timely answer. Within 14 days of being served with the answer, the bicyclist serves an amended complaint.

Was the bicyclist's amended complaint permitted?

(A) No, because it was served more than 10 days after being served with the answer.

(B) No, because the answer had already been served.

(C) Yes, because it was served no more than 30 days after being served with the answer.

(D) Yes, because it was served within 21 days after being served with the answer.

QUESTION 118

A motorcyclist is involved in an accident with a driver. The motorcyclist files a lawsuit based on negligence against the driver in federal court. The case proceeds to trial. The driver's lawyer properly requests that the court give a jury instruction on a particular matter. However, the judge does not permit the motorcyclist to object to the instruction outside of the jury's presence.

Was the court's decision regarding the objection proper?

(A) No, because objections to jury instructions are not permitted by the Rules.

(B) No, because the court must afford objecting counsel an opportunity to object outside of the jury's presence.

(C) Yes, because objections to jury instructions should only be made in the presence of the jury.

(D) Yes, because the judge has discretion in deciding how objections will be made.

QUESTION 119

A driver is involved in a collision on a highway with a trucker. The trucker files a lawsuit in federal court against the driver based on a claim of negligence. The driver answers the complaint, and the parties begin discovery. A genuine dispute exists as to whether the driver was speeding and crossed into the wrong lane at the time of the accident. To avoid a trial on the matter, the driver files a motion for summary judgment. The court grants the motion for summary judgment.

Which of the following is the best reason for why the court should not have granted the motion?

(A) A genuine dispute existed as to a material fact in the case.

(B) A motion for summary judgment may only be filed by the plaintiff.

(C) The driver filed the motion to obtain a judicial judgment and avoid trial.

(D) No genuine dispute existed as to any material fact in the case.

QUESTION 120

On January 1, the plaintiff served his complaint on the defendant. On February 1, the defendant filed his answer. The defendant admitted allegations 1 through 5, asserted his lack of sufficient knowledge to admit or deny allegations 6 through 10, and denied all of the other allegations in the complaint.

Did the defendant file a proper answer?

(A) Yes, because the answer was filed within one month of service of the complaint.

(B) No, because the answer did not admit or deny every allegation in the complaint.

(C) Yes, because the answer addressed all allegations in the complaint.

(D) No, because the answer was filed more than 21 days after service of the complaint.

QUESTION 121

A contractor agrees to remodel a homeowner's house. During the remodeling, one of the contractor's employees drops a hammer, which strikes and injures the homeowner's child. The homeowner sues the employee, the contractor, and the manufacturer of the hammer in federal court. Due to the complexity of the case, the court requires the jury to make a special written finding upon each issue of fact.

What type of verdict did the jury return?

(A) general verdict

(B) basic verdict

(C) special verdict

(D) inconsistent verdict

QUESTION 122

A customer was injured after slipping and falling at a grocery store. The customer brought a suit for negligence against the grocery store in a federal district court. The court possessed subject-matter jurisdiction over the case, and personal jurisdiction over the parties. At trial, the customer proffered evidence of a witness. The witness testified that, shortly after learning of the injury, he saw a grocery store employee applying a flooring solution to the area where the accident occurred. The witness testified that the bottle of the flooring solution had the words: "Extra Grip Solution for Preventing Slips."

The grocery store's attorney instinctively thought something was objectionable, although he did not object to the testimony when it was introduced. He assigned a law clerk to research the issue because he did not want to be wrong in front of the judge. The law clerk discovered a ground for objection after a few days of research. The attorney asserted the objection, with particularity, to the introduction of the evidence. The jury found in favor of the customer and the court entered judgment accordingly.

Can the grocery store challenge the admission of the testimony on appeal?

(A) No, because the objection was not made contemporaneously to the ruling.

(B) No, because the judge's determination was a non-final order.

(C) Yes, because the objection was made with particularity.

(D) Yes, because the potential error could have changed the outcome of the jury verdict.

QUESTION 123

A lawyer signed and filed a complaint in which she sought compensatory and punitive damages. Binding case law has established that punitive damages are not allowed under the facts that gave rise to the lawsuit. The lawyer knew about the case law that held that punitive damages were not allowed, but requested the damages anyway. The lawyer reasoned that her client was very sympathetic, so she should try to get punitive damages despite the binding case law.

Should the attorney be sanctioned?

(A) No, because she had a non-frivolous argument for the extension, modification, or reversal of existing law.

(B) Yes, because she violated Rule 11 by presenting a request for punitive damages that was not warranted by existing law.

(C) No, because she can seek any damages for her client that she would like.

(D) Yes, because she violated Rule 11 by seeking both compensatory and punitive damages.

QUESTION 124

A wooden peg manufacturer in State A is the primary manufacturer of wooden pegs used by a toy manufacturer in State B. The wooden peg manufacturer is aware that most, if not all, of the wooden pegs it sells to the toy manufacturer will be used in toys sold in State B. The wooden peg manufacturer advertises its products on a website that is accessible worldwide, and it also advertises the wooden pegs it makes in Toy Manufacturer's Monthly, a magazine published and distributed in State B. The peg manufacturer also solicits business in State B by sending sales agents into the State to secure additional manufacturing contracts. Unfortunately, the wooden pegs sold by the peg manufacturer to the toy manufacturer contained a toxic chemical that caused several hundred children in State B to become seriously ill after playing with the toys that were manufactured in State B and sold in State B. A lawsuit is filed in a State B court, and the peg manufacturer is named as a defendant in the case.

Does the court have personal jurisdiction over the peg manufacturer?

(A) No, because placing the wooden pegs into the stream of commerce is insufficient to establish personal jurisdiction over the manufacturer.

(B) No, because the toy manufacturer would be the proper defendant in the action, not the peg manufacturer.

(C) Yes, because the peg manufacturer was aware that its pegs would be sold in State B, and the peg manufacturer directed acts toward State B showing intent to serve State B's marketplace.

(D) Yes, because the peg manufacturer advertises its products on a website that is accessible in the forum state.

QUESTION 125

A motorcyclist is driving carefully on a highway. A vacationer, who is driving a large RV, is texting on a cellphone and looking at a map while driving. The vacationer does not notice that the RV has crossed over into oncoming traffic. The motorcyclist sees the RV in the oncoming lane and swerves to avoid a collision. If the motorcyclist hadn't swerved, the motorcyclist and RV would have had a head-on collision. However, by swerving, the motorcyclist loses control of the motorcycle and crashes into a bicyclist, who is injured in the crash. The bicyclist files a complaint in federal court, suing the vacationer on a claim of negligence. The vacationer serves a timely answer. The parties engage in several months of discovery. One week prior to trial, and nearly two months after completion of discovery, the bicyclist seeks to amend the complaint. The vacationer does not consent to an amendment, and the bicyclist then seeks the court's permission to amend the complaint.

Should the court permit the bicyclist to amend the complaint?

(A) No, because amending the complaint would likely cause undue prejudice to the vacationer.

(B) No, because the driver failed to file an amended complaint within 14 days of service of the answer.

(C) Yes, because courts must grant leave to amend when leave is requested prior to trial.

(D) Yes, because the plaintiff is master of the complaint and may amend a complaint as a matter of right.

QUESTION 126

A contractor agrees to remodel a homeowner's house. During the remodeling, one of the contractor's employees drops a hammer, which strikes and injures the homeowner's child. The homeowner sues the employee and the contractor in federal court on a negligence theory. The case proceeds to trial. After instructing the jury, the judge states to the jury, "Thank you for your service today. I know you will carefully consider the evidence, testimony, and law on which you have been instructed. Please remember when you are considering these things, that if that employee had acted reasonably, the child would not have been injured, and you wouldn't be here today."

Was the judge's statement to the jury proper?

(A) No, because the judge did not give that statement at the beginning of the jury instructions.

(B) No, because the judge may not express an opinion regarding the evidence when charging the jury.

(C) Yes, because it was the judge's fair comment and opinion of the evidence.

(D) Yes, because the judge is the trier of fact and must instruct the jury as to the court's opinion regarding the evidence.

QUESTION 127

A driver is involved in a collision on a highway with a trucker. The trucker files a lawsuit based on a claim of negligence against the driver in federal court. The driver answers the complaint, and the parties begin discovery. There is no doubt that the driver was involved in the collision with the trucker, though the driver believes the accident was not due to negligence. To avoid a trial on the matter, the driver files a

motion for summary judgment. The court finds that a genuine dispute of fact exists as to whether the driver was wearing a yellow polo shirt or a yellow button-down dress shirt at the time of the accident. Therefore, on that basis alone, the court denies the motion for summary judgment.

Was the court's reasoning proper?

(A) No, because a dispute of fact existed.

(B) No, because the fact in dispute was not material.

(C) Yes, because the driver filed the motion to avoid a trial.

(D) Yes, because the jury could reasonably return a verdict for the trucker.

QUESTION 128

The defendant's lawyer filed 10 documents, including the answer and affirmative defenses, requests for admission, and 3 motions, without signing any of the documents. The plaintiff's lawyer then filed a motion for sanctions. In his motion, the plaintiff's lawyer requested that the court impose sanctions on the defendant's lawyer for failing to sign every pleading, motion, or paper, as required by Rule 11.

Should the court deny the motion for sanctions?

(A) Yes, because the defendant's lawyer did not violate Rule 11.

(B) No, because the motion described the specific conduct alleged to have violated Rule 11.

(C) Yes, because the plaintiff's lawyer

failed to serve the motion on the defendant's lawyer.

(D) No, because the challenged filing was not withdrawn or appropriately corrected.

QUESTION 129

A motorcyclist is involved in an accident with a driver. The motorcyclist files a lawsuit based on negligence against the driver in federal court. The case proceeds to a jury trial. The court permits the jury to enter a verdict and also provide written answers to interrogatories addressed to important fact issues in the case.

Did the court violate the Rules in regard to the verdict procedure?

(A) No, because the court may permit any procedure it deems appropriate in any given case.

(B) No, because the court may submit general verdict forms to the jury, along with written questions on fact issues.

(C) Yes, because the court may not submit general verdict forms to the jury, along with written questions on fact issues.

(D) Yes, because a jury may not provide written answers to interrogatories.

QUESTION 130

A consumer from State A filed a products liability action in federal court against a manufacturer incorporated and with its principal place of business in State B. The con¬sumer claimed that a flaw in the manufacturer's product had resulted in

severe injuries to the consumer. The consumer's complaint demanded damages in the amount of $250,000. A witness gave testimony during the trial that the product malfunctioned during normal use by the consumer. Based largely on the testimony of the witness, the jury entered a verdict for the consumer.

Upon reviewing the case, the attorney for the manufacturer noticed that the witness' name was not spelled correctly in the trial record. The attorney appealed the trial court's decision, arguing that the decision must be overturned because of the error.

Should the appellate court hear the appeal?

(A) Yes, because the error had a substantial effect on the outcome of the trial.

(B) No, because an error made by a trial court is not sufficient reason for an appeal.

(C) No, because the error would not have affected the trial's result.

(D) Yes, because an appellate court must hear an appeal if an error is made by the trial court.

QUESTION 131

A sophisticated businessman from State A desired to open a franchise of a restaurant chain owned by a corporation, and he filed an application for the franchise in the corporation's district office in State A. In order to open a franchise, the businessman completed several training sessions sponsored by the corporation, including a week-long conference provided at the corporation's headquarters in State B. Eventually, the businessman entered into a contract with the corporation. The contract permitted the businessman to open a franchise in State A. The contract further provided that the parties' relationship was established in State B and that State B's law governed the contractual relationship. After opening the franchise, the businessman struggled to make a profit due to an unexpected downturn in State A's economy, and he was unable to meet his contractual obligations to the corporation. The corporation filed a breach of contract lawsuit in State B against the businessman. The businessman objected to personal jurisdiction in State B.

Will the businessman's challenge to the court's jurisdiction be successful?

(A) No, because the contract provided that State B's law governed the contractual relationship, which is sufficient to establish minimum contacts with State B.

(B) No, because the businessman was sophisticated, and he engaged in a substantial and continuous business relationship with the corporation, and he received fair notice that he could be subject to personal jurisdiction in State B.

(C) Yes, because the businessman operates the franchise in State A, and State A is where the corporation's district office is located.

(D) Yes, because his failure to meet his contractual obligation was due to an unexpected decline in the economy.

QUESTION 132

An entrepreneur and a business enter into a contractual relationship. Several months after the contract was entered, the entrepreneur becomes aware of facts indicating that the business is failing to meet its contractual obligations. The entrepreneur sues the business in federal court on a breach of contract claim. After the statute of limitations expires, the entrepreneur amends the complaint, adding a claim of fraud based on the business's statements during the contract negotiations.

Is the entrepreneur's amended complaint permitted?

(A) No, because the statute of limitations expired.

(B) No, because the claim of fraud arose from the same transaction that gave rise to the breach of contract claim, and therefore, both claims should have been brought at the same time.

(C) Yes, even though the statute of limitations has expired, the claim will be treated as if it had been filed on the date of the original complaint.

(D) Yes, because the entrepreneur is master of the complaint and may amend the complaint at any time.

QUESTION 133

A driver is involved in a collision on a highway with a trucker. The trucker files a lawsuit based on a claim of negligence against the driver in federal court. The driver answers the complaint, and the parties begin discovery. Subsequently, the trucker files a motion for summary judgment. The court considers the motion and draws all inferences from the record, including from deposition testimony, in favor of the trucker. After careful consideration, the court denies the motion.

Did the court properly consider the motion?

(A) No, because it reviewed deposition testimony when considering the motion.

(B) No, because it drew inferences in favor of the trucker.

(C) Yes, because it drew inferences in favor of the trucker.

(D) Yes, because it reviewed deposition testimony when considering the motion.

QUESTION 134

The plaintiff's lawyer failed to sign two motions he filed with the court. After the court saw that the motions lacked an attorney's signature, the court directed the plaintiff's lawyer to show cause, in writing within 20 days, why it had not violated Rule 11. After the plaintiff's lawyer filed its response, the court imposed sanctions.

Did the court properly impose sanctions?

(A) No, because the defendant's lawyer did not file a motion seeking sanctions.

(B) Yes, because a court can impose sanctions for violations of Rule 11 on its own initiative.

(C) Yes, because the plaintiff's lawyer failed to sign two motions.

(D) No, because the court did not have a hearing before imposing sanctions.

QUESTION 135

A motorcyclist is involved in an accident with a driver. The motorcyclist files a lawsuit based on negligence against the driver in federal court. The case proceeds to a jury trial. The jury's general verdict and written answers are consistent. However, the court declines to approve a judgment based on the verdict and answers and requires the jury to further consider them.

Was it permissible for the court to reject the verdict and written answers?

(A) No, because the general verdict and written answers were consistent.

(B) No, because a court may never require the jury to further consider its answers and verdict.

(C) Yes, because the court is in the best position to evaluate the facts, evidence, and law.

(D) Yes, because a jury's finding is merely a non-binding recommendation to the court.

QUESTION 136

An employee for a private company, who resides in State A, sued the owner of the building where the employee works in federal court for negligence. The owner was a State B corporation, with its principal place of operations located in State B. The complaint alleges that the employee was injured by a light fixture that fell from the ceiling in the building.

At the bench trial, the court permitted testimony, proffered by the employee, that there had been several previous accidents in the same building. The judge found for the employee, and the company appealed. One of the company's arguments on appeal is that the testimony about the previous accidents should have been excluded as irrelevant and highly prejudicial.

Which standard of review applies to this argument?

(A) Abuse of Discretion

(B) De Novo

(C) Clearly Erroneous

(D) Preservation of Error

QUESTION 137

A proceeding is commenced in a federal court in State A to determine the ownership of a parcel of land located in State A. The action is not based on the seizure of the property through attachment or garnishment. Reasonable notice of the proceeding was given to all possible interest holders. The court finds that it has jurisdiction over the property, and it makes a determination in which it adjudicates the entire world's rights in relation to the parcel of land.

What is the most appropriate term for the type of jurisdiction, if any, that the court exercised in this case?

(A) Quasi in rem jurisdiction

(B) *In rem* jurisdiction

(C) *In properteris* jurisdiction

(D) The court did not have jurisdiction to render a decision in this case.

QUESTION 138

Pat, a motorcyclist, is involved in a serious crash with a van driven by Dave, the sole occupant of the vehicle. Dave was texting while driving the van. Donna is the owner and insurer of the van. Pat, through the assistance of legal counsel, contacts Donna's insurance provider and the parties agree to a settlement. In that settlement case, Donna is mistakenly named as the driver of the van. Aware that the statute of limitations is about to expire, Pat files a suit in federal court based on the driver's negligence in order to recover for personal injuries. However, the complaint names only Donna as a defendant, and Donna is named as the driver of the van. After the statute of limitations for the claim expires, Pat learns that Dave was driver of the van. Pat amends the complaint, substituting Dave as the defendant, and the next day, Dave is served with the complaint. Dave moves to dismiss the case, arguing that the statute of limitations has run, and therefore, the claim against him is too late.

Should the court grant the motion to dismiss?

(A) No, because the amended complaint is based on the same conduct that gave rise to the original complaint, Dave received notice, and Dave knew that but for Pat's misidentification of the driver in the complaint, the action would have been served earlier.

(B) No, because a plaintiff may amend a complaint anytime before trial.

(C) Yes, because Pat was negligent in not properly filing a timely complaint.

(D) Yes, because the statute of limitations expired.

QUESTION 139

A mechanic installs a new set of brakes on a driver's BMW. After leaving the mechanic's shop, the brakes fail to work on the BMW, and the driver veers off the road and crashes into a tree. The driver sues the mechanic in federal court, claiming that the mechanic was negligent. The driver's complaint alleges $85,000 in damages. After pleadings have concluded, the driver files a motion for summary judgment. The driver cites to specific portions of depositions and documents in the record in support of the driver's assertion that a material fact cannot be genuinely disputed.

Was it proper for the driver to include citations to the record with the motion?

(A) No, because a motion for summary judgment must consist of only the motion itself, with no additional citations to the record.

(B) No, because the citations to depositions and documents amount to an ex parte communication to the court.

(C) Yes, because all parts of the record would be admissible at trial.

(D) Yes, because a party who asserts that a material fact cannot be genuinely disputed must support its assertion by citing to specific portions of materials in the record.

QUESTION 140

A motorcyclist is involved in an accident with a driver. The motorcyclist files a lawsuit based on negligence against the driver in federal court. The case proceeds to a jury trial, and the jury is called upon to provide written answers to questions and enter a general verdict. The jury's written answers are consistent, but one of them is inconsistent with the general verdict. The court concludes that the Rules require the court, without having any discretion in the matter, to order a new trial because of the inconsistent written answer.

Did the court properly apply the Rules?

(A) No, because written answers may be used in conjunction with a general verdict.

(B) No, because the court believed it had no discretion in the matter.

(C) Yes, because the court was required to order a new trial.

(D) Yes, because the jury may only enter a general verdict.

QUESTION 141

A party served a motion for sanctions on the opposing party alleging that the opposing party violated Rule 11 by filing fifty separate motions seeking thousands of documents. The party alleged that these motions were filed only to harass and increase the costs of litigation in a simple contract dispute. The court held a hearing, and allowed the opposing party an opportunity to explain why sanctions should not be imposed.

The court imposed sanctions against the attorney of record as well as the attorney's law firm.

Did the court properly impose sanctions against the attorney and the firm?

(A) Yes, because the court held a hearing before imposing sanctions.

(B) No, because the court cannot impose sanctions against an entire law firm when only one lawyer violated Rule 11.

(C) Yes, because the court can impose sanctions against both the attorney and the firm.

(D) No, because the alleged actions do not constitute a violation of Rule 11.

QUESTION 142

A student files a complaint against a private university in a federal district court. The court possesses subject-matter jurisdiction over the case and personal jurisdiction over the parties. The student alleges that she was injured while she was on a campus tour. The university conducts campus tours every other week during the months of September through March.

The university offered evidence from several witnesses that the student was not in the tour on the date she alleged she was injured. The student offered testimony from the student's best friend, who testified that she was on the campus tour with the student.

After a long bench trial, the judge entered a judgment for the student. The university appeals the judgment. The university's argument on appeal is that the judge made an error in finding that the student was on the campus tour.

What standard of review applies to the university's argument?

(A) De Novo

(B) Clearly Erroneous

(C) Harmless Error Rule

(D) Abuse of Discretion

QUESTION 143

In the proper court in State A, a plaintiff who does not have a lawyer files a complaint against a defendant from State B. The plaintiff is a citizen of State A. The complaint is based on a claim of negligence, and the plaintiff seeks $100,000 in damages. The plaintiff presents a summons that is in proper form to the clerk of court for the clerk's signature. The clerk signs, seals, and issues the summons to the plaintiff. The plaintiff asks the clerk if there is anything else that needs to be done to commence the lawsuit against the defendant. The clerk, who has diligently watched every episode of Law and Order, says, "No. Your case is filed, and that's all you have to do. Just sit back and wait to get the defendant's answer to your complaint."

Should the plaintiff follow the clerk's advice?

(A) No, because the plaintiff should prepare for oral arguments in order to prove the amount of damages.

(B) No, because the defendant has not been given reasonable notice of the lawsuit.

(C) Yes, because the clerk signed, sealed, and issued the summons to the plaintiff.

(D) Yes, because the plaintiff filed the complaint with the proper court in State A, and the clerk properly signed, sealed, and issued the summons to the plaintiff.

QUESTION 144

A supervisor at a company berates an employee with gender-based slurs and sexist remarks. The employee sues the supervisor and the company. After the employee's complaint is filed, the supervisor fires the employee, telling the employee, "That'll teach you to sue us! Good luck finding another job!" Without leave of court, the employee files a supplemental claim against the supervisor and company, alleging wrongful termination.

Is the employee's supplemental pleading permitted?

(A) No, because the employee did not obtain leave of court to file the supplemental pleading.

(B) No, because the employee did not obtain the consent of the adverse parties.

(C) Yes, because the claim arises from the same set of events that gave rise to the initial complaint.

(D) Yes, a plaintiff may file a supplemental pleading as a matter of right.

QUESTION 145

A motorcyclist is involved in an accident with a driver. The motorcyclist files a lawsuit based on negligence against the driver in federal court. The case proceeds to a jury trial, and the jury is called upon to provide written answers to questions and enter a general verdict. However, the jury's written answers are inconsistent with each other, and one of them is inconsistent with the general verdict.

What, if anything, must the court do?

(A) Nothing, because the court entered a general verdict.

(B) The court must not enter a judgment.

(C) The court must enter a judgment consistent with the general verdict and the answers that are not inconsistent with the verdict.

(D) The court must disregard the jury's finding and decide the matter as if it had been a bench trial.

QUESTION 146

A party served a motion for sanctions on an opposing party alleging that the opposing party violated Rule 11 by bringing a frivolous claim in their complaint. The court directed the opposing party to show cause, in writing within 20 days, why they had not violated Rule 11 and why sanctions should not be imposed. After reviewing the opposing party's response, the court entered an order finding that the claim was frivolous and thus, violated Rule 11. The court directed the opposing party to withdraw the frivolous claim and ordered the opposing party to pay a fee to the court.

Did the court impose proper sanctions for a violation of Rule 11?

(A) No, because the court cannot impose a fee or fine for violating Rule 11.

(B) No, because the court cannot both direct the party to correct the violation of Rule 11 and impose a fine.

(C) Yes, because the court can impose non-monetary directives and order the party to pay a penalty for violating Rule 11.

(D) Yes, because the court can impose any sanction it wants after finding a violation of Rule 11.

QUESTION 147

In the proper federal court in State A, a plaintiff from State A files a complaint against a defendant from State B. The complaint is based on a claim of negligence, and the plaintiff seeks $100,000 in damages. The plaintiff presents a summons that is in proper form to the clerk of court for the clerk's signature. The clerk is new to the job, but the clerk signs, seals, and issues the summons to the plaintiff. The summons and complaint are personally served on the defendant within the forum state 79 days after the filing of the complaint. The defendant believes that the summons and complaint were served beyond the time limit for service, and files a motion to dismiss the complaint.

Should the court grant the motion to dismiss?

(A) No, because the defendant was served before the 90-day time limit expired.

(B) No, because the defendant was served before the 120-day time limit expired.

(C) Yes, because the defendant was not served within the 60-day time limit.

(D) Yes, because the defendant was not served within the 30-day time limit.

QUESTION 148

A supervisor at a company berates an employee with gender-based slurs and sexist remarks. The employee sues the supervisor and the company. After the employee's complaint is filed, the supervisor fires the employee, telling the employee, "That'll teach you to sue us! Good luck finding another job!" Without leave of court, the employee files a supplemental claim against the supervisor and company, alleging wrongful termination.

Is the employee's supplemental pleading permitted?

(A) No, because the employee did not obtain leave of court to file the supplemental pleading.

(B) No, because the employee did not obtain the consent of the adverse parties.

(C) Yes, because the claim arises from the same set of events that gave rise to the initial complaint.

(D) Yes, a plaintiff may file a supplemental pleading as a matter of right.

QUESTION 149

A mechanic installs a new set of brakes on a driver's BMW. After leaving the mechanic's shop, the brakes fail to work on the BMW, and the driver veers off the road and crashes into a tree. The driver sues the mechanic in federal court, claiming that the mechanic was negligent. The driver's complaint alleges $85,000 in damages. After pleadings have concluded, the driver files a motion for summary judgment. The driver cites to specific portions of depositions in the record in support of the driver's assertion that a material fact cannot be genuinely disputed. The mechanic objects to the motion, arguing that the potential evidence cited as support would not be admissible at trial.

Is the mechanic's objection authorized in this context?

(A) No, because the court record in its entirety is admissible, no objection is necessary or permitted.

(B) No, because the court must consider the motion in the light most favorable to the movant.

(C) Yes, because a party can object that the potential evidence cited as support for a motion for summary judgment would not be admissible at trial.

(D) Yes, because it is improper for the movant to cite to depositions in a motion for summary judgment.

QUESTION 150

A contractor agrees to remodel a homeowner's house. During the remodeling, one of the contractor's employees drops a hammer, which strikes and injures the homeowner's child. The homeowner sues the contractor in federal court on a negligence theory. The case proceeds to trial, and a judgment is entered in favor of the homeowner. Twenty days after entry of the judgment, the contractor files a motion to alter the judgment.

Was the contractor's motion timely?

(A) No, because a party making a motion to alter or amend a judgment must file the motion within 7 days after entry of the judgment.

(B) No, because a party making a motion to alter or amend a judgment must file the motion within 14 days after entry of the judgment.

(C) Yes, because a party making a motion to alter or amend a judgment must file the motion within 28 days after entry of the judgment.

(D) Yes, because a party making a motion to alter or amend a judgment must file the motion within 60 days after entry of the judgment.

QUESTION 151

A party served a motion for sanctions on an opposing party alleging that the opposing party violated Rule 11 by bringing a frivolous lawsuit. The party requesting sanctions waited the required 21 days and then filed the motion with the court. The opposing party filed a response in opposition, and argued that there was recent case law that explicitly allowed for the lawsuit. The opposing party alleged that the party who brought the motion simply was not aware of the new case law.

The court denied the motion for sanctions, finding that the motion was not warranted in light of the recent case law allowing for the lawsuit. The court awarded the opposing party reasonable expenses and attorney's fees incurred as a result of defending against the motion.

Did the court properly award expenses and attorney's fees?

(A) No, because the court can only award expenses or attorney's fees to the party who brought the motion.

(B) No, because the court did not first find that the party bringing the motion for sanctions had filed a frivolous motion in light of recent case law.

(C) Yes, because the court can award reasonable expenses and attorney's fees to the prevailing party.

(D) Yes, because the opposing party failed to correct the complained of action within 21 days.

QUESTION 152

In the proper federal court in State A, a plaintiff from State A files a complaint against a defendant from State B. In a written notice addressed to the defendant and sent by first class mail, the plaintiff notifies the defendant of the commencement of the action and requests that the defendant waive service of the summons. The notice includes a copy of the complaint and informs the defendant that complying with the request will constitute a waiver of defenses relating to service of process, but non-compliance will cause the defendant to incur the costs incurred in effecting service of the summons. The notice states that the defendant has 30 days from the date the request was sent to return the waiver. The defendant receives and reads the notice. The defendant says, "There's no way I'm going to make it easy for these guys to sue me. Let them try to find me and serve me with

their summons, if they think they can." The defendant then throws the notice in the trash and doesn't return the waiver. Two months after the filing of the complaint, the plaintiff causes service of process to be completed on the defendant.

Will the defendant be responsible for the costs incurred in effecting the service of process?

(A) No, because the plaintiff did not give the defendant a reasonable time to return the waiver.

(B) No, because it was improper for the plaintiff to request that the defendant waive service of process.

(C) No, because the notice of waiver of service of process was sent in the mail instead of personal service.

(D) Yes, because the defendant's request was proper, and the defendant does not have good cause for the failure to comply with the request.

QUESTION 153

A trucker is traveling at a high rate of speed over icy roads. The trucker loses control of the truck and is involved in an accident with a driver. The driver's attorney prepares a complaint alleging that the trucker negligently operated the truck and caused $100,000 in damages. The driver asks the attorney if the driver must sign the complaint. The attorney says, "Oh no, you don't want your signature on this thing. I'm not signing it either. Your name is in the caption at the top, and that's sufficient. Besides, I know the judge. I don't need to sign this complaint." The attorney files the unsigned complaint.

Was the attorney's statement correct?

(A)   No, the attorney violated Rule 12.

(B)   No, the attorney violated Rule 11.

(C)   Yes, because the caption is sufficient to verify the complaint.

(D)   Yes, because the attorney knows the judge.

QUESTION 154

A computer geek invents and patents an unbreakable screen for smartphones. Without the geek's knowledge, an unscrupulous corporation begins manufacturing smartphones that use the geek's design for smartphone screens. The geek sues the corporation in federal court on a claim of patent infringement. After depositions are completed in the case, the corporation files a motion for summary judgment, and it cites materials in the record in support of its motion. After considering the cited materials, as well as interrogatory answers that were not cited in the motion, the court denies the motion.

Was the court permitted to consider the interrogatory answers?

(A)   No, because when considering a motion for summary judgment, the court may not consider materials that were not cited by a party.

(B)   No, because when considering a motion for summary judgment, the court may not consider interrogatory answers.

(C)   Yes, because when considering a

motion for summary judgment, the court may consider materials in the record that were not cited by a party.

(D)   Yes, because when considering a motion for summary judgment, the court may consider materials in the record not cited by a party, except for electronically stored information.

QUESTION 155

A driver and a trucker are involved in an accident on a state road. The driver sues the trucker in federal court, alleging that the trucker's negligence caused the accident. The driver seeks $80,000 in damages. The case proceeds to trial, and the jury returns a verdict in favor of the driver and awards the driver $350,000 in damages. The court believes that the verdict is excessive and that a new trial should be granted for that reason only.

What may the court recommend to the parties?

(A)   Remittitur, which is the reduction of an award for damages.

(B)   Additur, which is the reduction of an award for damages.

(C)   That the driver pay, in the interests of justice and fairness, the trucker's costs and expenses of litigation due to the extraordinary jury finding.

(D)   A new trial.

QUESTION 156

An attorney filed his client's complaint in federal district court, but failed to sign the complaint. The attorney had the client sign the complaint, but decided he simply did not want to sign the document. The attorney then filed two motions to compel production of records and six requests for admission. The attorney again had his client sign the documents, but decided not to sign the documents himself because he enjoyed aggravating opposing counsel and knew not signing the documents would achieve that goal.

Could the attorney be subjected to disciplinary action?

(A) Yes, because the attorney willfully failed to sign every pleading, motion, and other paper.

(B) No, because the attorney only had to sign the complaint, but not the other documents.

(C) Yes, because the attorney intended to aggravate opposing counsel by not signing the documents.

(D) No, because the client signed all the documents.

QUESTION 157

An inventor from the western district of State A holds a patent for a device that increases fuel economy in gasoline-fueled combustion engines. The inventor runs a small manufacturing shop in the eastern district of State B. An opportunist from the northern district of State C learns of the inventor's device and begins manufacturing and selling an identical device, marketing it within the northern district of State C as the opportunist's own invention.

The inventor sues the opportunist in federal

court in the northern district of State C. The inventor's complaint sought $500,000 in damages and alleged patent infringement under federal law. The opportunist believes venue is improper and moves to dismiss the case.

Should the court grant the motion to dismiss?

(A) No, because the opportunist lives in the northern district of State C.

(B) No, because in a federal question case, venue is proper in any federal district court.

(C) Yes, because the inventor is domiciled in the western district of State A.

(D) Yes, because the inventor manufactures the device in State B, where the facts giving rise to the claim arose.

QUESTION 158

A painter enters into a contract with a homeowner to paint the homeowner's house. After the painter has completed painting the house, the homeowner says, "I don't think I like this color anymore, and I want to hire a different painter. I'm not paying you." The painter sues the homeowner, and the complaint seeks relief for breach of contract. The homeowner files a motion to dismiss, which the court denies. The homeowner, extremely upset at having to defend a lawsuit, tells his attorney to "do whatever it takes to make the painter's life miserable. I'll pay you double your hourly rate to make him squirm." The lawyer, acting on what he believes to be his client's best interests, files two more motions to dismiss, each alleging the same grounds as the initial motion to dismiss. The lawyer knows that even though the motions will be denied, it will cause the painter to incur more legal fees and will delay the proceedings.

Should the lawyer be sanctioned?

(A) No, because the lawyer acted on what he believed to be his client's best interests.

(B) No, because filing the repetitive motions to dismiss was a reasonable tactical decision designed to wear down the opposing party.

(C) Yes, because the motions were filed for an improper purpose.

(D) Yes, because a lawyer may not charge double the lawyer's normal hourly rate.

QUESTION 159

A computer geek invents and patents an unbreakable screen for smartphones. Without the geek's knowledge, an unscrupulous corporation begins manufacturing smartphones that use the geek's design for smartphone screens. The geek sues the corporation in federal court on a claim of patent infringement. The geek files a motion for summary judgment and includes an affidavit from a friend of the geek. The content in the affidavit is not based on the personal knowledge of the friend, but the affidavit is properly sworn.

Should the court consider the facts alleged in the affidavit when deciding whether to grant or deny the motion for summary judgment?

(A) No, because the affidavit is not based

on personal knowledge.

(B) No, because the court may not consider affidavits when deciding whether to grant or deny motions for summary judgment.

(C) Yes, because the affidavit is properly sworn.

(D) Yes, because the court must consider alleged facts, even if not admissible in evidence, when considering a motion for summary judgment.

QUESTION 160

An inventor holds a patent for a device that increases fuel economy in gasoline-fueled combustion engines. An opportunist learns of the inventor's device and begins manufacturing and selling an identical device, marketing it as the opportunist's own invention. The inventor sues the opportunist in federal court on a claim of patent infringement. The case proceeds to a bench trial. After the close of evidence, the judge sets forth the court's findings of fact separately from conclusions of law. The judge does not make its findings of fact in a written order.

Did the court properly set forth the findings of fact?

(A) No, because a jury must make findings of fact.

(B) No, because the court did not present the findings of fact in a written order.

(C) Yes, because the court may set forth the findings of fact separately from conclusions of law.

(D) Yes, because the court must set forth the findings of fact separately from conclusions of law.

QUESTION 161

The plaintiff filed a complaint in federal district court alleging that the defendant breached an implied covenant of good faith and fair dealing in a contract between the parties. In that same complaint, the plaintiff also raised an unjust enrichment claim.

The defendant filed a motion to dismiss arguing that the plaintiff's complaint must be stricken because he cannot allege both a breach of contract claim and an unjust enrichment claim.

Is the defendant correct?

(A) Yes, because the plaintiff cannot bring two causes of action in one complaint.

(B) Yes, because the complaint violates the Election of Remedies doctrine.

(C) No, because a pleading may be inconsistent or alternative.

(D) No, because the plaintiff could recover for both breach of contract and unjust enrichment.

QUESTION 162

A driver from the southern district of State A is involved in an accident in the northern district of State A with a trucker from the southern district of State B and a motorcyclist from the southern district of State C. The driver believes the trucker and the motorcyclist were racing at the time of the accident, and he brings a diversity suit

against the trucker and the motorcyclist in federal court in the northern district of State A.

Is venue proper?

(A) No, because the motorcyclist lives in State C and the trucker lives in State B.

(B) No, because the driver lives in the southern district of State A, and the accident occurred in the northern district of State A.

(C) Yes, because the accident occurred in the northern district of State A.

(D) Yes, because venue would be proper in any federal court in State A, B, or C, on the facts in this case.

QUESTION 163

A wealthy homeowner hires a lawyer to bring a claim against a contractor. The homeowner tells the lawyer that the contractor was supposed to install an in-ground swimming pool, and that the parties had a contract stating that the installation would be complete by Labor Day and would cost $100.00. The homeowner tells the lawyer, "That dirty rat of a contractor finished the project a day late and insisted the price was $10,000, not $100.00." The lawyer asks the homeowner if there was any written paperwork documenting the contractual arrangement, and the homeowner says, "Yeah, but I threw it away. The price wasn't stated correctly in it. Too many zeros after the number one, you know?" The homeowner leans closer to the lawyer and whispers, "Look, I did agree to pay $10,000, and the pool is beautiful, but I really don't like this contractor. I don't like the way he looked at my wife when he was working. Can't you just file a claim and give him a scare? Tell the court I want $100,000 in damages because the contractor checked out my wife when he was working on my pool." The lawyer knows the homeowner's claim does not have merit, but nevertheless, the lawyer takes the case and collects a sizeable retainer from the homeowner. The lawyer files a carefully worded complaint against the contractor, alleging the facts as told to him by the homeowner.

Are sanctions appropriate?

(A) No, because there is no indication that the wife provided a sworn affidavit alleging that the contractor looked at her.

(B) No, because the pleading was carefully typed.

(C) Yes, because the pleading presented a baseless claim.

(D) Yes, because a lawyer should not use facts relayed by a client.

QUESTION 164

A driver is involved in a collision on a highway with a trucker. The trucker files a lawsuit based on a claim of negligence against the driver in federal court. The driver answers the complaint, and the parties begin discovery. Subsequently, the trucker files a motion for summary judgment and cites to depositions in the record. After careful consideration of the motion and the record, the court denies the motion with a signed, written order that identifies the parties and the motion, and which concisely states: "Motion for Summary Judgment DENIED."

Was the court's denial of the motion proper?

(A) No, because the court considered the record and did not decide the motion solely on the face of the pleadings.

(B) No, because the court did not provide reasons for the denial.

(C) Yes, because the court carefully considered the motion and the record.

(D) Yes, because the court entered a signed, written order identifying the parties and the motion.

QUESTION 165

An inventor holds a patent for a device that increases fuel economy in gasoline-fueled combustion engines. An opportunist learns of the inventor's device and begins manufacturing and selling an identical device, marketing it as the opportunist's own invention. The inventor sues the opportunist in federal court on a claim of patent infringement. The court grants the opportunist's motion for summary judgment; however, the court does not include conclusions of law in its order granting the motion.

Did the court err by failing to include conclusions of law in its order?

(A) No, because the judge is not required to set forth conclusions of law in an order granting a motion for summary judgment.

(B) No, because the judge need never set forth conclusions of law in an order granting a motion.

(C) Yes, because the judge is required to set forth conclusions of law in an order granting a motion for summary judgment.

(D) Yes, because a judge is required to set forth conclusion of law in any order the judge enters that grants a motion.

QUESTION 166

An attorney filed a complaint in federal district court on behalf of his client. Attached to the complaint was an affidavit signed by the plaintiff in which he swore under oath that the facts alleged in the complaint were true. The defendant's attorney filed an answer in which he responded to the allegations in the complaint. The attorney decided not to have the answer notarized nor attach an affidavit signed under oath by the defendant, reasoning that such was not required.

Was the defendant's attorney correct?

(A) No, because responsive pleadings must always be verified.

(B) Yes, because it is never required to have a responsive pleading verified.

(C) No, because the complaint was verified, all responsive pleadings also had to be verified.

(D) Yes, because it is within the attorney's discretion whether to have a pleading verified or not.

QUESTION 167

A driver from the northern district of State A is involved in an accident there with a trucker from the southern district of State B and a motorcyclist from the northern district of State B. The driver believes the trucker and the motorcyclist were racing at the time of the accident, and he brings a diversity suit against the trucker and the motorcyclist in federal court in the northern district of State B. The trucker moves to dismiss the case, arguing that venue is not proper.

Should the court grant the trucker's motion?

(A) No, because venue would be proper in either the southern or northern district of State B.

(B) No, because venue would be proper in the eastern, western, northern, or southern district of State B.

(C) Yes, because the trucker does not live in the same district as the motorcyclist.

(D) Yes, because the accident occurred in the northern district of State A.

QUESTION 168

A plaintiff files a complaint alleging that the defendant failed to meet contractual obligations. The defendant's attorney files a baseless counterclaim in bad faith. On its own motion, after giving the defendant notice and an opportunity to be heard, the court imposes sanctions against the defendant and the defendant's attorney.

Did the court exceed the scope of its authority in imposing sanctions on the defendant and the defendant's attorney?

(A) No, because sanctions may only be imposed on the court's own initiative.

(B)   No, because the court may impose sanctions on its own initiative.

(C)   Yes, because the court may not impose sanctions on its own initiative.

(D)   Yes, because the court imposed sanctions on the defendant when it was the defendant's attorney who filed the baseless counterclaim.

QUESTION 169

A driver is involved in a collision on a highway with a trucker. The trucker files a lawsuit based on a claim of negligence against the driver in federal court. The driver answers the complaint, and the parties' complete discovery. Subsequently, the trucker files a motion for summary judgment and cites to depositions in the record. After careful consideration of the motion and the record, the court partially grants the motion with respect to one of the trucker's claims. The trucker is infuriated, and says, "The court can't do this! The court can't partially grant my motion! It's all or nothing!"

Is the trucker correct concerning the court's ruling?

(A)   No, because a court may partially grant a motion for summary judgment as to certain claims or defenses.

(B)   No, because the driver limited the court's access to the record by citing only to depositions.

(C)   Yes, because the court may only fully grant or fully deny a motion for summary judgment.

(D)   Yes, because the trucker is the plaintiff

in the lawsuit.

QUESTION 170

A motorcyclist is involved in an accident with a driver. The motorcyclist files a lawsuit based on negligence against the driver in federal court. The case proceeds to a bench trial, and the court finds in favor of the motorcyclist. The driver files a timely notice of appeal. The appellate court finds that the trial court's finding of fact was unreasonably erroneous, and the appellate court sets aside the trial court's findings.

Did the appellate court apply the proper standard in making its decision?

(A)   No, because an appeals court will only set aside a judicial finding of fact if it is clearly erroneous.

(B)   No, because an appeals court will only set aside a judicial finding of fact if it is per se erroneous.

(C)   Yes, because an appeals court will only set aside a judicial finding of fact if it is unreasonably erroneous.

(D)   Yes, because an appeals court may always set aside a judicial finding of fact if it is unreasonably or potentially erroneous.

QUESTION 171

A plaintiff filed a 20-paragraph complaint. In paragraphs 1 through 6, the plaintiff presented the party names and relationships, and alleged that the court had jurisdiction over the matter. In paragraphs 7 through 10, the plaintiff presented his breach of contract cause of action and supporting facts. In paragraphs 11 through 13, the plaintiff presented his claim alleging conversion. In paragraphs 14 through 20, the plaintiff presented his requests for relief, in which he sought both injunctive and monetary relief.

In his answer, the defendant admitted the allegations in paragraphs 1 and 2. The defendant failed to respond to the allegations in paragraphs 3 and 4. He asserted that he lacked sufficient knowledge to respond to the allegations in paragraphs 5 and 6. The defendant denied the allegations in paragraphs 7 through 20.

Did the defendant file a proper answer?

(A) No, because the defendant did not admit or deny every allegation in the complaint.

(B) No, because the defendant did not admit, deny, or allege lack of sufficient knowledge to respond to every allegation in the complaint.

(C) Yes, because the defendant addressed the allegations in paragraphs 1, 2, and 5 through 20, and the allegations in paragraphs 3 and 4 will be deemed admitted.

(D) Yes, because the defendant denied the two causes of action, which is sufficient.

QUESTION 172

A driver from the northern district of State A is involved in an accident there with a trucker from the southern district of State B and a motorcyclist from the northern district of State B. The driver believes the trucker

and the motorcyclist were racing at the time of the accident, and he brings a diversity suit against the trucker and the motorcyclist in federal court in the northern district of State A. There were two witnesses to the accident, one of whom lives in the northern district of State B. The federal court in State A is further from the defendants' homes than the federal court in the northern district of State B. Frustrated with having to defend a lawsuit, and knowing it will take much time out of his schedule to travel to State A regarding the case, the motorcyclist files a motion to transfer the case to the federal district court in the northern district of State B. In his motion, he argues that the northern district in State B will be more convenient to the parties and witnesses.

May the court grant the motion?

(A) No, because venue would not be proper in the northern district of State B.

(B) No, because the claim arose in the northern district of State A and was properly initiated in that venue.

(C) Yes, because the initial choice of venue was improper.

(D) Yes, because the motorcyclist lives in the northern district of State B and the trucker lives in the southern district of State B.

QUESTION 173

A defendant, who is being sued on a claim of copyright infringement, files a motion for sanctions against the plaintiff. The defendant alleges that the plaintiff's claim is frivolous and was filed for purposes of harassment. The defendant does not serve the motion on the plaintiff.

Should the court deny the defendant's motion?

(A) No, because the plaintiff did not object to the motion.

(B) No, because it alleges that the plaintiff's claim was filed for purposes of harassment.

(C) Yes, because the defendant did not serve the defendant with the motion and wait 21 days before filing the motion with the court.

(D) Yes, because the defendant did not serve the defendant with the motion and wait seven days before filing the motion with the court.

QUESTION 174

A plaintiff sues a defendant on a claim of copyright infringement in federal court. The plaintiff seeks $1,250,000 in damages. Before discovery has been completed, the defendant moves for summary judgment. The plaintiff cannot present facts that would justify its opposition to the motion for summary judgment, so the plaintiff submits an affidavit detailing the need for further discovery to avoid judgment for the defendant. Consequently, instead of ruling on the motion, the court defers considering the motion until later in the case.

Was it proper for the court to defer ruling on the motion?

(A) No, because courts, in the interest of judicial economy, must issue a ruling on a motion's merits in a timely manner.

(B) No, because by deferring ruling on the motion, the court showed bias toward the defendant.

(C) Yes, because the plaintiff seeks over one million dollars in damages.

(D) Yes, because the plaintiff needed further discovery to avoid judgment for the defendant.

QUESTION 175

A painter, who is driving a van, is involved in an accident with a driver. The painter files a lawsuit based on negligence against the driver in federal court. A final judgment on the merits is entered in favor of the painter. Later, the driver files a claim in federal court against the painter based on a breach of contract theory. The driver alleges the painter breached a contract concerning the painting of the driver's house. The painter moves to dismiss the case, arguing that the doctrine of claim preclusion forbids the litigation.

Should the court grant the motion to dismiss?

(A) No, because the cases do not involve the same cause of action.

(B) No, because the prior judgment was not rendered by a court of competent jurisdiction.

(C) Yes, because a final judgment on the merits exists in the prior action.

(D) Yes, because the same parties exist in both lawsuits and a final judgment on the merits exists in the prior action.

QUESTION 176

The plaintiff filed a complaint in federal district court and served it on the defendant. The defendant filed and served an answer 15 days later. Another 15 days later, the defendant filed and served an amended answer.

Was the amendment of the answer proper?

(A) Yes, because an answer can be amended at any time.

(B) Yes, because an answer can be amended once within 21 days after serving it.

(C) No, because any amendments had to be filed within 21 days of service of the complaint.

(D) No, because an answer cannot be amended once it is filed.

QUESTION 177

A corporation has its main office and principal place of business in the northern district of State A and is incorporated in the southern district of State B. The corporation does not have any business or contact with the other districts in State A. The corporation enters into a contract with an individual from the southern district of State B. The contract was signed and entered into by the parties at the corporation's main office. Five months into the contractual relationship, the corporation is unable to meet the requirements of the contract, and the individual brings a diversity action in federal court in the southern district of State A. The corporation moves to dismiss the action on the basis that it was filed in an improper venue.

Should the court grant the motion to dismiss?

(A) Yes, because venue would only be proper in the southern district in State B because it is the state of incorporation.

(B) Yes, because the plaintiff brought the case in the wrong venue.

(C) No, because the plaintiff brought the case in the proper venue.

(D) No, because the contract was signed and entered into in State A, thereby making venue proper in any district in that State.

QUESTION 178

A painter enters into a contract with a homeowner to paint the homeowner's house. After the painter has completed painting the house, the homeowner says, "I don't think I like this color anymore, and I want to hire a different painter. I'm not paying you." The painter sues the homeowner, and the complaint seeks relief for breach of contract. The homeowner files a motion seeking sanctions against the painter for filing the breach of contract claim. The homeowner's motion states that "the painter is a horrible painter and therefore the breach of contract claim should be rendered moot and the painter should be sanctioned for bringing the claim in the first place." Three weeks after the painter is served with the homeowner's motion seeking sanctions, the homeowner files the motion with the court. After holding a hearing on the motion, the court denies the motion and awards the painter the attorney fees incurred in opposing the motion.

Was the court's award of fees to the painter improper?

(A) No, because the painter prevailed on the motion.

(B) No, because the painter completed painting the house.

(C) Yes, because the painter did not file a counterclaim motion for sanctions against the homeowner.

(D) Yes, because the court may not award attorney fees to a party defending a motion for sanctions.

QUESTION 179

A mechanic installs a new set of brakes on a driver's BMW. After leaving the mechanic's shop, the brakes fail to work on the BMW, and the driver veers off the road and crashes into a tree. The driver sues the mechanic in federal court, claiming that the mechanic was negligent. The driver's complaint alleges $85,000 in damages. Forty-five days after the close of all discovery, the driver files a motion for summary judgment.

Should the court find the motion timely?

(A) No, because it was filed more than 30 days after the end of discovery.

(B) No, because it was filed more than 40 days after the end of discovery.

(C) Yes, because it was filed within 60 days after the end of discovery.

(D) Yes, because it was filed within 90 days after the end of discovery.

QUESTION 180

The plaintiff filed a complaint in federal district court and served it on the defendant. The defendant filed and served an answer 15 days later. 14 days after that, the plaintiff filed and served an amended complaint.

Was the amendment of the complaint proper?

(A) No, because a complaint must be amended within 21 days after service of the complaint.

(B) Yes, because a complaint can be amended at any time.

(C) No, because a complaint can only be amended with leave of court.

(D) Yes, because the complaint was amended within 21 days after service of the answer.

QUESTION 181

A manufacturer is involved in a class action suit based on a products liability cause of action. A final judgment is entered against the manufacturer. Subsequently, a consumer, who chose not to join the class action, files a claim against the manufacturer that involves the same products liability issues. The manufacturer contends that the action is barred by the doctrine of issue preclusion.

Is the consumer's case barred by the doctrine of issue preclusion?

(A) No, because the consumer was not a party to the original lawsuit.

(B) No, because the doctrine of issue preclusion prevents a party from re-litigating claims that have been previously litigated and determined in a prior action.

(C) Yes, because the consumer had a full and fair opportunity to litigate the same issue in the prior action.

(D) Yes, because the consumer was not a party to the original lawsuit.

QUESTION 182

A plaintiff from State A files a complaint in federal court against a defendant from State A. The plaintiff's case is based exclusively on state law that could also support a federal claim. The plaintiff seeks $80,000 in damages. The defendant files a motion to dismiss the case, arguing that the federal court does not have jurisdiction over the case.

Should the court grant the motion to dismiss?

(A) No, because the case is based on state law that could also support a federal claim.

(B) No, because the case is based on state law that could also support a federal claim, and the damages sought satisfy the amount in controversy requirement.

(C) Yes, because the case is based on state law that could also support a federal claim.

(D) Yes, because although the case is based on state law that could also

support a federal claim, the amount in controversy requirement necessary for federal question jurisdiction is not satisfied.

QUESTION 183

A plaintiff files a complaint alleging that the defendant failed to meet contractual obligations. The defendant's attorney files a baseless counterclaim in bad faith. The plaintiff properly files a motion for sanctions against the defendant. After hearing the matter, the court imposes sanctions against the defendant's lawyer and law firm. No other attorneys from the lawyer's firm appeared in court or filed motions in the case.

Was it proper for the court to impose sanctions on the law firm?

(A) No, because a court may sanction a lawyer, but not the lawyer's law firm.

(B) No, because no other lawyer from the firm appeared in court or filed motions in the case.

(C) Yes, because a court may sanction the lawyer and the lawyer's law firm.

(D) Yes, because the plaintiff filed a motion for sanctions, which is the only way for a defendant to be sanctioned by a court.

QUESTION 184

A driver is involved in a collision on a highway with a trucker. The trucker files a lawsuit based on a claim of negligence against the driver in federal court. The driver answers the complaint, and the parties complete discovery and proceed to a trial by jury. After the close of the trucker's evidence, the driver moves for judgment as a matter of law. The court considers the motion and, while weighing the evidence that had been presented to the jury, the court finds that two of the trucker's witnesses lacked credibility. The court grants the driver's motion.

Was the court's ruling proper?

(A) No, because the case had not yet been presented to the jury.

(B) No, because in reaching its decision, the court weighed the evidence and determined the credibility of witnesses.

(C) Yes, because in reaching its decision, the court weighed the evidence and determined the credibility of witnesses.

(D) Yes, because the case had not yet been presented to the jury.

QUESTION 185

A plaintiff files a claim in state court in State A based on the law of State A. The plaintiff has no desire to litigate the matter in federal court, and the plaintiff's complaint asserts, in good faith, that a federal defense the defendant may raise is insufficient to defeat the plaintiff's claim. The defendant, who is from State B, wants to remove the case to federal court in State B.

Would removal of the case to the federal court in State B be proper?

(A) No, because the complaint asserts that a federal defense that the defendant may raise is insufficient to defeat the claim.

(B) No, because cases based on state law must be litigated in federal court.

(C) Yes, because the complaint asserts that a federal defense the defendant may raise is insufficient to defeat the claim.

(D) Yes, because it was improper for the plaintiff to attempt to prevent removal of the case to federal court.

QUESTION 186

The plaintiff filed a complaint in federal district court and served it on the defendant. The defendant filed and served an answer. Twenty-five days later, the plaintiff's attorney called the defendant's attorney and asked for his permission to file an amended complaint. The defendant's attorney orally agreed to allow the plaintiff to file an amended complaint. The plaintiff filed an amended complaint.

Did the plaintiff properly amend his complaint?

(A) Yes, because the adverse party agreed to allow the amendment.

(B) No, because he failed to obtain either leave of court or written consent of the adverse party.

(C) Yes, because he amended his complaint within 30 days of service of the answer.

(D) No, because he had to file any amendment within 21 days after service of the answer.

QUESTION 187

A plaintiff files a complaint alleging that the defendant failed to meet contractual obligations. The defendant's attorney files several baseless motions in bad faith. The plaintiff properly files a motion for sanctions

against the defendant. After hearing the matter, the court imposes sanctions against the defendant, including an order that the defendant pay a penalty into court.

Was the court's order permitted?

(A) No, because the court may not impose sanctions against a party prior to trial.

(B) No, because a court may not impose a sanction requiring a party to pay a penalty into court.

(C) Yes, because when a court finds that sanctions are appropriate, the court must require the sanctioned party to pay a penalty into court.

(D) Yes, because a court may impose a sanction requiring a party to pay a penalty into court.

QUESTION 188

A driver is involved in a collision on a highway with a trucker. The trucker files a lawsuit based on a claim of negligence against the driver in federal court. The driver answers the complaint, and the parties complete discovery and proceed to a trial by jury. After the close of the trucker's evidence, the driver moves for judgment as a matter of law. The court considers the motion and finds there is no legally sufficient evidentiary basis for the jury to find in favor of the trucker. The court grants the motion.

Did the court apply the proper standard in granting the motion?

(A) No, because the court did not determine the credibility of witnesses.

(B)   No, because the court did not weigh the evidence.

(C)   Yes, because the court found that there was no way the jury could find for the trucker.

(D)   Yes, because the court replaced the jury's view of the evidence with that of its own.

QUESTION 189

A driver from State A was operating a 1963 Corvette Stingray sports car on a highway in State B and was involved in a crash with a motorcyclist from State B. The motorcyclist was miraculously unhurt in the crash. The driver believed that the accident was caused by the motorcyclist's recklessness, and the driver filed a negligence claim in federal court in State B, seeking $75,500 from the motorcyclist for the damage sustained to the driver's car. The driver prevailed in the lawsuit and received a judgment for $74,250. There had been no indication on the face of the pleadings that the driver would receive less than the amount sought. After the judgment is entered, the motorcyclist filed a motion challenging the subject-matter jurisdiction of the court on the basis that the amount in controversy was not satisfied.

Will the motorcyclist prevail in his challenge to the court's jurisdiction?

(A)   No, because the amount in controversy requirement was satisfied in the driver's complaint.

(B)   No, because subject-matter jurisdiction cannot be challenged once the court has entered a judgment in the case.

(C)   Yes, because the driver's award of damages did not satisfy the amount in controversy requirement.

(D)   Yes, because the amount in controversy was not diverse at the commencement of the action.

QUESTION 190

A trucker is traveling at a high rate of speed over icy roads. The trucker loses control of the truck and is involved in an accident with a driver. The driver files a claim based on negligence in federal court. The complaint alleges that the trucker negligently operated the truck and caused $100,000 in damages. The trucker serves a timely answer. Subsequently, without an order from the court, the driver files a reply to the answer.

Was the driver's reply permitted?

(A)   No, because the court did not order the driver to reply.

(B)   No, because the trucker did not file a motion for a reply.

(C)   Yes, because a plaintiff must always file a reply to the defendant's answer.

(D)   Yes, because a plaintiff may file a reply to an answer at the plaintiff's discretion.

QUESTION 191

A plaintiff sues a defendant on a claim of negligence in federal court. The plaintiff seeks $1,250,000 in damages. The case proceeds to a jury trial. During the course of the trial, various witnesses testify for the plaintiff, including a witness who had been convicted of a crime involving dishonesty in the past. After the case is submitted to the jury, the defendant moves for a judgment as a matter of law.

Which of the following best explains why the court should not grant the motion?

(A) A motion for a judgment as a matter of law is permissible in bench trials, but not in jury trials.

(B) A witness for the plaintiff has been convicted of a crime involving dishonesty in the past.

(C) A motion for judgment as a matter of law may only be filed by a plaintiff.

(D) The motion is untimely.

QUESTION 192

A taxi driver from State A entered into a written agreement with a contractor from State B in which the contractor agreed to remodel the taxi driver's home, which is located in State A. The contractor completed the work, but the taxi driver failed to pay the contractor as required by the written agreement. Two months after the taxi driver's failure to pay the contractor for his work, the contractor and the taxi driver were involved in an accident on a highway in State B. The accident was unrelated to the taxi driver's failure to pay the contractor. The contractor sued the taxi driver in federal court for breach of contract and sought $80,000 in damages. The taxi driver filed a counterclaim against the contractor for $100,000 in damages, alleging that the contractor's negligence caused the accident on the highway. The contractor moved to dismiss the taxi driver's claim for lack of subject-matter jurisdiction.

Should the court grant the contractor's motion to dismiss?

(A) No, because the taxi driver's claim is a compulsory counterclaim.

(B) No, because the taxi driver's claim is a permissive counterclaim.

(C) Yes, because the taxi driver's claim is a de-minimis counterclaim.

(D) Yes, because the taxi driver's claim does not arise under federal law.

QUESTION 193

On July 4, a driver from State A was operating a 1963 Corvette Stingray sports car on a highway in State B and was involved in a crash with a motorcyclist from State B. The driver was texting at the time of the crash. The driver believed that the accident was caused by the motorcyclist's recklessness, and the driver filed a negligence claim in federal court in State B, seeking $85,000 from the motorcyclist for the damage sustained to the driver's car. The case proceeded to trial, and ultimately the jury found that the motorcyclist was negligent. The motorcyclist believed that the driver was negligent due to the driver texting at the time of the crash. A few months later, the motorcyclist, believing the time for justice is at hand, sues the driver in federal court in State B. The complaint alleges that the driver was negligent and caused the crash that occurred on July 4, and the motorcyclist seeks $77,000 in damages. The court declines to hear the motorcyclist's case and dismisses it with prejudice.

Was it proper for the court to dismiss the motorcyclist's claim with prejudice?

(A) No, because the plaintiff may choose when to file a complaint, as long as the statute of limitations has not expired.

(B) No, because there is evidence suggesting that the driver was negligent, and therefore, the claim is not baseless.

(C) Yes, because the motorcyclist was negligent, and therefore, the claim is baseless.

(D) Yes, because the claim arose out of the same occurrence that was the subject matter of the opposing party's claim.

QUESTION 194

A plaintiff sues a defendant on a claim of negligence in federal court. The plaintiff seeks $100,000 in damages. The case proceeds to a jury trial. The defendant moves for a judgment as a matter of law before the case is submitted to the jury. The court denies the motion. The jury returns a verdict in favor of the plaintiff. Thirty days after the judgment is entered, the defendant files a renewed motion for a judgment as a matter of law on grounds asserted in its initial motion.

Why should the court not consider the motion?

(A) The court already denied the initial motion.

(B) The defendant filed the renewed motion after the jury returned the verdict.

(C) The defendant filed the renewed motion 30 days after the judgment.

(D) The defendant failed to file the motion within 15 days of the judgment.

QUESTION 195

A patient from State A sues a doctor from State B in state court in State B. The patient's complaint seeks $100,000 damages for the doctor's alleged negligence. On the advice of the doctor's attorney, the doctor decides that the suit will be better defended in federal court in State B. Twenty days after service of the initial complaint, the doctor files a notice of removal containing a short and plain statement of the grounds for removal, together with a copy of all process, pleadings, and orders served upon the doctor. Five days after being served with the removal notice, the patient moves to remand the case from the federal court in State B to the state court in State B.

Will the case be remanded to the state court?

(A) No, because the doctor properly filed a notice of removal.

(B) No, because remand is improper in diversity jurisdiction cases.

(C) Yes, because the patient did not raise a federal claim.

(D) Yes, because removal was improper.

QUESTION 196

A vacationer is driving a large RV and texting on a cellphone. The vacationer does not notice that the RV has crossed over into oncoming traffic. A motorcyclist, who is exceeding the speed limit, sees the RV in the oncoming lane and swerves to avoid the RV.

If the motorcyclist hadn't swerved, the motorcyclist and RV would have had a head-on collision. However, by swerving, the motorcyclist loses control of the motorcycle and crashes into a bicyclist, who is injured in the crash. The bicyclist files a complaint in federal court, suing the vacationer and the motorcyclist on claims of negligence. The motorcyclist files a claim against the vacationer, also alleging that the vacationer was negligent.

Which of the following describes the nature of the motorcyclist's claim?

(A)   negligence claim

(B)   collateral claim

(C)   cross-claim

(D)   co-defendant claim

QUESTION 197

A plaintiff sues a defendant on a claim of negligence in federal court. The plaintiff seeks $100,000 in damages. The case proceeds to a jury trial. The jury returns a verdict in favor of the plaintiff. Twenty-five days after the judgment is entered, the defendant files a motion for a new trial.

What may the court do when considering the motion?

(A)   Weigh the evidence.

(B)   Dismiss the motion because it was not preserved with a pre-verdict motion for a new trial.

(C)   Dismiss the motion because it was filed more than 15 days after the judgment.

(D)   Ignore the jury's wisdom.

QUESTION 198

A patient from State A sues a doctor from State B in state court in State A. The patient's complaint seeks $100,000 damages for the doctor's alleged negligence regarding treatment the doctor administered in State A to the patient. The doctor wants to remove the case to federal court in State A. Consequently, 22 days after service of the initial complaint on the doctor, the doctor files a notice of removal containing a short and plain statement of the grounds for removal, together with a copy of all process, pleadings, and orders served upon the doctor.

Is removal to the federal court in State A proper?

(A)   No, because although the doctor filed a notice of removal, the doctor did not first file a motion to remove the case to the federal court in State A.

(B)   No, because the doctor removed the case more than 20 days after being served with the initial complaint.

(C)   Yes, because the doctor properly filed the notice of removal.

(D)   Yes, because claims in which the relief sought exceeds $75,000 must be litigated in federal court due to the amount in controversy.

QUESTION 199

A musician enters into a contractual relationship with a management company and a record label. The contract governs royalties from sales of music, as well as production cost advances for recording albums, and a requirement that the musician record three albums of new material in the next five years. The contract also contains terms and obligations that affect the management company, including the direct payment from the record label to the management company of a percentage of royalties from album sales. The musician seeks rescission of the contract on grounds that the record label made material misrepresentations during the contract negotiations that occurred among the parties. The musician sues the record label in federal court. The court dismisses the case.

Was it proper for the court to dismiss the case?

(A) No, because the musician is master of the complaint and is entitled to sue whomever is alleged to have made material misrepresentations during the contractual negotiations.

(B) No, because the management company was a dispensable party.

(C) Yes, because the management company was an indispensable party.

(D) Yes, because requiring three albums of new material within five years is not materially unreasonable.

QUESTION 200

A driver is involved in a collision on a highway with a trucker. The trucker files a lawsuit based on a claim of negligence against the driver in federal court. The driver answers the complaint, and the parties complete discovery and proceed to a trial by jury. The jury enters a verdict in favor of

the trucker, and judgment is entered. The driver files a motion for a new trial, and the court grants the motion.

Which of the following explains why the court granted the motion?

(A) The court found that, although it wasn't a miscarriage of justice, the jury's verdict was contrary to the weight of the evidence.

(B) The court found that the trucker's witnesses lacked credibility, and therefore, the evidence was sharply in conflict.

(C) The court found potential error that might have affected the trial's outcome.

(D) The court found that the award of damages was excessive.

QUESTION 201

A trucker from State A is involved in an accident in State B with a driver from State B. The driver sustains physical injuries and damage to his car in the crash. A passenger from State A was riding with the driver at the time of the crash, but the passenger was unhurt and suffered no damages. The driver files a lawsuit against the trucker in state court in State B based on a claim of negligence, claiming $100,000 in damages. The driver does not want to litigate the matter in federal court, so to avoid federal jurisdiction, the driver joins the passenger to the lawsuit. The trucker files a timely and proper notice of removal to federal court in State B.

May the trucker remove the case to federal court in State B?

(A) No, because the driver properly added a non-diverse party in order to defeat diversity jurisdiction.

(B) No, because the trucker is not a resident of State B.

(C) Yes, because the driver improperly added a non-diverse party in order to defeat diversity jurisdiction.

(D) Yes, because most, if not all, cases can be removed to federal court upon the filing of a timely and proper notice of removal to federal court.

QUESTION 202

A cattle rancher and a dairy farmer each own land situated downstream from a factory. For a period of several days, the factory produces emissions and waste runoff that flows into the stream. The farmer's cows become sick, and many die after drinking from the stream. The rancher's cattle become sick and weak, and the rancher experiences a loss of sales. The factory becomes aware of the contamination, and within one week, the factory is able to stop ongoing contamination of the stream. Nevertheless, the rancher and farmer sue the factory in a single action in which the complaint alleges that the factory's negligence caused the rancher $110,000 in damages and caused the farmer $90,000 in damages.

Is it permissible for the rancher and farmer to sue the factory in this case?

(A) No, because the farmer is not an indispensable party.

(B) No, because plaintiffs may not join together in suing a single defendant.

(C) Yes, because the rancher and farmer asserted a right to relief that arose out of the same event, with a common question of law or fact.

(D) Yes, because any plaintiff may always join with another plaintiff in a lawsuit.

QUESTION 203

A driver is involved in a collision on a highway with a trucker. The trucker files a lawsuit based on a claim of negligence against the driver in federal court. The driver answers the complaint, and the parties complete discovery and proceed to a trial by jury. The jury enters a verdict in favor of the trucker, and judgment is entered. Ten days after the verdict and judgment is entered, the driver becomes aware of facts showing that during voir dire a juror did not disclose the juror's continuing romantic relationship with the trucker.

What should the driver do?

(A) Move for change of venue.

(B) Move for judgment as a matter of law.

(C) Move for a new trial.

(D) Move for an ex parte hearing with the judge to explain the inherent bias of the juror's misconduct.

QUESTION 204

A trucker from State A was involved in an accident in State B with a driver from State B. The driver sustained physical injuries and damage to his car in the crash, but the total amount of the driver's damages is less than $70,000. A passenger, who is from

State B, was riding with the driver at the time. The passenger suffered no more than $10,000 in damages. The driver filed a lawsuit against the trucker in state court in State B based on a claim of negligence. The driver was concerned the trucker might attempt to remove the case to the federal court in State B, so for the purpose of preventing removal, the driver did not join the passenger to the lawsuit, and the driver's complaint seeks less than the jurisdictional amount necessary to satisfy the amount in controversy for federal diversity jurisdiction.

Are the driver's actions proper in attempting to prevent removal of the case to federal court?

(A) No, because it is improper to deliberately prevent removal of a case to federal court when the defendant is not a resident of the forum state.

(B) No, because although it may be proper to deliberately prevent removal of a case to federal court in some cases, the driver filed his complaint fraudulently in order to prevent removal.

(C) Yes, because the accident occurred in State B.

(D) Yes, because a plaintiff may prevent removal by not pleading damages sufficient to allow removal and not joining a diverse party.

QUESTION 205

A fast-food restaurant hired a contractor to install new siding on the outside of the restaurant. The contractor hired a laborer to install the siding. The contractor knows that the laborer has been known to drink a "liquid lunch" of several beers. While

working on the siding on the restaurant, the laborer backs the contractor's truck full of new siding into a customer's car during the afternoon. The customer's car, a new Corvette, is destroyed in the accident. The customer seeks $80,000 in damages, but is unsure of who may be sued. After consulting an attorney who provides pro bono services, the customer files a single action based on negligence in federal court against the contractor and the laborer.

Is the customer's lawsuit against the contractor and laborer permissible?

(A) No, because the laborer drove the truck while intoxicated.

(B) No, because plaintiffs must choose a single defendant when filing a lawsuit.

(C) Yes, because the plaintiff is master of the complaint and may always join any defendant to an action, regardless of whether the claims arise from a single transaction.

(D) Yes, because the claim arises from a single transaction with a common issue of fact or law.

QUESTION 206

A mechanic installs a new set of brakes on a driver's BMW. After leaving the mechanic's shop, the brakes fail to work on the BMW, and the driver veers off the road and crashes into a tree. The driver sues the mechanic in federal court, claiming that the mechanic was negligent. The driver's complaint alleges $85,000 in damages. The case proceeds to a trial by jury. The jury finds for the driver and awards $80,000 in damages. Two months after the judgment is entered, the mechanic hires an expert BMW brake technician to examine the BMW's brakes. The expert would have been available to inspect the BMW before trial, but the mechanic chose not to use the expert's services. The BMW has not been driven since the accident. The expert technician examines the BMW and prepares a report indicating that the mechanic's brake installation was not faulty. The mechanic, ecstatic for having obtained this new information, files a Rule 60 motion for relief from the final judgment on the grounds that newly discovered evidence requires relief.

Should the court grant the motion?

(A) No, because the evidence could have been obtained with due diligence.

(B) No, because a Rule 60 motion cannot be granted on a claim of newly discovered evidence.

(C) Yes, because the failure to obtain the expert's report was due to excusable neglect.

(D) Yes, because an expert prepared the report.

QUESTION 207

A patient from State A sues a doctor from State B in state court in State A. The patient's complaint seeks $100,000 damages for the doctor's alleged negligence regarding treatment the doctor administered in State A to the patient. The doctor wants to remove the case to federal court in State A. Consequently, 20 days after service of the initial complaint on the doctor, and before the doctor has answered the complaint or presented defenses, the doctor files a notice of removal containing a short and plain statement of the grounds for removal,

together with a copy of all process, pleadings, and orders served upon the doctor. The doctor begins preparing an answer to the complaint and plans to file it 30 days after having removed the case to federal court. Ten days after the doctor files the notice of removal, the patient requests the court to enter a default judgment.

Has the doctor's plan regarding the filing of his answer created exposure to a risk of a default judgment?

(A) No, because the doctor filed a timely notice of removal.

(B) No, because the doctor planned to answer the complaint 30 days after removing the case to federal court.

(C) Yes, because the doctor planned to answer the complaint 30 days after removing the case to federal court.

(D) Yes, because the doctor filed a fraudulent notice of removal.

QUESTION 208

An elderly owner of a parcel of land is involved in a legal dispute with a neighbor over the boundaries of the parcel of land. Although the owner has hired an experienced attorney, the owner's adult son, who is to receive the parcel of land upon the owner's death, is worried over what may happen to his inheritance as a result of the legal proceedings.

Which of the following choices is the son's best argument as to how he may participate in the ongoing litigation?

(A) The son may assist his father, the owner, as pro se co-counsel.

(B) The son has a right to intervene in the action in order to protect his inheritance interest that may be affected by the litigation.

(C) The son has a right to file an amicus curiae brief on behalf of his father, the owner.

(D) The son may observe the proceedings in the courtroom, but he may have no participation in the case.

QUESTION 209

A mechanic installs a new set of brakes on a driver's BMW. After leaving the mechanic's shop, the brakes fail to work on the BMW, and the driver veers off the road and crashes into a tree. The driver sues the mechanic in federal court, claiming that the mechanic was negligent. The driver's complaint alleges $85,000 in damages. The case proceeds to a trial by jury. The jury finds for the driver and awards $85,000 in damages. A clerical mistake on the written judgment indicates that the award of damages was $8,500. A week after entry of the erroneous written judgment, the court, on its own motion, corrects the judgment to reflect the jury award of $85,000.

Was it proper for the court to correct the judgment?

(A) No, because an error in a judgment may not be corrected, absent consent of the parties.

(B) No, because the court may not correct a mistake in a judgment on its own initiative.

(C) Yes, because the court may correct a mistake in a judgment on its own

initiative.

(D) Yes, because 30 days had not yet expired since the judgment was entered.

QUESTION 210

While traveling for the first time in State A, a vacationer from State B is involved in a car accident in State A with a driver from State A. The vacationer files a negligence claim in federal court in State B, seeking $80,000 in damages. The vacationer, knowing that the driver needs a new car, sends the driver a notice that the driver has won a contest in State B. The notice states that the prize for winning the contest is a new Cadillac, which must be accepted in person. The vacationer does not intend to give the driver a prize, but the vacationer hopes the driver will travel to State B so that the driver can be served with process in State B. The driver does not know that the vacationer is responsible for the notice, and the driver travels to State B for the purpose of accepting the prize. However, upon arrival in State B at the location specified in the prize notice, the driver is served with process. Disgusted and angry after being served with process, the driver immediately leaves State B and says, "That was my first and last trip to that awful state!"

Does the court have personal jurisdiction over the driver?

(A) No, because the driver was not served with process in the driver's state of domicile.

(B) No, because the vacationer lured the driver into the forum state.

(C) Yes, because the driver was involved

in an accident with the vacationer, who is domiciled in State B.

(D) Yes, because the driver was served with process in the forum state.

QUESTION 211

A trucker, who works for a trucking company, is texting on a cellphone while driving the company's truck. The trucker does not notice that the truck has crossed over into oncoming traffic. A motorcyclist sees the trucker in the oncoming lane and swerves to avoid a crash. If the motorcyclist hadn't swerved, the motorcyclist and trucker would have had a head-on collision. However, by swerving, the motorcyclist loses control of the motorcycle and crashes into a tree. The motorcyclist sustains serious physical injuries in the crash and sues the company. The company brings a third-party complaint against the trucker based on a claim for indemnity.

What is the name of the process by which the company added the truck driver to the lawsuit?

(A) Impleader

(B) Intervention

(C) Interpleader

(D) Interlocker

QUESTION 212

A mechanic installs a new set of brakes on a driver's BMW. After leaving the mechanic's shop, the brakes fail to work on the BMW, and the driver veers off the road and crashes into a tree. The driver sues the mechanic in federal court, claiming that the mechanic was negligent. The driver's complaint alleges $85,000 in damages. The case proceeds to a trial by jury. The jury finds for the driver and awards $80,000 in damages. Ninety-five days after entry of the judgment, the mechanic files a Rule 60 motion based on a claim of misconduct of the driver.

May the court consider the motion?

(A) No, because it was filed more than 30 days after the entry of the judgment.

(B) No, because it was filed more than 90 days after the entry of the judgment.

(C) Yes, because it was filed less than two years after the entry of the judgment.

(D) Yes, because it was filed less than four months after the entry of the judgment.

QUESTION 213

A patient from State A sues a doctor from State C in state court in State B. The patient's complaint seeks $100,000 damages for the doctor's alleged negligence. On the advice of the doctor's attorney, the doctor decides that the suit will be better defended in federal court in State B. Twenty days after service of the initial complaint, the doctor files a notice of removal containing a short and plain statement of the grounds for removal, together with a copy of all process, pleadings, and orders served upon the doctor. Sixty days after being served with the removal notice, the patient moves to remand the case from the federal court in State B to the state court in State B.

Should the federal court grant the motion for remand?

(A) No, because the doctor may only remove the case to federal court in State C.

(B) No, because the patient filed the motion for remand more than 30 days from being served with the removal notice.

(C) Yes, because the patient filed the motion for remand within 90 days from being served with the removal notice.

(D) Yes, because removal was improper.

QUESTION 214

A trucker, who works for a trucking company, is texting on a cellphone while driving the company's truck. The trucker does not notice that the truck has crossed over into oncoming traffic. A motorcyclist sees the trucker in the oncoming lane and swerves to avoid a crash. If the motorcyclist hadn't swerved, the motorcyclist and trucker would have had a head-on collision. However, by swerving, the motorcyclist loses control of the motorcycle and crashes into a tree. The motorcyclist sustains serious physical injuries in the crash and sues the company. Ten days after the company serves the answer, the company—without leave of court—serves the truck driver with a third-party complaint based on indemnity.

Was it proper for the company to serve the truck driver with the third-party complaint?

(A) No, because the company did not first obtain leave of court to serve the complaint.

(B) No, because more than 7 days had elapsed since the company served its answer.

(C) Yes, because 14 days had not yet elapsed since the company served its answer.

(D) Yes, because 30 days had not yet elapsed since the company served its answer.

QUESTION 215

A mechanic installs a new set of brakes on a driver's BMW. After leaving the mechanic's shop, the brakes fail to work on the BMW, and the driver veers off the road and crashes into a tree. The driver sues the mechanic in federal court, claiming that the mechanic was negligent. The amount of medical expenses for the driver is in dispute; however, the parties agree that replacement value for the BMW is $77,000. After pleadings have concluded, the driver files a motion for summary judgment. The court denies the motion, but the court issues an order establishing the amount of damages as to the replacement value of the BMW.

Was it proper for the court to issue the order establishing damages?

(A) No, because the court did not grant the motion for summary judgment.

(B) No, because a court may not issue an order establishing a material fact in the case.

(C) Yes, because if a court does not grant a motion for summary judgment, the court may issue an order establishing a material fact that is not genuinely in dispute.

(D) Yes, because the replacement value of the BMW exceeded the amount in controversy requirement.

QUESTION 216

A guitar teacher from State A teaches students from his home. To facilitate public interest in music in general, the guitar teacher also operates and owns a website that showcases some of the guitar teacher's original musical compositions, which viewers of the website can stream via the internet; however, no information can be downloaded or uploaded to the website. The website also contains information on the history and development of the guitar, and it includes a short instructional video on how to string and tune a guitar. The website has a biography page that includes a list of the guitar teacher's musical accomplishments, and it also states that the guitar teacher "operates a small guitar tutoring studio from home." The website contains the guitar teacher's contact information. A prospective student from State B locates the website while searching for guitar teachers on the internet. While trying to tune a guitar in State B while watching the instructional video, one of the guitar's strings breaks and slices the cornea of the prospective student's eye, resulting in the need for medical treatment. The prospective student files a lawsuit based on a claim of negligence against the guitar teacher in federal court in State B, claiming $85,000 in damages. The guitar teacher challenges the federal court's personal jurisdiction.

Will the guitar teacher be successful in challenging the federal court's personal jurisdiction?

(A) No, because the website can be accessed anywhere, thereby exposing the guitar teacher to personal jurisdiction in any forum where the website is accessed.

(B) No, because the guitar teacher negligently operated the website.

(C) Yes, because there is no evidence that the guitar teacher negligently operated the website.

(D) Yes, because the website is passive.

QUESTION 217

A trucker from State A, who works for a trucking company from State B, is texting on a cellphone while driving the company's truck. The trucker does not notice that the truck has crossed over into oncoming traffic. A motorcyclist from State A sees the trucker in the oncoming lane and swerves to avoid a crash. If the motorcyclist hadn't swerved, the motorcyclist and trucker would have had a head-on collision. However, by swerving, the motorcyclist loses control of the motorcycle and crashes into a tree. The motorcyclist sustains serious physical injuries in the crash and sues the company in federal court. The company timely serves the truck driver with a third-party complaint based on indemnity. The trucker files a motion to dismiss on the ground that the court does not have subject-matter jurisdiction over the claim because there is no diversity jurisdiction.

Should the court grant the trucker's motion to dismiss?

(A) No, because the third-party claim falls within the federal court's supplemental jurisdiction.

(B) No, because by filing the motion to

dismiss the trucker consented to the court's subject-matter jurisdiction, thereby waiving that defense.

(C)   Yes, because both the trucker and the motorcyclist are from State A.

(D)   Yes, because the company's third-party claim does not raise a federal question.

QUESTION 218

A patient from State A sues a doctor from State B in federal court in State B. The patient's complaint seeks $100,000 damages for the doctor's alleged negligence. Sixty days after filing the complaint, the patient personally serves the doctor with the complaint by visiting the doctor's office in State B and handing the summons and complaint to the doctor.

Was service of the summons and complaint proper?

(A)   No, because the service was untimely.

(B)   No, because the patient personally handed the summons and complaint to the doctor.

(C)   Yes, because the service was timely.

(D)   Yes, because the patient personally handed the summons and complaint to the doctor.

QUESTION 219

In an isolated area of the United States, a cattle rancher and a dairy farmer each own land situated downstream from a factory. For a period of several days, the factory produces emissions and waste runoff that flows into the stream. The farmer's cows become sick, and many die after drinking from the stream. The rancher's cattle become sick and weak, and the rancher experiences a loss of sales. The factory becomes aware of the contamination, and within one week, the factory is able to stop further contamination of the stream. The rancher and the dairy farmer are the only parties who suffer a loss due to the temporary contamination of the stream's water. The rancher and the dairy farmer believe that the factory's negligence caused the contamination.

May the rancher and the dairy farmer bring a class action lawsuit against the factory?

(A)   No, because joinder is not impractical.

(B)   No, because the claim will be based on negligence.

(C)   Yes, because common questions of law and fact exist between the rancher and the dairy farmer.

(D)   Yes, because the rancher and dairy farmer will share the same legal theory of recovery (i.e., negligence).

QUESTION 220

An inventor from State A holds a patent for a device that increases fuel economy in gasoline-fueled combustion engines. An opportunist from State B learns of the inventor's device and begins manufacturing and selling an identical device, marketing it as the opportunist's own invention.

The inventor files a complaint against the opportunist in federal court in State B. The inventor's complaint sought $500,000 in damages and alleged patent infringement under federal law. Three months after the filing of the complaint, the opportunist is served with the summons and complaint while on vacation in State C enjoying the profits from the sale of the device. The summons and complaint were personally served on the opportunist by the inventor's 18-year old cousin from Pennsylvania, who has no stake in the inventor's claim.

Has the opportunist received proper notice?

(A) No, because the opportunist was served with the summons and complaint in State C, which is outside the personal jurisdiction of the forum court in State B.

(B) No, because the inventor's cousin served the complaint and summons.

(C) Yes, even though the opportunist was served with the summons and complaint in State C, which is outside the personal jurisdiction of the forum court.

(D) Yes, even though the service was untimely, the inventor had good cause for the late service due to the opportunist's vacation in another forum.

QUESTION 221

A brother, sister, and nephew each claim sole entitlement to the proceeds of an insurance policy. The insurance company is concerned about who is the proper beneficiary. On the advice of counsel, the insurance company files a lawsuit requiring the brother, sister, and nephew to assert their respective claims in a lawsuit.

Which of the following is correct?

(A) The insurance company is a stakeholder in a severance action.

(B) The insurance company is a stakeholder in an interpleader action.

(C) The court should dismiss the case because the insurance company may not file a lawsuit requiring the brother, sister, and nephew to assert their respective claims in a lawsuit.

(D) The insurance company has filed a class action against the brother, sister, and nephew.

QUESTION 222

A driver from State A was operating a 1963 Corvette Stingray sports car on a highway in State A and was involved in a crash with a motorcyclist from State B, which is located 150 miles from State A. Besides the driver and motorcyclist, there was one witness to the accident, a truck driver from State B. The motorcyclist was injured in the crash, and State B's police and paramedics responded to the scene. The paramedics treated the motorcyclist, and the motorcyclist was hospitalized in State B as a result of the accident. The motorcyclist believed that the accident was caused by the driver's recklessness, and the motorcyclist filed a negligence claim against the driver in federal court in State A, seeking $80,000 in damages. The federal court in State A dismissed the case.

Which of the following is the best explanation for why the court dismissed the case?

(A) The court applied the doctrine of forum casus fortuitous.

(B) The court applied the doctrine of forum in curia.

(C) The court applied the doctrine of forum in loco parentis.

(D) The court applied the doctrine of forum non conveniens.

QUESTION 223

The prospective plaintiffs in a class action seek recovery based on a products liability theory against a manufacturer of car seats for babies. In attempting to certify the class action, the plaintiffs demonstrate that common questions of law and fact exist among the members of the class and that the sheer number of class members would make joinder of all plaintiffs impractical. The attorney selected to represent the plaintiffs in the class action is a newly licensed attorney in the first year of law practice. The attorney has no prior experience with class actions.

Must the court take any action regarding the attorney?

(A) No, because the court may not become involved in a plaintiff's selection of attorney in a class action.

(B) No, because the attorney is a licensed member of the bar.

(C) Yes, because the court must ensure that the counsel for the class is experienced and qualified to carry out the litigation.

(D) Yes, because the constitutional

standard of strict scrutiny must be applied.

QUESTION 224

A cartoonist from State A creates a series of unique characters and properly obtains the copyright for the characters. The cartoonist uses the characters in a comic strip printed in a widely circulated newspaper. The characters also appear in the electronic, on-line version of the newspaper. A struggling filmmaker from State A sees the cartoonist's work in the electronic version of the newspaper and uses the characters in a short film, which ultimately is picked up by a major studio in State A and released in theaters. The cartoonist learns of the film and sues the filmmaker and the film studio in federal court in State A. The complaint is based on federal copyright law. The filmmaker moves to dismiss the case for lack of federal subject-matter jurisdiction. The basis of the motion is that the parties lack diversity of citizenship.

Should the court grant the motion to dismiss?

(A) No, because the complaint states a claim based on federal law.

(B) No, because the filmmaker may not challenge the federal court's jurisdiction until discovery is complete.

(C) Yes, because the parties do not have diversity of citizenship.

(D) Yes, because copyright claims may not be litigated in federal court.

QUESTION 225

A trucker is traveling at a high rate of speed during a rainstorm. The trucker loses control of the truck and is involved in an accident with a driver. A motorcyclist, who was parked under an overpass waiting for the storm to pass, saw the accident occur. The motorcyclist speaks with law enforcement and paramedics who arrive on the scene. The driver files a claim based on negligence in federal court. The complaint alleges that the trucker negligently operated the truck and caused $100,000 in damages. The driver wants to depose the motorcyclist, so he calls the motorcyclist on the phone to set a time and place for the deposition. The driver and his attorney meet with the motorcyclist and conduct a deposition. The deposition is not conducted in the courthouse. After the deposition, the driver's attorney provides a transcript of the motorcyclist's sworn deposition testimony to the trucker, who is surprised to learn that the motorcyclist has been deposed.

Was the deposition proper?

(A) No, because the driver did not give reasonable notice to the trucker.

(B) No, because the deposition took place outside of court.

(C) Yes, because the motorcyclist was under oath.

(D) Yes, because a transcript of the deposition was provided to the trucker.

QUESTION 226

A plaintiff sues a defendant on a claim based on state law that could also support a federal claim. The plaintiff, however, relies exclusively on state law to present the claim. The amount in controversy is $100,000.

On these facts, would a federal court have federal question subject-matter jurisdiction over the case?

(A) No, because the claim does not satisfy the Well-Pleaded Diversity Rule.

(B) No, because the plaintiff relied exclusively on state law to present the claim.

(C) Yes, because although the claim is based on state law, it could also support a federal claim.

(D) Yes, because the amount in controversy exceeds the required jurisdictional amount.

QUESTION 227

A computer geek invents and patents an unbreakable screen for smartphones. Without the geek's knowledge, an unscrupulous corporation begins manufacturing smartphones that use the geek's design for smartphone screens. The geek sues the corporation in federal court on a claim of patent infringement. The geek wants the corporation to produce certain documents in discovery.

What should the geek do to obtain the desired information?

(A) Serve a subpoena ad testificandum on the corporation.

(B) Serve a subpoena ad prosequendum on the corporation.

(C) Serve a subpoena quo warranto on the

corporation.

(D)   Serve a subpoena duces tecum on the corporation.

QUESTION 228

A plaintiff sues a defendant on a state-law cause of action. In the complaint, the plaintiff anticipates a federal defense and properly asserts that the federal defense is not sufficient to defeat the plaintiff's claim.

On these facts, would a federal court have federal question subject-matter jurisdiction over the case?

(A)   No, because a federal defense is insufficient to confer federal question jurisdiction.

(B)   No, because the defendant has not yet had a fair opportunity to present the federal defense.

(C)   Yes, because a federal defense is always sufficient to invoke federal question jurisdiction.

(D)   Yes, because federal courts have federal question jurisdiction over all claims that arise under state law, as long as the complaint is filed in federal court.

QUESTION 229

A trucker is traveling at a high rate of speed during a rainstorm. The trucker loses control of the truck and is involved in an accident with a driver. A motorcyclist, who was parked under an overpass waiting for the storm to clear, saw the accident occur. The motorcyclist speaks with law enforcement and paramedics who arrive on the scene. The driver would like to conduct a deposition of the motorcyclist before filing a case against the trucker.

May the driver seek a deposition of the motorcyclist?

(A)   No, because an actual case has not been filed in court.

(B)   No, because the motorcyclist is not a party to the case.

(C)   Yes, because the driver may file a verified petition for a pre-filing deposition in the federal court in the trucker's county of residence.

(D)   Yes, because a petitioner may depose any potential witness as a matter of right at any time without notice.

QUESTION 230

A magician from State A performs a magic show at a theater in State B. During the performance, the magician asks for a volunteer from the audience to assist with an illusion. An audience member, who is from State A, volunteers. While the volunteer is walking on the wooden stage, the volunteer trips on a board that has become loose. The volunteer falls and sustains a broken wrist. The volunteer sues the theater manager, who is from State B, in federal court in State B on a claim based on negligence regarding the condition of the stage. The volunteer seeks $80,000 in damages. The theater manager moves to dismiss the case, arguing that the court does not have subject-matter jurisdiction because the magician and the volunteer do not have diversity of citizenship.

Should the court grant the theater's motion?

(A) No, because the volunteer and the theater manager have complete diversity of citizenship.

(B) No, because this case involves a federal question.

(C) Yes, because the magician and the volunteer are both from State A.

(D) Yes, because the amount in controversy is not satisfied and the magician and the volunteer are both from State A.

QUESTION 231

A trucker is traveling at a high rate of speed during a rainstorm. The trucker loses control of the truck and is involved in an accident with a driver. A motorcyclist, who was parked under an overpass waiting for the storm to clear, saw the accident occur. The motorcyclist speaks with law enforcement and paramedics who arrive on the scene. The driver would like to submit written questions to the motorcyclist in order to receive written answers under oath. Consequently, without leave of court, the driver serves the motorcyclist with interrogatories.

Did the driver follow proper procedure?

(A) No, because interrogatories may only be served on a party.

(B) No, because the driver did not obtain leave of court to file the interrogatories.

(C) Yes, because interrogatories may be

served on a party or potential witness.

(D) Yes, because interrogatories may only be served on a witness or potential witness.

QUESTION 232

A bicyclist from State A is involved in a collision with a jogger from State B, in State B. During the collision, the jogger sustains injuries when the bicyclist runs over the jogger's leg. Due to a rare medical condition, the jogger's leg fractures in an unusual manner during the collision, and the injury requires a surgical procedure. Subsequently, the jogger files a claim against the bicyclist in federal court in State A, alleging that the bicyclist's negligence caused the injuries. The jogger alleges that the damages total $75,000, plus $20,000 in interest and costs. The bicyclist moves to dismiss the case for lack of subject-matter jurisdiction.

Should the court grant the bicyclist's motion?

(A) No, because the parties are diverse, and the amount in controversy requirement is satisfied by the $75,000 total in damages.

(B) No, because the parties are diverse, and the interests and costs combined with the total damages exceed the amount in controversy.

(C) Yes, because the amount in controversy requirement is not satisfied.

(D) Yes, because the citizenship of the court and the bicyclist are not diverse.

QUESTION 233

A computer geek invents and patents an unbreakable screen for smartphones. Without the geek's knowledge, an unscrupulous corporation begins manufacturing smartphones that use the geek's design for smartphone screens. The geek sues the corporation in federal court on a claim of patent infringement. The corporation serves the geek with a set of interrogatories consisting of a total of 25 questions. The geek serves his answers to the interrogatories 25 days after having been served with the interrogatories.

Did the geek timely serve the answers to the interrogatories?

(A) No, because the answers were not served within 10 days of being served with the interrogatories.

(B) No, because the answers were not served within 14 days of being served with the interrogatories.

(C) Yes, because the answers were served within 30 days of being served with the interrogatories.

(D) Yes, because the answers were served within 60 days of being served with the interrogatories.

QUESTION 234

A carpenter from State A enters into a contract with a company, in which the carpenter is to be paid $40,000 to construct customized wood shelving units throughout the company's home office and principal place of business, located in State B. The carpenter completes the work, but the company fails to pay the carpenter as

required by the contract.

A plumber from State C enters a contract with the same company. The plumber, pursuant to the terms of the contract, is to be paid $50,000 to update the plumbing throughout the company's home office and principal place of business. The plumber completes the work, but the company fails to pay the plumber as required by the contract.

May the carpenter and the plumber aggregate their claims together and sue the company in federal court?

(A) No, the carpenter and the plumber may not aggregate their individual claims against the company, regardless of how similar the claims are.

(B) No, because the Federal Rules do not provide for aggregation of claims.

(C) Yes, because the claims are sufficiently related to permit aggregation.

(D) Yes, because aggregation is necessary to meet the amount in controversy requirement.

QUESTION 235

A trucker is traveling at a high rate of speed during a rainstorm. The trucker loses control of the truck and is involved in an accident with a driver. The driver files a claim in federal court alleging that the trucker's negligence caused the accident. The driver serves the trucker with a request for admission regarding an issue of fact. Forty-five days later, the trucker has not yet responded to the request for admission.

Will the issue of fact be construed as an

admission?

(A) No, because the trucker has 60 days in which to respond to a request for an admission.

(B) No, because failure to respond to a request for admission may not be construed as an admission.

(C) Yes, because failure to serve a response to a request for an admission within 30 days may be construed as an admission.

(D) Yes, because failure to serve a response to a request for an admission within 14 days may be construed as an admission.

QUESTION 236

A contractor from State A enters into a contract with a homeowner from State B in which the contractor agrees to build a guesthouse for the homeowner. The contractor fails to complete the project as required by the contract.

The homeowner runs a barbershop, as a sole proprietor. The contractor goes to the barbershop and, during a shave, he receives a serious cut that requires stitches. The injury is unrelated to the contract case.

The homeowner sues the contractor in federal court on a claim of breach of contract, seeking $80,000 in damages. The contractor files a counterclaim against the homeowner, based on negligence. The contractor's counterclaim alleges that the homeowner's negligence caused the cut that required stitches, and the contractor seeks $3,000 in damages.

Does the federal court have subject-matter jurisdiction over the contractor's claim?

(A) No, because the contractor did not file the initial lawsuit.

(B) No, because the contractor's permissive counterclaim does not independently fulfill the jurisdictional amount requirement.

(C) Yes, because the contractor's permissive counterclaim need not independently fulfill the jurisdictional amount requirement.

(D) Yes, because the contractor's claim is a compulsory counterclaim.

QUESTION 237

A computer geek invents and patents an unbreakable screen for smartphones. Without the geek's knowledge, an unscrupulous corporation begins manufacturing smartphones that use the geek's design for smartphone screens. The geek sues the corporation in federal court on a claim of patent infringement. The geek requests that the corporation produce certain electronically stored information relevant to the lawsuit. Without court order or agreement from the corporation, the request specifies that the corporation produce the same information in three formats: a USB thumb drive, an external hard drive, and on CD-ROM.

Must the corporation produce the requested information in the three formats specified by the geek?

(A) No, because the parties did not agree to the multiple formats, nor did the court order multiple formats for production.

(B) No, because a party may not request production of electronically stored information maintained in the course of business.

(C) Yes, because a party is required to produce electronically stored information in the formats specified by the party making the request when the information is relevant to the issues at stake in the lawsuit.

(D) Yes, because of the changing technological methods in which electronic information is stored, a party is required to produce electronically stored information in multiple formats to permit easy access by the requesting party.

QUESTION 238

A chiropractor from State A treats a patient from State B. Subsequent to the treatment, the patient suffers from debilitating pain. The patient seeks medical treatment elsewhere, and learns that the chiropractor likely caused a spinal injury. The patient sues the chiropractor in state court. The chiropractor properly files a notice of removal. Twenty-one days after the service of the notice of removal, the patient serves a demand for a trial by jury.

Did the patient timely serve the demand for a trial by jury?

(A) Yes, because the demand was served within 30 days after the chiropractor filed the notice of removal.

(B) Yes, because the demand was served

within 60 days after the chiropractor filed the notice of removal.

(C) No, because the demand was not served within 14 days of the service of the notice of removal.

(D) No, because the demand was not served within 7 days of the service of the notice of removal.

QUESTION 239

On July 4, a driver was operating a 1963 Corvette Stingray sports car on a highway and was involved in a crash with a motorcyclist. The driver was texting at the time of the crash. Several people witnessed the accident occur, including a passenger in the driver's Corvette. The motorcyclist believed that the accident was caused by the driver's negligence, and the motorcyclist filed a claim in federal court, seeking $175,000 from the driver for injuries sustained in the accident. During discovery, the motorcyclist did not request the names or contact information of persons likely to have discoverable information. Consequently, the driver did not disclose the name and contact information of the passenger.

Was the driver required to disclose the information?

(A) No, because the motorcyclist did not request the information and could have obtained it by the exercise of due diligence.

(B) No, because a party is not required to assist the opposing party in preparing for trial.

(C) Yes, because even without a request, a

party must produce the names and contact information of all persons likely to have discoverable information.

(D) Yes, but the driver need only produce the name of the passenger.

QUESTION 240

An artist who has relocated to State A is hired by a business owner from State B to paint a mural on a wall in the conference room of the business. The business owner desires to impress potential clients with the mural. The mural is planned to be a copy of Michelangelo's artwork in the Sistine Chapel. However, the artist fails to begin the project, deciding that painting is a waste of time and sculpting is a better outlet for creativity. The business owner sues the artist in State A in federal court, on a claim of breach of contract. The artist challenges the court's personal jurisdiction. After examining the artist's registrations, as well as property and tax records, the court finds that the artist is domiciled in State A, and therefore, the court has personal jurisdiction over the artist.

Was it proper for the court to consider the registrations and property and tax records?

(A) No, because a court may not examine property and tax records or registrations to determine domicile.

(B) No, because the court did not apply a subjective test to determine domicile.

(C) Yes, although it was unnecessary to do so because the artist had a physical presence in the state, which is sufficient in and of itself to establish

the court's personal jurisdiction.

(D) Yes, because a court examines property and tax records, registrations, and other relevant documents to determine if a state is a person's domicile.

QUESTION 241

On July 4, a driver was operating a 1963 Corvette Stingray sports car on a highway and was involved in a crash with a motorcyclist. The driver was texting at the time of the crash. Several people witnessed the accident occur, including a passenger in the driver's Corvette. The motorcyclist believed that the accident was caused by the driver's negligence, and the motorcyclist filed a claim in federal court, seeking $175,000 from the driver for injuries sustained in the accident. Sixty days before trial, the motorcyclist disclosed that an expert will testify for the motorcyclist at trial.

Was the motorcyclist's disclosure proper?

(A) No, because it was not made at least 90 days prior to trial.

(B) No, because it was not made at least 120 days prior to trial.

(C) Yes, because it was made within 90 days of the trial.

(D) Yes, because it was made within 120 days of the trial.

QUESTION 242

A musician sues a songwriter in federal court on a claim of copyright infringement.

At the beginning of the case, and without seeking affirmative relief, the songwriter appears in court and directly attacks the court's personal jurisdiction. The musician argues that, by voluntarily making an appearance in court, the songwriter submitted to the court's jurisdiction.

Did the songwriter submit to the court's jurisdiction?

(A) No, because in almost all jurisdictions, a party may directly attack the jurisdiction of the court at the beginning of the case without submitting to the court's jurisdiction.

(B) No, because a party may object to a court's personal jurisdiction at any time.

(C) Yes, because in almost all jurisdictions, a party may not directly attack the jurisdiction of the court at the beginning of the case without submitting to the court's jurisdiction.

(D) Yes, because the songwriter did not seek affirmative relief.

QUESTION 243

A trucker is traveling at a high rate of speed during a snowstorm. The trucker loses control of the truck and is involved in an accident with a driver. The driver files a claim based on negligence in federal court. The complaint alleges that the trucker negligently operated the truck and caused $100,000 in damages. The matter is set for trial, and 14 days before the trial, the trucker makes various pretrial disclosures, including the identity of and contact information for witnesses who may be called to testify at trial, the designation of the witnesses whose

testimony will be presented by deposition, along with a transcript of relevant portions of the depositions, and an identification of each document or exhibit that may be offered as evidence at trial.

Were the trucker's pretrial disclosures proper?

(A) No, because they were not made at least 60 days before trial.

(B) No, because they were not made at least 30 days before trial.

(C) Yes, because they were made at least 14 days before trial.

(D) Yes, because pretrial disclosures may be made any time before trial.

QUESTION 244

A chef owns and operates a restaurant in State A. The chef does not advertise the restaurant because it stays busy through word-of-mouth advertising. Nearly all of the restaurant's business is generated from the people who reside in the town in which the restaurant is located. A traveler from State B dines at the restaurant. The chef does not speak with the traveler, but the chef prepares the food that the traveler eats. Six hours after eating in the restaurant, while driving home to State B in an RV, the traveler gets sick and loses control of the RV after having just crossed over the state line. The RV crashes through a guardrail, overturns, and the traveler is injured. The traveler sues the chef in federal court in State B, alleging that the chef's negligence in preparing the food resulted in the traveler's food poisoning, which caused the traveler to get sick and crash the RV, causing the injuries. The chef challenges the court's personal jurisdiction.

Will the chef's challenge to the court's personal jurisdiction be successful?

(A) No, because the chef did not ask the traveler if he was from State B.

(B) No, because the chef did not have sufficient minimum contacts with State B, to reasonably require the chef to appear and defend the lawsuit there.

(C) Yes, because by serving food to the traveler, the chef submitted to the court's personal jurisdiction.

(D) Yes, because the parties are diverse.

QUESTION 245

A jogger is running on a street in a quiet residential area. A motorcyclist is traveling at a high rate of speed and sees the jogger, who is directly in the path of the motorcycle. The motorcyclist swerves to avoid the jogger and loses control of the motorcycle. The motorcyclist veers into the oncoming lane and crashes into a driver of a compact car. The motorcyclist is unhurt in the crash, but the driver is injured when the motorcycle impacts the car. The driver files a lawsuit based on negligence against the motorcyclist in federal court, alleging that the motorcyclist's negligence caused $90,000 in damages. During discovery, the driver does not disclose relevant information that might lead to admissible evidence. The driver reasoned that because the relevant information itself would not be admissible at trial, it did not need to be disclosed.

Did the driver follow proper procedure?

(A) No, because the information is relevant

and might lead to discovery of admissible evidence.

(B) No, because the driver must disclose all relevant information, including attorney work-product.

(C) Yes, because, although the information is relevant, it would not be admissible at trial.

(D) Yes, because a defendant need only disclose information that the plaintiff requests.

QUESTION 246

An online seller from State A sells various products and owns and operates a website that is accessible worldwide. The online seller routinely sells products through the website to residents of State B, and a large portion of those sales are generated by marketing emails sent by the seller to residents of State B. The emails contain a link to the website. The website permits potential customers to view images of the items for sale, and customers can enter their contact, address, and credit card information on the website. A resident of State B accesses the online seller's website in State B and purchases a product. The product malfunctions, and the resident is injured. The resident sues the manufacturer of the product, as well as the online seller, in federal court in State B. The online seller challenges the court's personal jurisdiction.

Will the challenge to the court's personal jurisdiction be successful?

(A) No, because the online seller owns and operates the website.

(B) No, because the website is not passive,

and the online retailer seeks business with State B's residents.

(C) Yes, because the online seller is from State A and is not incorporated in State B.

(D) Yes, because the resident of State B did not access the website while being physically present in State A.

QUESTION 247

An inventor holds a patent for a device that increases fuel economy in gasoline-fueled combustion engines. An opportunist learns of the inventor's device and begins manufacturing and selling an identical device, marketing it as the opportunist's own invention. The inventor sues the opportunist in federal court on a claim of patent infringement. During discovery, the opportunist files a motion to limit discovery on the ground that the expense of the proposed discovery outweighs its likely benefit. After hearing the motion, the court agrees with the opportunist's assertions regarding the proposed discovery.

Should the court grant the opportunist's motion?

(A) No, because the expense of discovery may not be used as an excuse to not disclose information to the opposing party.

(B) No, because a court may not limit the scope of discovery absent agreement of the parties.

(C) Yes, because the expense of the proposed discovery outweighs its likely benefit.

(D) Yes, though the court is not required to grant the motion under the circumstances.

QUESTION 248

A plaintiff from State A sues a defendant from State B in federal court in State C. The complaint is based on a tort allegedly committed by the defendant in State C. State C has a "long-arm" statute that provides that a person's commission of a tort within the state subjects the person to the personal jurisdiction of the state's courts. The defendant challenges the federal court's personal jurisdiction, on the basis that the state's long-arm statute does not apply to the federal case.

Will the defendant's challenge be successful?

(A) No, because the general federal long-arm statute applies to this case.

(B) No, because a federal court may use the long-arm statute of the forum state in which it is located.

(C) Yes, because the general federal long-arm statute does not apply to this case.

(D) Yes, because a federal court may not use the long-arm statute of the forum state in which it is located.

QUESTION 249

A trucker who works for a trucking company is traveling at a high rate of speed during a snowstorm while working for the company. The trucker loses control of the truck and is involved in an accident with a driver. The company prepares a report to address a threat of imminent litigation with the driver regarding the accident. Two weeks after the report is completed, the driver files a claim in federal court against the company. The driver seeks $100,000 from the company for damages sustained in the accident. During discovery, the company refuses to disclose the report, claiming that it is not discoverable.

Is the company correct in its assertion that the report is not discoverable?

(A) No, because it is relevant information pertaining to the accident.

(B) No, because the lawsuit was not pending at the time the report was completed.

(C) Yes, because the company need only disclose the report upon motion by the driver.

(D) Yes, because the report was prepared to address a threat of imminent litigation.

QUESTION 250

A sophisticated business owner enters into a contract with a customer. The business owner's team of attorneys drafted the contract. The customer has no significant business or contract experience and was not represented by an attorney during the contract negotiations. The contract contains a forum-selection clause, which states that any legal dispute that arises between the parties will be litigated in State A. State A is the state in which the business owner resides, and that is the only connection of the forum to the contract. The customer lives in State B, which is located 1,600 miles from State A.

A legal dispute arises between the parties, and the business owner files a lawsuit against the customer in State A, as provided by the forum-selection clause. The customer challenges the court's personal jurisdiction. The business owner argues that the court should exercise personal jurisdiction over the customer because the existence of the forum-selection clause in the contract is dispositive of the issue.

Will the customer's challenge to the court's personal jurisdiction be successful?

(A) No, because the existence of a forum-selection clause in a contract is dispositive of the issue.

(B) No, because by challenging the court's jurisdiction, the customer submitted to personal jurisdiction.

(C) Yes, because forum-selection clauses are prohibited.

(D) Yes, because the existence of the forum-selection clause is not dispositive of the issue.

QUESTION 251

A trucker is traveling at a high rate of speed during a snowstorm. The trucker loses control of the truck and is involved in an accident with a driver. The driver files a claim in federal court alleging that the driver's negligence caused the accident and $100,000 in damages to the driver. The trucker had made several transcribed statements about the accident that the driver possesses. The trucker requests copies of those statements from the driver, but the driver refuses to disclose the statements. The trucker files a motion requesting the court to order the driver to disclose the statements.

Should the court grant the motion?

(A) No, because it was the trucker's responsibility to ensure access to the trucker's own statements.

(B) No, because the statements may not have been made in anticipation of litigation.

(C) Yes, and the trucker may be awarded expenses incurred in the filing of the motion.

(D) Yes, but the trucker may not be awarded expenses incurred in the filing of the motion.

QUESTION 252

A driver is involved in an auto accident in State A, with a traveler from State B. The driver initiates an action, in federal court in State C, by seizing property located in State C by means of attachment. Eventually, the case is resolved with a judgment in favor of the plaintiff. The judgment is limited to the value of the property that was seized.

Which of the following choices best identifies the type of jurisdiction exercised as to the traveler?

(A) In personam

(B) In rem

(C) Quasi in rem

(D) Quasi in personam

QUESTION 253

A defendant involved in a claim of patent infringement obtains a court order that requires the plaintiff to disclose certain materials that the plaintiff prepared in anticipation of litigation. The court granted the motion because it found that the materials were otherwise discoverable, the defendant had substantial need for the materials to prepare its case, and the defendant would have been unable, without undue hardship, to obtain the substantial equivalent of the materials by other means.

Which of the following is correct?

(A) The court erred in granting the motion because materials prepared in anticipation are not discoverable.

(B) The court erred in granting the motion because the materials were otherwise discoverable.

(C) The court erred in granting the motion because the defendant could have obtained the substantial equivalent of the materials by other means.

(D) Although it was permissible for the court to grant the motion, the court must protect against disclosure of the mental impressions and conclusions of the plaintiff's lawyer.

QUESTION 254

A contractor from State A enters into a contract with a homeowner from State B, in which the contractor agrees to build a guesthouse for the homeowner. The contractor fails to complete the project as required by the contract, and the homeowner files a complaint in federal court. However, the contractor does not have an attorney. The contractor calls his cousin Vinny, who is studying to be a lawyer, for advice. Vinny tells the contractor that it is necessary for a copy of the complaint and summons to be served on the homeowner. The contractor asks Vinny how service of process is accomplished, and Vinny says, "That's simple. All you need to do is personally take the complaint and summons to the homeowner yourself. That's called personal service." Based on this advice, the contractor personally takes the summons and complaint to the homeowner and delivers the documents into the homeowner's hands.

Was the homeowner properly served with the complaint and summons?

(A) No, because the contractor personally served the complaint and summons.

(B) No, because the contractor should have merely taped the documents to the homeowner's front door.

(C) Yes, because the plaintiff must serve the defendant with the complaint and summons.

(D) Yes, because a defendant in a lawsuit must receive service of process by delivery of the documents in person.

QUESTION 255

A driver was operating a 1963 Corvette Stingray sports car on a highway and was involved in a crash with a motorcyclist. The driver was texting at the time of the crash. The motorcyclist believed that the accident was caused by the driver's negligence, and the motorcyclist filed a claim in federal court, seeking $175,000 from the driver for

injuries sustained in the accident. The motorcyclist hires an expert to testify at trial. The motorcyclist's lawyer and the expert witness communicate through e-mails. One e-mail, dated June 11, concerns the compensation to be paid to the expert for the expert's testimony as well as data provided by the lawyer that the expert considered in forming opinions.

During discovery, is the motorcyclist required to disclose the June 11 e-mail to the driver?

(A) No, because the e-mail was a communication between the motorcyclist's lawyer and the expert witness.

(B) No, because an e-mail is not a physical document.

(C) Yes, because the e-mail concerned compensation for the expert's testimony and data provided by the lawyer that the expert considered in forming opinions.

(D) Yes, because it is improper for an expert to be compensated for testifying.

QUESTION 256

A motorist from State A and a traveler from State B are involved in a collision on a highway in State C. At the time of the accident, the traveler was texting on a cellphone. The motorist files a lawsuit based on negligence, in federal court in State A. The traveler is personally served with the complaint and summons in State B. The traveler challenges the service of process, arguing that the service occurred outside of the court's scope of personal jurisdiction.

Will the traveler's challenge to the service of process be successful?

(A) No, because the traveler had notice of a potential lawsuit due to the traveler's unreasonable act of texting while driving.

(B) No, because service of process may occur outside of the court's scope of personal jurisdiction.

(C) Yes, because service of process may not occur outside of the court's scope of personal jurisdiction.

(D) Yes, because service of process must occur in the forum state and must be accomplished by certified mail.

QUESTION 257

A driver was operating a 1963 Corvette Stingray sports car on a highway and was involved in a crash with a motorcyclist. The driver was texting at the time of the crash. The motorcyclist believed that the accident was caused by the driver's negligence, and the motorcyclist filed a claim in federal court, seeking $175,000 from the driver for injuries sustained in the accident. After researching several accident reconstruction experts, the motorcyclist's lawyer hires one of the experts to serve as a consultant, solely for trial preparation. The expert is not expected to be called as a witness at trial. The expert is aware of various facts in the case and develops several opinions regarding the matter.

During discovery, must the motorcyclist disclose the facts known by the expert and the expert's opinions?

(A) No, because the expert was hired solely for trial preparation and is not expected to testify at trial.

(B) No, because the expert's opinions are not tangible, discoverable materials.

(C) Yes, because a party is entitled to discovery regarding facts known and opinions held by the opposing party's expert.

(D) Yes, because the expert was employed solely for trial preparation and is not expected to testify at trial.

QUESTION 258

A baker, who is a sole proprietor, enters into a contract with a grocer, who is the owner and sole proprietor of a small grocery store, to deliver fresh baked goods to the store by 6 A.M. every day except Sundays. The baker lives in the eastern district of State A and operates the bakery in that same district. The grocer lives in the southern district of State B and operates the grocery store in the western district of State B. The contract negotiations and contract signing took place in the western district of State B. The baker meets his contractual obligations, but the grocer fails to pay the baker as required by the contract. The contract does not include a forum selection clause. The baker wants to file a lawsuit based on breach of contract.

Where would venue be proper?

(A) Venue would be proper only in the western district of State B.

(B) Venue would be proper only in the southern district of State B.

(C) Venue would be proper in State A because the baker lives in State A.

(D) Venue would be proper in the southern or western district of State B.

QUESTION 259

A patient sues a doctor in federal court on a claim of medical malpractice. During discovery, the doctor seeks information from the patient that the patient believes is protected from disclosure as material prepared in anticipation of trial. The patient expressly makes a claim that the material is not discoverable and refuses to disclose the material.

Did the patient follow proper procedure by withholding the materials?

(A) No, because generally, materials that are prepared in anticipation of trial are not protected from discovery.

(B) No, because the patient did not describe the nature of the materials in a way that would permit the doctor to assess the claim.

(C) Yes, because to take any further action would inevitably disclose the privileged information.

(D) Yes, because a plaintiff need not disclose materials to a defendant.

QUESTION 260

A customer, who is a resident of a town in the western district of State A, slips and falls on the floor of a hobby shop located in the western district of State A. A witness, who also is a resident of the western district of State A, saw the customer fall. The owner of the hobby shop lives in the western district of State A. The customer files a

claim against the owner in federal court in the southern district of State A. That federal court, on its own motion, transfers venue to the federal court in the western district of State A.

Was it permissible for the court to transfer venue?

(A) No, because the only remedy for improper venue is dismissal, not transfer.

(B) No, because the court may not, on its own motion, transfer venue.

(C) Yes, because the court may, on its own motion, transfer venue.

(D) Yes, because the only way for venue to be transferred is through a sua sponte motion by the court.

QUESTION 261

A computer geek invents and patents an unbreakable screen for smartphones. Without the geek's knowledge, an unscrupulous corporation begins manufacturing smartphones that use the geek's design for smartphone screens. The geek sues the corporation in federal court on a claim of patent infringement. The geek wants the corporation to produce certain materials in discovery. Without certifying that the corporation conferred or attempted to confer with the geek about the issue, the corporation files a motion for a protective order on the basis that some of the materials sought by the geek contain trade secrets.

Is the corporation's motion properly before the court?

(A) No, because the corporation did not

certify that the corporation, in good faith, conferred or attempted to confer with the geek to try to resolve the dispute over the materials.

(B) No, because the corporation wrongfully used the geek's design.

(C) Yes, because the geek may not seek the corporation's trade secrets during discovery.

(D) Yes, because the corporation need not certify that the corporation conferred or attempted to confer with the geek to try to resolve the dispute over the materials.

QUESTION 262

A plaintiff files a claim in federal court in the eastern district of State A against a defendant. Subsequently, the parties agree that it would be more convenient for the parties and witnesses, as well as promote the interests of justice, for the case to be brought in the western district of State A. However, the case could not have originally been filed in the western district. Nevertheless, the parties consent to a transfer of venue to the federal court in the western district, and the court transfers the case.

Was it proper for the court to transfer the case to the federal court in the western district of State A?

(A) No, because the case could not have originally been filed in the western district.

(B) No, because the parties to a lawsuit may not consent to a change of venue.

(C) Yes, because, whenever the parties

consent to a change of venue, the federal district court must transfer the case to any venue to which the parties have consented.

(D) Yes, because a federal district court may transfer a case to any venue to which the parties have consented, if the transfer would increase the convenience of parties and witnesses and promote the interests of justice.

QUESTION 263

A computer geek invents and patents an unbreakable screen for smartphones. Without the geek's knowledge, an unscrupulous corporation begins manufacturing smartphones that use the geek's design for smartphone screens. The geek sues the corporation in federal court on a claim of patent infringement. The geek wants the corporation to produce certain materials in discovery. The corporation files a motion for a protective order on the basis that some of the materials sought by the geek contain trade secrets. After carefully considering the motion, the court grants the motion and enters an order that forbids discovery of the trade secrets.

Was it proper for the court to have granted the motion?

(A) No, because the corporation is the defendant in the case.

(B) No, because a court may not order that trade secrets not be disclosed.

(C) Yes, because a court may require that trade secrets not be revealed.

(D) Yes, because the corporation is the defendant in the case.

QUESTION 264

A trucker is traveling at a high rate of speed over icy roads. The trucker loses control of the truck and is involved in an accident with a driver. The driver files a claim based on negligence in federal court. The complaint alleges that the trucker negligently operated the truck and caused $100,000 in damages. The driver serves the trucker with a set of interrogatories, to which the trucker timely answers. After answering, new information comes to light that impacts the trucker's previous disclosures.

Must the trucker take any action regarding the new information?

(A) No, because the driver did not receive permission from the court to serve the trucker with an additional set of interrogatories.

(B) No, because the trucker does not have a duty to amend its answers to the interrogatories.

(C) Yes, because the trucker has a duty to amend its answers to the interrogatories.

(D) Yes, because the trucker was negligent.

Civil Procedure

Answer Key and Explanations

1.	B	47.	D	93.	D
2.	A	48.	B	94.	C
3.	C	49.	B	95.	C
4.	C	50.	C	96.	B
5.	A	51.	B	97.	C
6.	A	52.	D	98.	B
7.	B	53.	A	99.	D
8.	A	54.	B	100.	D
9.	C	55.	A	101.	B
10.	A	56.	C	102.	B
11.	A	57.	B	103.	B
12.	A	58.	D	104.	B
13.	D	59.	C	105.	D
14.	C	60.	B	106.	B
15.	C	61.	A	107.	B
16.	B	62.	C	108.	D
17.	C	63.	C	109.	C
18.	B	64.	D	110.	A
19.	D	65.	B	111.	D
20.	C	66.	C	112.	A
21.	B	67.	C	113.	A
22.	A	68.	B	114.	B
23.	D	69.	C	115.	C
24.	A	70.	C	116.	D
25.	A	71.	D	117.	D
26.	B	72.	D	118.	B
27.	A	73.	C	119.	A
28.	C	74.	D	120.	D
29.	A	75.	A	121.	C
30.	B	76.	A	122.	A
31.	B	77.	D	123.	B
32.	C	78.	A	124.	C
33.	D	79.	C	125.	A
34.	B	80.	D	126.	B
35.	D	81.	A	127.	B
36.	C	82.	D	128.	C
37.	A	83.	B	129.	B
38.	B	84.	D	130.	C
39.	C	85.	B	131.	B
40.	A	86.	C	132.	C
41.	A	87.	D	133.	B
42.	D	88.	C	134.	B
43.	C	89.	C	135.	A
44.	B	90.	D	136.	A
45.	C	91.	B	137.	B
46.	B	92.	C	138.	A

139.	D	185.	A	231.	A
140.	B	186.	B	232.	C
141.	C	187.	D	233.	C
142.	B	188.	C	234.	A
143.	B	189.	A	235.	C
144.	A	190.	A	236.	B
145.	B	191.	D	237.	A
146.	C	192.	B	238.	C
147.	B	193.	D	239.	C
148.	A	194.	C	240.	D
149.	C	195.	D	241.	A
150.	C	196.	C	242.	A
151.	C	197.	A	243.	B
152.	D	198.	C	244.	B
153.	B	199.	C	245.	A
154.	C	200.	D	246.	B
155.	A	201.	C	247.	C
156.	A	202.	C	248.	B
157.	A	203.	C	249.	D
158.	C	204.	D	250.	D
159.	A	205.	D	251.	C
160.	D	206.	A	252.	C
161.	C	207.	C	253.	D
162.	C	208.	B	254.	A
163.	C	209.	C	255.	C
164.	B	210.	B	256.	B
165.	A	211.	A	257.	A
166.	C	212.	D	258.	D
167.	A	213.	B	259.	B
168.	B	214.	C	260.	C
169.	A	215.	C	261.	A
170.	A	216.	D	262.	D
171.	C	217.	A	263.	C
172.	D	218.	B	264.	C
173.	C	219.	A		
174.	D	220.	C		
175.	A	221.	B		
176.	B	222.	D		
177.	B	223.	C		
178.	A	224.	A		
179.	A	225.	A		
180.	D	226.	B		
181.	C	227.	D		
182.	C	228.	A		
183.	C	229.	C		
184.	B	230.	A		

QUESTION 1
ANSWER & EXPLANATION
Jurisdiction & Venue

(B)   No, because the inventor's claim arises under federal law.

The correct answer is B. A federal district court possesses limited original jurisdiction over a case arising under the United States Constitution, federal statutory or common law, and federal treaties. Article III requires that an actual "case or controversy" exist between the parties. A "case or controversy" involves a federal question only when a plaintiff's complaint states a claim or cause of action that involves federal law. Because the inventor's complaint alleges patent infringement, the claim arises under federal law. Consequently, the federal court has federal question jurisdiction.

Answer choice A is incorrect because there is no amount in controversy requirement for an action that is based on a federal question.

Answer choice C is incorrect because the claim does arise under federal law.

Answer choice D is incorrect because the opportunist's denial of the allegations in the complaint has no bearing on the court's subject-matter jurisdiction over the claim in this case.

Civil Procedure Outline § I (A)(1): Federal Question Jurisdiction

QUESTION 2
ANSWER & EXPLANATION
Pre-Trial Procedures

(A)   No, because the initial conference must take place at least 21 days before a scheduling conference.

The correct answer is A. In federal court actions, unless otherwise directed by the court, the parties must hold an initial conference to plan the discovery process as soon as practicable, or at least 21 days before a scheduling conference. At the initial conference, the parties must:

- consider claims and defenses, and the possibilities for settling or resolving the case;
- make or arrange for initial disclosures;
- discuss any issues regarding preserving discoverable information; and
- develop a discovery plan.

Civil Procedure Outline § III (E)(6) Discovery, Disclosure, and Sanctions: Required Initial Conference of the Parties

QUESTION 3
ANSWER & EXPLANATION
Law Applied by Federal Courts

(C) the law of State B because the work was performed in State B

C is the correct answer. This question tests the Erie doctrine as it applies to choice-of-law rules. Under the Erie doctrine, a federal court hearing a diversity case must apply the choice-of-law rules of the state in which it sits to determine which state's substantive law governs. In this instance, the federal court sits in State A, and under State A's common law, the substantive law of the state in which contract work is performed governs in contract dispute cases. Here, the work was performed in State B. Therefore, pursuant to the Erie doctrine, the federal court must apply the law of State B.

A is incorrect. While a federal court must apply the law of the state in which it sits, the Erie doctrine requires that it apply the choice-of-law rules and the state's common law. In this instance, the common law of State A required application of State B's substantive law in this contract dispute.

B is incorrect. The domiciles of the parties to the case have no bearing on what substantive law applies in a federal diversity case under the Erie doctrine.

D is incorrect. The substantive law of State A applies in this case pursuant to the Erie doctrine. Under State A's choice-of-law rules, the location of the work under the contract rather than the state of contract formation governs which laws apply.

Civil Procedure Outline § II(A)(2)(b): Choice-of-Law Rules of Forum State

QUESTION 4
ANSWER & EXPLANATION
Pre-Trial Procedures

(C) Yes, because the court found the TRO was necessary to prevent immediate irreparable injury.

The correct answer is C. A court may issue a TRO on an ex-parte basis (i.e., without the other party present) when necessary to prevent irreparable injury. Fed. R. Civ. P. 65(b). Because notice to the other party may not be required, a TRO is an extraordinary remedy. In this case, the facts state that the resident's complaint met all the requirements for seeking the TRO. Because the requirements were met, the relevant issue was whether the court could issue the TRO on an ex-parte basis. Because the facts indicate that the TRO is necessary to prevent immediate irreparable injury, the court properly issued the TRO. Accordingly, B is incorrect because the court was not required to give the construction company an opportunity to respond.

A is incorrect because it is not necessary to hold a hearing when the TRO is necessary to prevent immediate irreparable harm, as long as the requirements for obtaining the TRO are met.

D is incorrect because it is an incorrect statement. A TRO is an extraordinary remedy.

Civil Procedure Outline § III (A)(2)(a) Temporary Restraining Order

QUESTION 5
ANSWER & EXPLANATION
Jury Trails

(A)   No, because a party possesses a right to a jury trial in all actions at law for claims exceeding a claim amount of $20.

The correct answer is A. A party possesses a right to a jury trial in all actions at law (for damages) for claims exceeding a claim amount of $20. U.S. Const. amend. VII; Fed. R. Civ. P. 38(a). Pursuant to the Rules, any legal claims should be tried before any equitable claims are tried.

Civil Procedure Outline § IV A(1) Jury Trials: Right to a Jury Trial: General—Actions at Law

QUESTION 6
ANSWER & EXPLANATION
Motions

(A)   No, because the trucker filed an answer.

The correct answer is A. The defense of lack of personal jurisdiction is waived if not asserted in the first responsive motion or pleading. Because the trucker filed his answer and did not raise the defense of lack of personal jurisdiction at that time, the defense is waived.

B is incorrect because it ignores the rules regarding waiver.

C is incorrect because it is the fact that the trucker failed to raise the defense that resulted in waiver.

D is incorrect because the trucker failed to raise the defense in the first responsive pleading.

Civil Procedure Outline § V (A)(1)(b)(1)(a) Pretrial Motions: Waivable Defenses: Lack of Personal Jurisdiction

QUESTION 7
ANSWER & EXPLANATION
Pre-Trial Procedures

(B)   No, because the report should have been filed within 14 days after the initial conference.

The correct answer is B. Within 14 days after the initial conference, the parties must submit a written report to the court outlining the discovery plan.

Civil Procedure Outline § III (E)(6)(a) Discovery, Disclosure, and Sanctions: Required Initial Conference of the Parties: Discovery Plan

QUESTION 8
ANSWER & EXPLANATION
Verdicts and Judgments

(A)   No, because the clerk's entry of default is not a judgment.

The correct answer is A.

If a defendant fails to timely respond to a complaint or otherwise defend in a case, a plaintiff can make an application to the clerk to file an entry of default. The plaintiff must attach an affidavit and any other proof relevant to the defendant's failure to respond to the suit to the application for entry of default. The entry of default is a preliminary step. The clerk examines the docket and papers in the plaintiff's filing to determine if there has been an answer or responsive pleading. The clerk may then enter the default. The entry of default is not a judgment. Once the plaintiff obtains the default, the plaintiff can apply to the court for a default judgment. There is no default judgment until the court orders it.

B, C, and D are incorrect because they are erroneous statements of law.

Civil Procedure Outline § VI A(1)(a)(1) Defaults and Involuntary Dismissals: Default Judgment: Motion for a Default Judgment: Entry of Default

QUESTION 9
ANSWER & EXPLANATION
Appealability and Review

(C)   Yes, because a party may appeal, as a matter of right, an interlocutory order or decree that grants an injunction.

The correct answer is C. As a general rule, an interlocutory order is not appealable. An interlocutory order is an order in a case that does not dispose of the case. For example, a ruling on the admissibility of a piece of evidence is an interlocutory order.

However, a party may appeal, as a matter of right, an interlocutory order or decree that:

- grants, continues, modifies, refuses, or dissolves an injunction;

- appoints a receiver, or refuses to wind-up a receivership or take steps to accomplish its purpose(s);

- determines the liabilities and rights of the parties to an admiralty case; or

- is final in a patent infringement action, except for an accounting.

Civil Procedure Outline § VII A(1) Availability of Interlocutory Review: Appeal in Specified Types of Cases

QUESTION 10
ANSWER & EXPLANATION
Jurisdiction and Venue

(A)   No, because although the opposing parties are citizens of different states, the amount in controversy is $75,000.

The correct answer is A. In order for federal courts to possess original jurisdiction over parties of diverse state citizenship, the amount in controversy must exceed $75,000, exclusive of interest and costs. If the amount in controversy is $75,000 or less, diversity jurisdiction does not exist. Here, the amount in controversy equals $75,000, but does not exceed it. Therefore, although the opposing parties are citizens of different states, the amount in controversy does not satisfy the required jurisdictional amount.

B is incorrect because even though the negligence claim does not raise a question under federal law, a federal court may have diversity of citizenship jurisdiction over a negligence case if the parties are diverse and the amount in controversy exceeds $75,000, exclusive of interest and costs.

C is an incorrect statement of law.

D is incorrect because the amount in controversy must exceed $75,000.

Civil Procedure Outline § I (A)(2): Diversity of Citizenship Jurisdiction

QUESTION 11
ANSWER & EXPLANATION
Pre-Trial Procedures

(A)   No, because the parties had not yet held an initial conference.

The correct answer is A. A party cannot seek discovery from any source before the required initial conference of the parties, other than in proceedings exempted from initial disclosure, or when allowed by stipulation or court order. Discovery can be made in any sequence unless otherwise ordered by the court for any parties' or witnesses' convenience or where the interests of justice dictate. Also, discovery by one party does not require any other party to delay its discovery.

B is incorrect because discovery can be made in any sequence unless otherwise ordered by the court for any parties' or witnesses' convenience or where the interests of justice dictate.

C and D are incorrect because they ignore the above rules.

Civil Procedure Outline § III (E)(7) Discovery, Disclosure, and Sanctions: Timing and Order of Discovery

QUESTION 12
ANSWER & EXPLANATION
Law Applied to Federal Courts

(A)   the corporation, because the president signed her name correctly.

A is the correct answer. This question tests the Erie doctrine. Under the Erie doctrine, a federal court hearing a diversity case must apply the statutory and common law of the state in which it sits. Here, the court sits in State B. State B's common law permits a court to validate a contract if it can determine the signatory's identity from context. Because the president signed her name correctly, the court can determine her identity and will hold for the corporation.

B is incorrect. If the court had been unable to determine the president's identity, statutory law would have governed despite the corporation's bylaws.

C is incorrect. The federal court was required to apply State B's common law under the Erie doctrine.

D is incorrect. Pursuant to Erie, there is no federal common law for diversity cases.

Civil Procedure Outline § II(A)(2)(a): Erie Doctrine

QUESTION 13
ANSWER & EXPLANATION
Pre-Trial Procedures

(D)   The inventor did not set out specific facts in his complaint showing that immediate and irreparable injury will result to the inventor before the opportunist can be heard.

The correct answer is D.   To obtain an ex-parte TRO, the moving party must meet three conditions: (1) Irreparable Injury—In a verified complaint or by affidavit (under oath), the moving party must set out specific facts that show that immediate and irreparable injury will result to the moving party before the adverse party can be heard in opposition; (2) Efforts Made—The moving party must certify to the court, in writing, the efforts made to give the notice and the reasons supporting the claim that notice should not be required; and (3) Security—The moving party must provide a bond to the court in such a sum as the court deems proper to compensate the adverse party in the event that the TRO is wrongfully entered.   In this case, the inventor failed to state specific facts in his complaint.

A is incorrect because it is an incorrect statement of law.

B is incorrect because a TRO is sought in emergency situations when notice to the other party is not feasible.   Therefore, a hearing is not necessary.

C is incorrect because it is not necessary for a judgment to be obtained before a TRO can be issued.

Civil Procedure Outline § III (A)(2)(a)(1)(a) Temporary Restraining Order: Irreparable Injury

QUESTION 14
ANSWER & EXPLANATION
Jury Trials

(C)   Yes, because a party asserting solely equitable claims or remedies does not have a right to a jury trial.

The correct answer is C.   A party asserting solely equitable claims or remedies does not have a right to a jury trial, but a party may possess both legal and equitable claims in one action.

Civil Procedure Outline § IV A(2) Jury Trials: Right to a Jury Trial: Equitable Claims

QUESTION 15
ANSWER & EXPLANATION
Motions

(C)   Yes, because the defense was not raised in the trucker's initial motion.

The correct answer is C. The defense of improper venue is waived if not raised in the first responsive motion or pleading. In this case, the trucker waived the defense when he did not raise it in his initial motion in which he raised the defense of insufficient service of process.

A is incorrect because, although the defense of improper venue can be raised in a motion or answer, the trucker failed to raise the defense in the first motion.

B is an incorrect statement of law.

D is incorrect because the defense of improper venue must be raised in the first responsive motion. The trucker failed to raise the defense when he raised the defense of insufficient service of process.

Civil Procedure Outline § V (A)(1)(b)(1)(b) Pretrial Motions: Waivable Defenses: Improper Venue

QUESTION 16
ANSWER & EXPLANATION
Pre-Trial Procedures

(B)   No, because the attorney did not provide the attorney's address.

The correct answer is B. All initial and pretrial disclosures, and every request, response, or objection must be signed by at least one attorney of record, or by the party if unrepresented. The signature must also include the signer's address, e-mail address, and telephone number.

A is incorrect because the doctor is represented by an attorney.

C is incorrect because in cases where a party is unrepresented, the party must sign.

D is incorrect because it ignores the requirement that the signer's address be included.

Civil Procedure Outline § III (E)(8) Discovery, Disclosure, and Sanctions: Signing Disclosures and Discovery Requests

QUESTION 17
ANSWER & EXPLANATION
Verdicts and Judgments

(C) Yes, because the claim was for a definite identifiable amount of money damages.

The correct answer is C. If the claim is for a sum certain (a definite identifiable amount of money damages), the plaintiff may present an affidavit detailing the sum certain to the clerk, and the clerk can enter a default judgment.

A and D are incorrect because they are erroneous statements of law.

B is incorrect because the developer's failure to respond to the complaint was what permitted the entry of default and subsequent default judgment.

Civil Procedure Outline § VI A(1)(a)(2)(a) Defaults and Involuntary Dismissals: Default Judgment: Motion for a Default Judgment: Judgment: Sum Certain

QUESTION 18
ANSWER & EXPLANATION
Appealability and Review

(B) The judge may certify a controlling question of law for appellate review if an immediate appeal may materially advance the ultimate termination of the litigation.

The correct answer is B. A party may also take a certified appeal when a trial judge decides to certify a "controlling question of law" for appellate review for the reason that an immediate appeal "may materially advance the ultimate termination of the litigation." 28 U.S.C. § 1292(b).

A, C, and D are incorrect statements of law.

Civil Procedure Outline § VII A(2) Availability of Interlocutory Review: Discretionary Appeal of Certified Question of Law

QUESTION 19
ANSWER & EXPLANATION
Jurisdiction and Venue

(D) Yes, because the opposing parties are citizens of different states, and the amount in controversy is $100,000.

The correct answer is D. For diversity jurisdiction purposes, when an executor of a decedent's estate is a defendant, the executor is "deemed to be a citizen only of the same state as the decedent" when the executor represents the decedent in litigation. 28 U.S.C. § 1332(c)(2). Although the executor is domiciled in the same state as the driver, the executor is deemed to be a citizen only of State B for the purposes of the lawsuit. Therefore, diversity of citizenship exists. Because the amount in controversy exceeds $75,000, and because the parties are diverse, the court has jurisdiction over the case.

A is incorrect because, as explained above, diversity of citizenship exists in this case.

B is incorrect because even though the negligence claim does not raise a question under federal law, a federal court may have diversity of citizenship jurisdiction over a negligence case if the parties are diverse and the amount in controversy exceeds $75,000, exclusive of interest and costs.

C is an incorrect statement of law.

Civil Procedure Outline § I (A)(2): Diversity of Citizenship Jurisdiction

QUESTION 20
ANSWER & EXPLANATION
Pre-Trial Procedures

(C)   Yes, because the attorney did not sign it.

The correct answer is C. All initial and pretrial disclosures, and every request, response, or objection must be signed by at least one attorney of record, or by the party if unrepresented. The signature must also include the signer's address, e-mail address, and telephone number. If a discovery qualifying document is not signed, the other party has no duty to act on it. The court may strike it unless a signature is promptly provided.

A and B are incorrect because they ignore the requirement that the request should have been signed.

D is incorrect because it is an erroneous statement of law. A party may make a request for admission—i.e., a written statement served by one party, on another party, requesting that the responding party admit or deny the truth of a statement.

Civil Procedure Outline § III (E)(8)(b) Discovery, Disclosure, and Sanctions: Signing Disclosures and Discovery Requests: Consequences of Not Signing Discovery Qualifying Document

QUESTION 21
ANSWER & EXPLANATION
Law Applied by Federal Courts

(B)   The court should apply State C negligence law.

B is the correct answer. This question tests the effect of a venue change under the Erie doctrine. Under the Erie doctrine, a federal court hearing a diversity case must apply the statutory and common law of the state in which it sits. A transfer of a civil action under the federal venue transfer statute does not alter the state rule that would have been applied by the original court. In this case, the action was originally filed in a federal court sitting in State C, but was transferred to State B. Because the original court would have followed the law of the state in which it sat, State C, the transferee court must also apply the law of State C.

A is incorrect. There is no federal common law of state law matters.

C is incorrect. As explained above, the law the transferor court would have applied will govern when an action is transferred.

D is incorrect. A court would violate the Erie doctrine by selecting the law it felt was most appropriate because it would effectively be developing its own choice-of-law rule.

Civil Procedure Outline § II(A)(2)(c): Erie Doctrine and Effect of Venue Transfer

QUESTION 22
ANSWER & EXPLANATION
Pre-Trial Procedures

(A)   No, because the inventor did not certify to the court the efforts made to give notice to the opportunist and why such notice should not be required.

The correct answer is A. To obtain an ex-parte TRO, the moving party must meet three conditions: (1) Irreparable Injury—In a verified complaint or by affidavit (under oath), the moving party must set out specific facts that show that immediate and irreparable injury will result to the moving party before the adverse party can be heard in opposition; (2) Efforts Made—The moving party must certify to the court, in writing, the efforts made to give the notice and the reasons supporting the claim that notice should not be required; and (3) Security—The moving party must provide a bond to the court in such a sum as the court deems proper to compensate the adverse party in the event that the TRO is wrongfully entered. In this case, the inventor failed to certify to the court what efforts were made to give notice and reasons supporting the claim that notice should not be required.

B is incorrect because a TRO is sought in emergency situations when notice to the other party is not feasible. Therefore, a hearing is not necessary.

C and D are incorrect because, although those statements could be true, the inventor failed to meet the conditions necessary to obtain a TRO.

Civil Procedure Outline § III (A)(2)(a)(1)(b) Temporary Restraining Order: Efforts Made

QUESTION 23
ANSWER & EXPLANATION
Jury Trials

(D)   Yes, because the jury trial demand was not filed within 14 days of the filing of the last pleading directed to the issue for which the basis of the right to a jury trial exists.

The correct answer is D. A party must file a jury trial demand within 14 days of the filing of the last pleading that is directed to the issue for which the basis of the right to a jury trial exists. Fed. R. Civ. P. 38(b). Otherwise, the right to a trial by jury is waived.

Civil Procedure Outline § IV A(3) Jury Trials: Right to a Jury Trial: Waiver of the Right to a Jury Trial

QUESTION 24
ANSWER & EXPLANATION
Motions

(A)   No, because the driver waived the defense of insufficient process.

The correct answer is A. The defense of insufficient process is waived if not raised in the first responsive motion or pleading. Because the driver filed an answer and did not raise the defense, the defense was waived.

B is incorrect because it is an erroneous statement of law.

C is incorrect because the driver failed to raise the defense in the first responsive pleading (i.e., in this case, the answer).

D is incorrect because, although the attorney may have had a good faith belief that the motion was meritorious, the defense was not timely raised in the first responsive pleading.

Civil Procedure Outline § V (A)(1)(b)(1)(c) Pretrial Motions: Waivable Defenses: Insufficient Process

QUESTION 25
ANSWER & EXPLANATION
Pre-Trial Procedures

(A)   No, because the signature also certifies that, among other things, the disclosure is complete.

The correct answer is A. All initial and pretrial disclosures, and every request, response, or objection must be signed by at least one attorney of record, or by the party if unrepresented. The signature must also include the signer's address, e-mail address, and telephone number. By signing, the person certifies that:

*   a disclosure is complete and correct; and

*   a discovery request or response is consistent with the law, not requested for an improper purpose, and not unreasonably burdensome.

Civil Procedure Outline § III (E)(8)(a) Discovery, Disclosure, and Sanctions: Signing Disclosures and Discovery Requests: Person's Signature Certifies as to Disclosure, Request, Response

QUESTION 26
ANSWER & EXPLANATION
Verdicts and Judgments

(B)   No, because the geek did not apply to the court for a default judgment.

The correct answer is B. If the amount demanded is not a sum certain, the plaintiff must apply to the court for a default judgment. There must be a hearing where evidence regarding damages is offered. The hearing can be accomplished in some cases on documentary evidence such as affidavits. In this case, the geek should have applied to the court for a default judgment because the damages were not for a sum certain.

A is incorrect because the court, not the clerk, may hold a hearing.

C is incorrect because the court, not the clerk, may determine the damages.

D is incorrect because, although the corporation failed to answer the complaint, the geek should have applied to the court for a default judgment in this case where the damages were not for a sum certain.

Civil Procedure Outline § VI A(1)(a)(2)(b) Defaults and Involuntary Dismissals: Default Judgment: Motion for a Default Judgment: Judgment: Hearing on Damages

QUESTION 27
ANSWER & EXPLANATION
Appealability and Review

(A)   No, because the court has not yet entered a final judgment in the case.

The correct answer is A. As a general rule, an appeal can only be taken from a final judgment. A final judgment is a dispositive and controlling order that "ends the litigation on the merits and leaves nothing for the court to do but execute on the judgment." Catlin v. United States, 324 U.S. 229 (1945). An appeal from most pre-trial orders is considered interlocutory and not appealable as a final decision under the final judgment rule. An interlocutory order may, however, be subject to a collateral attack.

Civil Procedure Outline § VII B(1) Final Judgment Rule: Only Final Judgments are Appealable

QUESTION 28
ANSWER & EXPLANATION
Jurisdiction and Venue

(C)   Yes, because the parties were citizens of different states at the time the claim was filed.

The correct answer is C. Diversity subject-matter jurisdiction exists if: 1) the opposing parties are citizens of different states; and 2) the amount in controversy exceeds $75,000, exclusive of interests and costs. Citizenship is determined as of the time the action is commenced. In this case, although the parties were both citizens of State A at the time of the accident, at the time the action was commenced the motorcyclist had moved to State B with the intent to reside there permanently. Consequently, complete diversity of citizenship exists, and because the amount in controversy exceeds $75,000, the court will have subject-matter jurisdiction over the case.

A is incorrect because at the time of the commencement of the action diversity of citizenship existed.

B is incorrect because it is an inaccurate statement of law.

D is incorrect because it is an inaccurate statement of law.

Civil Procedure Outline § I (A)(a)(1): Diversity of Citizenship Jurisdiction

QUESTION 29
ANSWER& EXPLANATION
Pre-Trial Procedures

(A)   No, because the court may impose sanctions on the signer, the party on whose behalf the signer is acting, or both.

The correct answer is A. A trial court plays an integral role as the supervisor of discovery. A court may sanction parties or attorneys for unreasonable conduct during the discovery process. Fed. R. Civ. P. 37.

Civil Procedure Outline § III (E)(9) Discovery, Disclosure, and Sanctions: Sanctions for Discovery Violations

QUESTION 30
ANSWER & EXPLANATION
Law Applied by Federal Courts

(B)   The contract law of State B, because the case was originally filed in State B federal court.

B is the correct answer. This question tests the effect of a venue change under the Erie doctrine. Under the Erie doctrine, a federal court hearing a diversity case must apply the statutory and common law of the state in which it sits. A transfer of a civil action under the federal venue transfer statute does not alter the state rule that would have been applied by the original court. This rule applies even when the plaintiff initiates the transfer. Here, the civil case was originally filed in a State B federal court. When the case was transferred to a State C federal court, the transferee court was required to apply the state law that would have been applied by the transferor court. Because the State B court would have applied State B law under the Erie doctrine, the State C court was obligated to do so as well.

A is incorrect. The plaintiff's citizenship would have no impact on which law the court would apply.

C is incorrect. The rule regarding applicable law in a venue transfer applies regardless of whether the plaintiff or defendant initiated the transfer.

D is incorrect. While the general rule under the Erie doctrine is that a federal court hearing a diversity action must apply the law of the state in which it sits, this rule is modified when the court received the case through a venue transfer.

Civil Procedure Outline § II(A)(2)(c): Erie Doctrine and Effect of Venue Transfer

QUESTION 31
ANSWER & EXPLANATION
Pre-Trial Procedures

(B)   No, because the inventor did not provide a bond to the court.

The correct answer is B.   To obtain an ex-parte TRO, the moving party must meet three conditions: (1) Irreparable Injury—In a verified complaint or by affidavit (under oath), the moving party must set out specific facts that show that immediate and irreparable injury will result to the moving party before the adverse party can be heard in opposition; (2) Efforts Made—The moving party must certify to the court, in writing, the efforts made to give the notice and the reasons supporting the claim that notice should not be required; and (3) Security—The moving party must provide a bond to the court in such a sum as the court deems proper to compensate the adverse party in the event that the TRO is wrongfully entered.   In this case, the inventor failed to provide a bond.

A, C, and D are incorrect because those choices ignore the inventor's failure to provide a bond to the court.

Civil Procedure Outline § III (A)(2)(a)(1)(c) Temporary Restraining Order: Security

QUESTION 32
ANSWER & EXPLANATION
Jury Trials

(C)   Yes, because the jury trial demand was filed within 14 days of the filing of the last pleading directed to the issue for which the basis of the right to a jury trial exists.

The correct answer is C.   A party must file a jury trial demand within 14 days of the filing of the last pleading that is directed to the issue for which the basis of the right to a jury trial exists.   Fed. R. Civ. P. 38(b).   Otherwise, the right to a trial by jury is waived.

Civil Procedure Outline § IV A(3) Jury Trials: Right to a Jury Trial: Waiver of the Right to a Jury Trial

QUESTION 33
ANSWER & EXPLANATION
Pre-Trial Procedures

(D)   Yes, because a court may direct parties to appear before the court for a pre-trial conference for the purpose of discouraging wasteful pre-trial activities.

The correct answer is D. A court may direct the parties or attorneys to appear before it for a pre-trial conference for several purposes including:

-      expediting the disposition of the action,

-      establishing early and continuing control so that the case will not be protracted because of lack of management,

-      discouraging wasteful pre-trial activities,

-      improving the quality of the trial through more thorough preparation, and

-      facilitating the settlement of the case.

The judge possesses discretion in planning and conducting the conference. Appearance of counsel at a pre-trial conference ordered by a federal district court is mandatory, although the Rules do not compel the court to conduct such a conference in every case. *Identiseal Corp. v. Positive Identification Sys., Inc.,* 560 F.2d 298 (7th Cir. 1977).

A is incorrect because it is an erroneous statement of law.

B is incorrect because the court may direct the parties or attorneys to appear before it for a pre-trial conference to establish early and continuing control so that the case will not be protracted because of lack of management.

C is incorrect because the court need not conduct a pre-trial conference in every case.

Civil Procedure Outline § III (G)(1) Pre-Trial Conference and Order: Pre-Trial Conference: Objectives of Conference

QUESTION 34
ANSWER & EXPLANATION
Motions

(B) No, because the defense was waived.

The correct answer is B. The defense of insufficient service of process is waived if not raised in the first responsive motion or pleading. In this case, the defendant failed to raise the defense in the initial motion. Consequently, the defendant waived the defense.

A is incorrect because this answer choice wrongfully implies that because the plaintiff personally served the defendant with the summons and complaint, the defendant cannot raise the defense of insufficient service of process.

C is incorrect because the defense was waived, not preserved.

D is incorrect because, although it was improper for the plaintiff to personally serve the summons and complaint, the defendant waived the defense, as stated above.

Civil Procedure Outline § V (A)(1)(b)(1)(d) Pretrial Motions: Waivable Defenses: Insufficient Service of Process

QUESTION 35
ANSWER & EXPLANATION
Verdicts and Judgments

(D)   Yes, because if the party against whom the default judgment is sought has appeared, the party must be given at least seven days' notice for the hearing.

The correct answer is D. If the party against whom the default judgment is sought has appeared, the party must be given at least seven days' notice for the hearing.

Civil Procedure Outline § VI A(1)(a)(2)(b)(i) Defaults and Involuntary Dismissals: Default Judgment: Motion for a Default Judgment: Judgment: Hearing on Damages: Notice to Defaulting Party

QUESTION 36
ANSWER & EXPLANATION
Appealability and Review

(C)   Yes, because a court may direct entry of a final judgment as to specific claims or parties, making a final judgment on the severed claim appealable.

The correct answer is C. In a case that involves multiple claims or parties, a court may direct entry of a final judgment as to specific claims or parties (less than all), making a final judgment on the severed claim appealable. The court may sever the claims for appeal if it finds no just reason for delay. Fed. R. Civ. P. 54(b). If the trial court does not sever a judgment, the claim will not be subject to appeal until entry of a final judgment in the case.

Civil Procedure Outline § VII B(1)(a) Final Judgment Rule: Only Final Judgments are Appealable: Court May Sever Multi-Party or Multi-Claim Judgments

QUESTION 37
ANSWER & EXPLANATION
Jurisdiction and Venue

(A) No, because subject-matter jurisdiction cannot be consented to or waived by the parties.

The correct answer is A. Subject-matter jurisdiction cannot be consented to or waived by the parties. In this case, the parties are not diverse, and that jurisdictional defect cannot be cured by a party's consent to jurisdiction.

B is incorrect because a claim based in products liability may be properly brought before a federal court if the requirements of diversity jurisdiction are satisfied.

C is incorrect because it is misstatement of law.

D is incorrect because diversity jurisdiction requires that the parties be of diverse state citizenship and the amount in controversy must exceed $75,000. Here, the amount in controversy is satisfied, but both the customer and the corporation are citizens of State A. The federal court's location is not a relevant factor in determining subject-matter jurisdiction. The corporation's consent to federal jurisdiction does not overcome the lack of diversity of citizenship.

Civil Procedure Outline § I (A): Diversity of Citizenship Jurisdiction

QUESTION 38
ANSWER & EXPLANATION
Pre-Trial Procedures

(B) Patty, because she is authorized to enter into stipulations and make admissions.

The correct answer is B. At least one of the attorneys for each party participating in a pre-trial conference must possess the authority to enter into stipulations and to make admissions regarding all matters that the participants may reasonably anticipate to be discussed. Fed. R. Civ. P. 16(c). If appropriate, the federal district court may require that a party or its representatives be present or reasonably available by telephone in order to consider possible settlement of the dispute.

Civil Procedure Outline § III (G)(1)(b) Pre-Trial Conference and Order: Pre-Trial Conference: Authority of Counsel at Pre-Trial Conference

QUESTION 39
ANSWER & EXPLANATION
Law Applied by Federal Court

(C)   For State B, because State A was using more water than State B.

C is the correct answer. This question is testing the application of federal common law. Federal common law arises from federal courts interpreting federal constitutional provisions, statutes, or treaties, and is entitled to preclusive effect. Federal common law is followed in suits between states. Here, the suit involves a dispute between two states over shared water resources. Because the federal courts have developed common law interpreting federal statutes, the court should apply the federal common law. The result would be to hold for State B and enjoin State A from using more than its equitable share of the water.

A and B are incorrect. When a federal court is hearing a dispute between two states, federal common law will have a preclusive effect. Both of these answers involve application of competing state law.

D is incorrect. The federal court will not be swayed by a compelling state interest when federal common law addresses the question.

Civil Procedure Outline § II(B)(1): Federal Common Law of Federal Law

QUESTION 40
ANSWER & EXPLANATION
Pre-Trial Procedures

(A)   No, because the duration of the TRO is 21 days.

The correct answer is A. The Rules limit TROs to 14 days, absent good cause.

B is incorrect because a TRO is sought in emergency situations when notice to the other party is not feasible. Therefore, a hearing is not necessary.

C is incorrect because there is no indication that good cause exists to extend the TRO beyond 14 days.

D is incorrect because the TRO was for longer than the Rules permit, as stated above.

Civil Procedure Outline § III (A)(2)(a)(2) Temporary Restraining Order: Duration

QUESTION 41
ANSWER & EXPLANATION
Jury Trials

(A)   Juan, Mary, and Bill are all disqualified from serving on a jury.

The correct answer is A. A person can serve on a jury unless the person

- is not a United States citizen,

- is under 18 years of age,

- is illiterate,

- is not fluent in English,

- is mentally or physically infirm, or

- has a criminal record.

28 U.S.C. § 1865(b).

In this case, Juan is disqualified because he is not a United States citizen. Mary is disqualified because she is under 18 years of age. Bill is disqualified because he has a criminal record.

Civil Procedure Outline § IV B(1)(a)(1) Selection and Composition of Juries: Jury Selection: Considerations Regarding Prospective Jurors: Grounds for Disqualification from Serving on Jury

QUESTION 42
ANSWER & EXPLANATION
Motions

(D)   Yes, because the driver raised the defense.

The correct answer is D. Lack of subject-matter jurisdiction is a non-waivable defense. It can never be waived, and therefore, it may be asserted at any time.

A, B, and C are incorrect because the defense of lack of subject-matter jurisdiction can be raised at any time.

Civil Procedure Outline § V (A)(1)(b)(2)(a) Pretrial Motions: Non-Waivable Defenses: Lack of Subject-Matter Jurisdiction

QUESTION 43
ANSWER & EXPLANATION
Pre-Trial Procedures

(C)   Yes, because the notice of dismissal was filed before the driver served an answer.

The correct answer is C. An action may be dismissed without court order:

•   by the plaintiff alone by filing a notice of dismissal at any time before the adverse party serves an answer or a motion for summary judgment (whichever comes first); or

•   by stipulation of dismissal signed by all parties who have appeared in the action.

Otherwise, the part(ies) seeking dismissal must obtain a court order. Unless otherwise stated, the first such dismissal is without prejudice. The second dismissal of an action based on or including the same claim may act as a judgment on the merits.

A is incorrect because the plaintiff may not file a notice of dismissal if the opposing party has filed a motion for summary judgment.

B and D are incorrect because they are incorrect statements of law.

Civil Procedure Outline § III (F)(1) Adjudication without a Trial: Voluntary Dismissal of Claim

QUESTION 44
ANSWER & EXPLANATION
Verdicts and Judgments

(B)   No, because the trucker did not demonstrate good cause or a reasonable excuse for failure to answer the complaint.

The correct answer is B. A party may file a motion to set aside a default or default judgment. The court will grant the motion if the movant:

•   demonstrates good cause or a reasonable excuse for failure to timely plead or otherwise defend the lawsuit; and

•   states ultimate facts in support of a meritorious defense to a default.

In this case, although the trucker stated ultimate facts in support of a meritorious defense to the default, the trucker did not demonstrate good cause or a reasonable excuse for failure to timely plead or otherwise defend the lawsuit.

Civil Procedure Outline § VI A(1)(a)(3)(a) Defaults and Involuntary Dismissals: Default

Judgment: Motion for a Default Judgment: Setting Aside Default: Good Cause and Meritorious Defense

QUESTION 45
ANSWER & EXPLANATION
Appealability and Review

(C)   Yes, because the collateral order exception to the final judgment rule applies.

The correct answer is C. The United States Supreme Court has held that the determination of some questions that are collateral to other rights which are asserted in an action may be too important to be deferred for appellate review until after the whole case is adjudicated. The small category of interlocutory orders that are appealable as collateral orders must satisfy three criteria:

- the court's order must finally dispose of a disputed question;

- the question must be completely collateral to the cause of action; and

- the order that relates to the question must involve an important right that would be "lost, probably irreparably," if review of the question had to wait until after a final judgment occurred.

Cohen v. Beneficial Indus. Loan Corp., 337 U.S. 541 (1949).

"To come within the small class of decisions excepted from the final judgment rule by Cohen, the order must conclusively determine the disputed question, resolve an important issue completely separate from the merits of the action, and be effectively unreviewable on appeal from a final judgment." Coopers & Lybrand v. Livesay, 437 U.S. 463 (1978).

A and B are incorrect because they ignore the above rules.

D is incorrect because the fact that the ruling was adverse to the plaintiff does not state the most accurate reason as to why the plaintiff may appeal the order.

Civil Procedure Outline § VII B(2) Final Judgment Rule: Collateral Order Exception

QUESTION 46
ANSWER & EXPLANATION
Jurisdiction and Venue

(B)   No, because diversity of citizenship does not exist.

B is the correct answer. Diversity subject-matter jurisdiction exists if: 1) the opposing parties are citizens of different states; and 2) the amount in controversy exceeds $75,000, exclusive of interests and costs. There is no diversity jurisdiction when any party on one side of a dispute is a citizen of the same state as any party on the opposing side of the dispute. A person is a citizen of the state in which he or she is domiciled. A corporation may be a citizen in two states. A corporation is a citizen of the state in which it is incorporated. A corporation is also a citizen of the state in which it has its principal place of business. In this case, the corporation is a citizen of State C, where it is incorporated, as well as State A, where it has its principal place of business. Because the contractor is also a citizen of State A, diversity of citizenship does not exist, and therefore, the federal court does not have jurisdiction in this case.

A is incorrect because both the contractor and the corporation are citizens of State A. Therefore, complete diversity of citizenship does not exist.

C is incorrect because, although the amount in controversy requirement is satisfied, the parties' citizenship is not completely diverse.

D is incorrect because there is no indication that the claim in this fact pattern arises under federal law.

Civil Procedure Outline § I (A)(2)(a)(1): Diversity of Citizenship Jurisdiction

QUESTION 47
ANSWER & EXPLANATION
Pre-Trial Procedures

(D) Yes, because unless otherwise stated, the first dismissal by court order is without prejudice.

The correct answer is D. An action may be dismissed without court order:

- by the plaintiff alone by filing a notice of dismissal at any time before the adverse party serves an answer or a motion for summary judgment (whichever comes first); or

- by stipulation of dismissal signed by all parties who have appeared in the action.

Otherwise, the part(ies) seeking dismissal must obtain a court order. Unless otherwise stated, the first such dismissal is without prejudice. The second dismissal of an action based on or including the same claim may act as a judgment on the merits.

Civil Procedure Outline § III (F)(1) Adjudication without a Trial: Voluntary Dismissal of Claim

QUESTION 48
ANSWER & EXPLANATION
Law Applied by Federal Courts

(B)   The court should quiet title in favor of the investor.

B is the correct answer. This question tests the application of federal common law in state courts. Federal common law of federal law has a preclusive effect. A state court must apply federal common law when deciding issues of federal law. Here, the state court is determining the correct redemption period under a federal statute. The federal courts have developed a common law permitting the shortening of the redemption period. Because the state court must apply the federal common law, it must find that the redemption period has expired and quiet title in favor of the investor.

A is incorrect. Although the case does involve a federal statute, it is primarily a state-law case involving state property law, so there is no obligation to transfer the case, especially without a motion.

C is incorrect. The state court is obligated to apply the federal common law, which shortens the redemption period.

D is incorrect. The state court is not permitted to select between the two sources of law but rather must apply the federal common law because it is deciding a federal issue.

Civil Procedure Outline § II(B)(1)(a): State Court Follows Federal Common Law

QUESTION 49
ANSWER & EXPLANATION
Pre-Trial Procedures

(B)   No, because the construction company was not provided with notice.

The correct answer is B. A preliminary injunction is an injunction entered, with notice to the opposing party, before a final determination of the case. Fed. R. Civ. P. 65(a). Generally speaking, the only practical difference between a TRO and a preliminary injunction is that a preliminary injunction is issued:

•   after a moving party provides notice to a non-moving party; and

•   after the non-moving party has an opportunity to be heard.

A, C, and D are incorrect because they ignore the requirement that the opposing party be given reasonable notice.

Civil Procedure Outline § III (A)(2)(b) Preliminary Injunction

QUESTION 50
ANSWER & EXPLANATION
Jury Trials

(C) Yes, because the court may ask questions of the prospective jurors and then permit the lawyers for the parties to ask supplemental questions.

The correct answer is C. The trial court may either question the prospective jurors or permit the parties or lawyers to question them. Fed. R. Civ. P. 47(a). If the court questions the jurors, then:

•   the court must permit the parties or their lawyer to ask supplemental questions; or

•   the court must ask supplemental questions it considers proper. Id.

Civil Procedure Outline § IV B(1)(b)(1)(a) Selection and Composition of Juries: Jury Selection: Jury Selection Process: Mechanics of Questioning

QUESTION 51
ANSWER & EXPLANATION
Motions

(B) No, because the defense may be raised at trial.

The correct answer is B. A party may move to dismiss an action on the ground that the party bringing an action has failed to state a claim. The defense of failure to state a claim is generally not waived if it is not asserted in a Rule 12 motion or in the defendant's answer. In fact, it may be raised in any pleading permitted or ordered, by motion for judgment on the pleadings, or at trial.

A is incorrect because the defense of failure to state a claim may be raised in any pleading permitted or ordered, by motion for judgment on the pleadings, or at trial.

C is incorrect because the defense of failure to state a claim may be raised prior to trial or during trial. D is incorrect because the defense of failure to state a claim does not have to be raised in the first responsive pleading.

Civil Procedure Outline § V (A)(1)(b)(2)(b) Pretrial Motions: Non-Waivable Defenses: Failure to State a Claim

QUESTION 52
ANSWER & EXPLANATION
Pre-Trial Procedures

(D)   Yes, although settlement is not technically an adjudication, settlement has the same effect when the parties enter into a consent judgment.

The correct answer is D. The parties to a case can agree to settle the case out of court. The parties may set forth and sign their settlement agreement in a consent judgment (a judgment by consent or stipulation), which the court signs, enters on the record, and may enforce as a judgment. Although settlement does not technically constitute adjudication, it can have the same effect when the parties enter into a consent judgment.

Civil Procedure Outline § III (F)(2) Adjudication without a Trial: Settlement and Consent Judgment

QUESTION 53
ANSWER & EXPLANATION
Verdicts and Judgments

(A)   No, because the default judgment precluded the motorcyclist from making claims that were subject to a compulsory counterclaim requirement.

The correct answer is A. In most states a default judgment precludes a losing party from raising defenses that could have been asserted in the lawsuit, or from making claims that were subject to a compulsory counterclaim requirement of law in that lawsuit. 3 *Moore's Federal Practice §* 13.14 (3d ed.). In this case, the motorcyclist's claim was a compulsory counterclaim (i.e., it arose from the same occurrence), and therefore, the default judgment prevents the motorcyclist from raising the claim.

Civil Procedure Outline § VI A(1)(a)(4) Defaults and Involuntary Dismissals: Default Judgment: Motion for a Default Judgment: Preclusive Effect of Default Judgment

QUESTION 54
ANSWER & EXPLANATION
Appealability and Review

(B)   No, because the motorcyclist did not preserve the matter for appeal.

The correct answer is B. An appellate court can only review matters presented on the trial record. A party must take steps to present matters in order to preserve trial error for appeal. Generally, a party must object to a ruling of a court that the objecting party considers erroneous in order to preserve the matter for appeal. The objection must be made:

- contemporaneously to the ruling; and

- with particularity regarding the grounds for the objection.

In this case, the motorcyclist failed to properly object to the admission of the evidence, and therefore, the issue was not preserved for appeal.

A, C, and D are incorrect because they ignore the above rules.

Civil Procedure Outline § VII C(1)(a) Scope of Review for Judge and Jury: Preservation of Error: Contemporaneous Objection and Offer of Proof

QUESTION 55
ANSWER & EXPLANATION
Jurisdiction and Venue

(A)   No, because the parties are diverse and the amount in controversy is satisfied.

The correct answer is A. If a plaintiff possesses two unrelated claims, which total over $75,000, against a single defendant, then the plaintiff may sue in federal court because the aggregate exceeds $75,000. Here, the aggregate of damages sought exceeds $75,000, and the parties are diverse. Therefore, the federal court has subject-matter jurisdiction.

B is incorrect because the fact that the accident occurred in the taxi driver's state of residence does not have any bearing on whether the federal court has subject-matter jurisdiction in this case.

C is incorrect because unrelated claims may be aggregated to satisfy the amount in controversy requirement.

D is incorrect because a party may aggregate unrelated claims to satisfy the amount in controversy requirement.

Civil Procedure Outline § I (A)(2)(b)(2): Aggregation of Claims

QUESTION 56
ANSWER & EXPLANATION
Pre-Trial Procedures

(C) Yes, because the driver did not obtain a judgment that was more favorable than the trucker's offer.

The correct answer is C. At least 14 days before the trial date, a defendant may serve upon a plaintiff, an offer of judgment against the defendant for a particular amount of money or property. If the plaintiff provides a written notice of acceptance within 14 days, then either party may file the offer and notice, and the court clerk will enter judgment. Fed. R. Civ. P. 68(a). If the plaintiff does not accept the offer, and does not obtain a judgment more favorable than the offer, then the plaintiff must pay the costs of the trial from when the defendant made the offer. Fed. R. Civ. P. 68(d).

Civil Procedure Outline § III (F)(3) Adjudication without a Trial: Offer of Judgment and Notice of Acceptance

QUESTION 57
ANSWER & EXPLANATION
Law Applied by Federal Courts

(B) Actual damages and attorney's fees.

B is the correct answer. This question tests the Erie doctrine as it applies to choice-of-law rules. Under the Erie doctrine, a federal court hearing a diversity case must apply the choice-of-law rules of the state in which it sits to determine which state's substantive law governs. In this instance, although there is complete diversity, and the amount in controversy is sufficient, the court has subject-matter jurisdiction because the issue is a federal question. Therefore, the court must apply the federal law, which permits actual damages and attorney's fees.

A is incorrect. Even if this were a diversity case, the court sits in State X, so State Y common law would not apply. This case is a federal case, though, thus federal law applies.

C is incorrect. This outcome would require the court to determine its own method of computation, which is not permitted.

D is incorrect. If the court was hearing this case as a diversity case, then it would be obligated under Erie to apply the common law of the state in which it sits. As mentioned above, the court is hearing a federal question and must apply federal law.

Civil Procedure Outline § I(2)(b): Choice-of-Law Rules of Forum State

QUESTION 58
ANSWER & EXPLANATION
Pre-Trial Procedures

(D)   Yes, because the resident made a strong showing that it would prevail on the merits, that the resident will suffer irreparable injury if the injunction is not granted, that the construction company will not be substantially harmed by the injunction, and public interest would favor preventing contamination of the water supply.

The correct answer is D. When determining whether to grant a preliminary injunction, a court may examine several factors.

(1)   Likelihood of Success on Merits: A court considering whether to enter a preliminary injunction may consider whether the moving party made a strong showing that it is likely to prevail on the merits.

(2)   Irreparable Injury: A court considering whether to enter a preliminary injunction may consider whether the moving party has shown that without such relief, it will suffer irreparable injury.

(3)   Harm to Others: A court considering whether to enter a preliminary injunction may consider whether the issuance of the injunction would substantially harm other interested parties.

(4)   Public Interest: A court considering whether to enter a preliminary injunction must conduct an examination of the public interest under the circumstances.

A, B, and C are incorrect because they state erroneous legal standards.

Civil Procedure Outline § III (A)(2)(b)(2) Preliminary Injunction: Factors Courts Generally Examine

QUESTION 59
ANSWER & EXPLANATION
Pre-Trial Procedures

(C)   The attorney may challenge the jury panel on the basis that it does not represent a fair cross section of the community.

The correct answer is C. At voir dire, a lawyer may object to the composition of the jury panel as not fulfilling constitutional or statutory prerequisites. For example, an attorney may challenge the jury panel on the basis that it does not represent a fair cross section of the community. 28 U.S.C. § 1870.

This question is loosely based on Edmonson v. Leesville Concrete Company, in which the United States Supreme Court held that race-based peremptory challenges are not permissible. 500 U.S. 614 (1991). Consequently, on the facts of this question, the attorney for the worker could challenge the jury panel on the basis that it does not represent a fair cross section of the community.

A is incorrect because an appeal would not be appropriate until the case is final. At this point, the trial has not yet occurred and no judgment has been entered, so appeal would be premature.

B is incorrect because it is an erroneous statement of law.

D is incorrect because the jury panel should represent a fair cross section of the community, not be empanelled in favor of one of the parties.

Civil Procedure Outline § IV B(1)(b)(1)(b) Selection and Composition of Juries: Jury Selection: Jury Selection Process: Challenge to Jury Panel

QUESTION 60
ANSWER & EXPLANATION
Motions

(B)   may use common sense and judicial experience to decide whether the claim for relief is plausible.

The correct answer is B. A federal court takes two steps when determining plausibility of a claim. First, the court identifies the legal conclusions and the factual allegations. The court must accept the well-pleaded factual allegations as true, but need not accept the legal conclusions as true. Second, the court determines whether the complaint states a *plausible* claim for relief based on the factual allegations. The court will make a context-specific analysis of whether a claim for relief is plausible based on the court's common sense and judicial experience.

A and D are incorrect because the court *must* accept the well-pleaded factual allegations as true.

C is incorrect because the court need not accept the legal conclusions as true.

Civil Procedure Outline § V (A)(1)(b)(2)(b)(1) Pretrial Motions: Non-Waivable Defenses: Failure to State a Claim: Determining Plausibility of Claim

QUESTION 61
ANSWER & EXPLANATION
Pre-Trial Procedures

(A) No, because the court did not require that the trucker and driver consider the use of alternative dispute resolution processes.

The correct answer is A. All federal district courts must require that litigants consider the use of alternative dispute resolution (ADR) processes in civil litigation. 28 U.S.C. § 652. A federal district court must provide for the confidentiality of ADR processes and prohibit disclosure of confidential ADR communications.

Civil Procedure Outline § III (F)(4) Adjudication without a Trial: Federal Alternative Dispute Resolution Act of 1998

QUESTION 62
ANSWER & EXPLANATION
Verdicts and Judgments

(C) Yes, because a defaulting party may challenge the jurisdiction of the court entering the default in the court where the judgment creditor attempts to enforce the judgment.

The correct answer is C. A default judgment has a preclusive effect if the court entering the default judgment possesses jurisdiction (subject matter and personal) of the case and the parties. The defaulting party may challenge the jurisdiction of the court entering the default in the court where the judgment-creditor attempts to enforce the judgment.

Civil Procedure Outline § VI A(1)(a)(4) Defaults and Involuntary Dismissals: Default Judgment: Motion for a Default Judgment: Preclusive Effect of Default Judgment

QUESTION 63
ANSWER & EXPLANATION
Appealability and Review

(C) Yes, because the driver made an offer of proof that demonstrated what the purported evidence was intended to prove.

The correct answer is C. If an objection to the admissibility of evidence is sustained, the non-objecting party is prevented from introducing that evidence at trial. Consequently, in order to challenge the ruling on appeal, the non-objecting party must make an offer of proof that demonstrates what the purported evidence was intended to prove. That party may present appellate arguments in support of the admissibility of the purported evidence.

Civil Procedure Outline § VII C(1)(a) Scope of Review for Judge and Jury: Preservation of Error: Contemporaneous Objection and Offer of Proof

QUESTION 64
ANSWER AND EXPLANATION
Jurisdiction and Venue

(D)   Yes, because the motorcyclist's claim is a compulsory counterclaim.

The correct answer is D. A counterclaim is a claim made by a defendant against a plaintiff. It may or may not arise from the same transaction or occurrence giving rise to the plaintiff's claim. If a counterclaim is compulsory (i.e., arising from the same transaction or occurrence), then it will fall within the jurisdiction of the court and may be heard regardless of the amount in controversy. Here, the parties are diverse and the plaintiff's claim satisfies the amount in controversy requirement. Because the motorcyclist's claim arises from the same occurrence (the accident), it falls within the jurisdiction of the court even though the damages sought by the motorcyclist do not exceed $75,000.

A is incorrect because the motorcyclist's claim is a compulsory counterclaim, and therefore, it may be heard regardless of the amount in controversy because the driver's claim exceeds $75,000.

B is an incorrect statement. The motorcyclist's claim is a compulsory counterclaim.

C is incorrect because the motorcyclist's claim is a compulsory counterclaim. It arose from the same occurrence as the driver's claim.

Civil Procedure Outline § I (A)(2)(b)(3): Counterclaims

QUESTION 65
ANSWER & EXPLANATION
Pre-Trial Procedures

(B)   No, because the doctor's attorney was absent.

The correct answer is B. If the federal district court holds a final pre-trial conference, it must be held as close to the time of trial as reasonable under the circumstances. Fed. R. Civ. P. 16(d). The participants at any such conference must formulate a plan for trial, including a program for facilitating the admission of evidence. The conference must be attended by at least one of the attorneys who will conduct the trial for each of the parties, and by any unrepresented parties. In this case, the doctor was represented by an attorney; therefore, the doctor's attorney was required to attend the conference.

Civil Procedure Outline § III (G)(1)(c) Pre-Trial Conference and Order: Pre-Trial Conference: Final Pre-Trial Conference

QUESTION 66
ANSWER & EXPLANATION
Law Applied by Federal Courts

(C) look at all relevant State M case law and determine how State M's highest court is likely to rule.

Because State M's comparative negligence statute is ambiguous, and the state's common law is not settled, the federal court is obligated to review all relevant state court decisions and determine how it believes the state's highest court would rule.

A is incorrect. There is no federal common law of comparative negligence. Also, even though the state law is ambiguous, the federal court is forbidden from creating its own federal common law to fill the gap.

B is incorrect. The court must determine whether State M's highest court is likely to adopt the approach in the last State M case or if it would rule otherwise.

D is incorrect. Under *Erie*, the federal court must apply the common law of the state in which it sits.

Civil Procedure Outline § II(A)(2)(a): Erie *Doctrine*

QUESTION 67
ANSWER & EXPLANATION
Pre-Trial Procedures

(C) Yes, because a pleading may be inconsistent or alternative.

The correct answer is C. A pleading may be inconsistent or alternative. The Rules reject the common law "Election of Remedies" doctrine. Under the common law, a plaintiff was required to choose a method of recovery for harm. Once a method of recovery was selected, the plaintiff could not assert an alternative or inconsistent method of recovery.

A and B are incorrect for the above reasons. D is incorrect because, although it is a correct factual statement, the better choice is answer choice C, which states the correct legal concept.

Civil Procedure Outline § III (B)(2)(b) Nature and Style of Pleadings: Pleading may be Inconsistent or Alternative

QUESTION 68
ANSWER & EXPLANATION
Jury Trials

(B) No, because a party may make an unlimited number of challenges for cause on grounds that a juror has a bias or relationship to a party.

The correct answer is B. Each party alternately strikes (or challenges) prospective jurors from the array until the number of jurors needed for the jury is reached. At *voir dire*, a lawyer may object to a prospective juror by making either a challenge for cause or a peremptory challenge.

A party may make an unlimited number of challenges for cause on grounds that a juror:

-     does not fulfill the statutory qualifications for jury duty; or

-     has a bias or relationship to a party or the case.

Civil Procedure Outline § IV B(1)(b)(1)(c)(i) Selection and Composition of Juries: Jury Selection: Jury Selection Process: Voir Dire: Challenge to Prospective Juror: Challenge for Cause

QUESTION 69
ANSWER & EXPLANATION
Motions

(C) Yes, because the inventor's complaint contained just enough facts to support a possible claim for relief.

The correct answer is C. A claim is plausible when the plaintiff pleads enough facts to permit the court to reasonably infer that the defendant is liable for the alleged misconduct. The complaint must state more than a mere possibility that the defendant did not act lawfully. For example, a court will grant a motion to dismiss for failure to state a claim if the plaintiff alleges enough facts of misconduct by the defendant to support a possible claim for relief, but not enough to support a plausible claim for relief. In this case, the facts state only that the inventor's complaint alleges "just enough" facts to support a possible claim for relief. Because there is no indication that the facts in the complaint support a *plausible* claim for relief, the court properly granted the motion to dismiss.

A is incorrect because the complaint must allege enough facts to support a plausible—not just possible—claim for relief.

B and D are incorrect because they ignore the requirement that the factual allegations in the complaint must support a plausible claim for relief.

Civil Procedure Outline § V (A)(1)(b)(2)(b)(1) Pretrial Motions: Non-Waivable Defenses: Failure to State a Claim: Determining Plausibility of Claim

QUESTION 70
ANSWER & EXPLANATION
Pre-Trial Procedures

(C) Yes, because the attorney was substantially unprepared to participate in the conference.

The correct answer is C. A court may issue such orders that are just, and among other options, may impose sanctions if:

- a party or the party's attorney fails to obey a scheduling or pre-trial order;

- no appearance is made on behalf of a party at a scheduling or pre-trial conference;

- a party or party's attorney is substantially unprepared to participate in the conference; or

- a party or party's attorney fails to participate in good faith.
Fed. R. Civ. P. 16(f).

A is incorrect because if a federal district court holds a final pre-trial conference, it must be held as close to the time of trial as reasonable under the circumstances.

B is incorrect because the attorney was required to attend the conference.

D is incorrect because the attorney for either party is required to be prepared to participate in the conference.

Civil Procedure Outline § III (G)(1)(e)(1) Pre-Trial Conference and Order: Pre-Trial Conference: Sanctions: Grounds for Sanctions

QUESTION 71
ANSWER & EXPLANATAION
Verdicts and Judgments

(D) Yes, because the trucker failed to comply with discovery orders and failed to attend pretrial conferences.

The correct answer is D. A federal court has the authority to sanction a litigant for a violation of the Rules. The most extreme sanction is entering a default judgment. For example, a court may enter a default judgment against a party who refuses to comply with critical discovery orders or fails to attend mandatory conferences. However, a default judgment as a sanction should only be entered in the most extreme circumstances.

A is incorrect because it ignores the fact that the trucker did not comply with discovery orders and failed to attend pre-trial conferences that were ordered by the court.

B is an incorrect statement of law.

C is incorrect because the trucker's failure to comply with discovery and failure to attend conferences are not admissions.

Civil Procedure Outline § VI A(1)(b) Defaults and Involuntary Dismissals: Default Judgment: Default as Sanction

QUESTION 72
ANSWER & EXPLANATION
Appealability and Review

(D) Yes, because the error constituted plain error.

The correct answer is D. Plain error is a flaw in the trial process that is so obvious that a failure of the parties or the court to notice and rectify it would seriously affect the fairness or integrity of the judicial proceedings. To rise to the level of plain error, an asserted error must:

- seriously affect a party's substantial rights; and

- cause an unfair prejudicial impact on the jury's deliberations.

The plain error exception to the contemporaneous objection rule is to be used sparingly, in only those circumstances in which a miscarriage of justice would otherwise result.

A is incorrect because it ignores the above rule and neglects the facts that indicate the error was plain error.

B is incorrect because hiring a new attorney does not bar a party from raising an issue on appeal.

C is incorrect because it is an erroneous statement of law.

Civil Procedure Outline § VII C(1)(a)(1) Scope of Review for Judge and Jury: Preservation of Error: Contemporaneous Objection and Offer of Proof: Plain Error Exception – Objection Is Not Required

QUESTION 73
ANSWER & EXPLANATION
Jurisdiction and Venue

(C)   Decline jurisdiction to hear the case because the case involves an alimony decree.

The correct answer is C. A federal court will decline jurisdiction over a case involving the issuance of a divorce, alimony, or a child custody decree.

A is incorrect because although the parties are diverse and the amount in controversy is satisfied, a federal court will decline jurisdiction over a case involving alimony.

B is incorrect because it is an incorrect statement of law.

D is incorrect because federal courts will decline jurisdiction over a case involving alimony.

Civil Procedure Outline § I (A)(2)(b)(5): Domestic Relations Exception

QUESTION 74
ANSWER & EXPLANATION
Pre-Trial Procedures

(D)   Yes, because the attorney repeatedly and willfully missed deadlines.

The correct answer is D. In lieu of, or in addition to any other sanction, a judge can require a party, attorney, or both, to pay the reasonable expenses incurred because of any noncompliance. Some other more severe sanctions include striking pleadings, entering a default judgment, or dismissing a lawsuit. The latter two sanctions generally are proper "only when [a litigant's] misconduct is serious, repeated, contumacious, extreme, or otherwise inexcusable." *Bachier-Ortiz v. Colon-Mendoza*, 331 F.3d 193 (1st Cir. 2003). Unless grounds exist to believe that lesser sanctions would not ensure obedience to the judge's order, such sanctions should be imposed prior to ordering more severe ones. *Berry v. CIGNA/RSI-CIGNA*, 975 F.2d 1188 (5th

Cir. 1992). Of course, sanctions can be challenged and reversed on appeal if they constitute an abuse of the judge's discretion in terms of whether they are just under the facts and their severity. *Link v. Wabash R.R. Co., 370 U.S. 626 (1962).*

Civil Procedure Outline § III (G)(1)(e)(2) Pre-Trial Conference and Order: Sanctions: Types of Sanctions

QUESTION 75
ANSWER & EXPLANATION
Law Applied by Federal Courts

(A)   for the banker, because the State L court would have applied State L law.

A is the correct answer. This question tests the *Erie* doctrine as it applies to choice-of-law rules. Under the *Erie* doctrine, a federal court hearing a diversity case must apply the choice-of-law rules of the state in which it sits to determine which state's substantive law governs. This rule was implemented to discourage forum shopping. Here, the court sits in State L, so it must apply State L's common law to decide the case.

B and C are incorrect. The citizenship of the parties has no bearing on which common law the court must apply.

D is incorrect. Although the case originated in state court, the federal court is still obligated to adhere to the *Erie* doctrine and apply the common law and the choice-of-law rules of the forum state.

Civil Procedure Outline § II(A)(2)(b): Choice-of-Law Rules of Forum State

QUESTION 76
ANSWER & EXPLANATION
Pre-Trial Procedures

(A) No, because it involved a special matter that should have been pleaded with particularity.

The correct answer is A. Special matters must be plead with particularity. Special matters include fraud, mistake, judgments, and special damages. In this case, the homeowner's pleading was brief. The complaint likely should have stated, among other things, where and when the fraudulent statements were made, how they were made, and it should have specified the injuries sustained.

B is incorrect because the Rules reject the common law Election of Remedies doctrine. Further, in this case, the homeowner did elect one remedy: fraud.

C is incorrect because mere notice pleading would be insufficient. Under the Federal Rules of Civil Procedure, "notice" pleading was traditionally required for stating a claim, under which a complaint merely had to provide the opposing party with notice of the nature of the claim. Currently, "plausibility" pleading is required for stating a claim, under which a complaint must now allege enough facts to state a plausible claim for relief.

D is incorrect because it ignores the requirement for particularity when pleading fraud.

Civil Procedure Outline § III (B)(2)(b) Nature and Style of Pleadings: Pleading Special Matters

QUESTION 77
ANSWER & EXPLANATION
Jury Trials

(D)   Yes, the court may take the prospective juror's statement into consideration.

The correct answer is D. If a potential juror states that he can fairly consider the evidence, a court may take the statement into consideration.

A is incorrect because it tends to suggest that the court could not consider the prospective juror's statement.

B is incorrect because it is not necessary for the prospective juror to submit a sworn affidavit when answering questions during *voir dire.*

C is incorrect because it is not necessary for a party to object to a prospective juror's statement in order for the court to consider it.

Civil Procedure Outline § IV B(1)(b)(1)(c)(ii) Selection and Composition of Juries: Jury Selection: Jury Selection Process: Voir Dire: Challenge to Prospective Juror: Peremptory Challenge

QUESTION 78
ANSWER & EXPLANATION
Motions

(A)   No, because the defense may be raised at trial.

The correct answer is A. The defense of failure to join an indispensable party may be raised in any pleading permitted or ordered, by motion for judgment on the pleadings, or at trial. The defense of failure to join an indispensible party is not waived if it is not asserted in a Rule 12 motion or in the defendant's answer.

B, C, and D are incorrect for the reason stated above.

Civil Procedure Outline § V (A)(1)(b)(2)(c) Pretrial Motions: Non-Waivable Defenses: Failure to Join an Indispensible Party

QUESTION 79
ANSWER & EXPLANATION
Pre-Trial Procedures

(C) Yes, because after receiving the parties' discovery reports, a federal district court must enter a scheduling order that limits the time to join other parties and to amend the pleadings, file motions, and complete discovery.

The correct answer is C. After receiving the parties' discovery reports, a federal district court *must* enter a scheduling order that limits the time to:

- join other parties and to amend the pleadings;

- file motions; and

- complete discovery.

Fed. R. Civ. P. 16(b).

Civil Procedure Outline § III (G)(2) Pre-Trial Conference and Order: Scheduling Orders

QUESTION 80
ANSWER & EXPLANATION
Verdicts and Judgments

(D) abuse of discretion

The correct answer is D. A party's appeal challenging a sanction of default judgment will be reviewed under an abuse-of-discretion standard. The court examines the severity of the sanction and surrounding circumstances, and may grant the appeal if the trial judge abused his discretion in entering the default judgment.

Civil Procedure Outline § VI A(1)(b) Defaults and Involuntary Dismissals: Default Judgment: Default as Sanction: Standard of Review

QUESTION 81
ANSWER & EXPLANATION
Appealability and Review

(A)   Harmless error rule

The correct answer is A. The harmless error rule provides that any error which does not affect the substantive rights of the parties cannot be the grounds for an appeal. Generally, the standard in a civil case is whether an erroneous charge of the jury or ruling of the court would likely have affected a trial's result.

Civil Procedure Outline § VII C(1)(b) Scope of Review for Judge and Jury: Preservation of Error: Harmless Error Rule

QUESTION 82
ANSWER & EXPLANATION
Jurisdiction and Venue

(D)   Yes, because claim one arises under federal law and claim two is part of the same case or controversy.

The correct answer is D. Under the doctrine of supplemental jurisdiction, certain new parties and new claims may be added to a case without satisfying an independent subject-matter jurisdiction test. In a civil action in which a district court has original jurisdiction, the district court also has supplemental jurisdiction over all other claims that are so related to claims in the action within such original jurisdiction that they form part of the same case or controversy. Here, the court has original jurisdiction over claim one because it arises under federal law. Because the facts of the question state that the state law claim is part of the same case or controversy as the federal claim, the court may exercise supplemental jurisdiction over the state law claim.

A and B are incorrect because an independent jurisdictional basis for the state law claim is not necessary for the court to have supplemental jurisdiction in this case.

C is incorrect because the fact that the defendant did not file a motion to dismiss has no bearing on whether the court has jurisdiction over the state law claim.

Civil Procedure Outline § I (A)(3): Supplemental Jurisdiction

QUESTION 83
ANSWER & EXPLANATION
Pre-Trial Procedures

(B) No, because a temporary restraining order cannot be issued for the period of time sought by the small business.

The correct answer is B. A temporary restraining order ("TRO") is limited to 14 days, absent good cause. Here, the small business seeks a TRO pending the outcome of the lawsuit, but good cause is not alleged. Therefore, the court would not order a TRO through the outcome of the litigation.

A is incorrect because a TRO can be issued on an *ex parte* basis when it is necessary to prevent irreparable injury. Fed. R. Civ. P. 65(b).

C is incorrect because to obtain an *ex parte* TRO, the moving party must meet three conditions. First, the moving party must set out specific facts, under oath, that show immediate and irreparable injury will result to them before the other party can be heard in opposition. Second, the moving party must certify to the court, in writing, the efforts made to give the notice and the reasons supporting the claim that notice should not be required. Finally, the moving party must provide a bond to the court in a sum that the court deems proper to compensate the other party should the TRO be wrongfully entered. C is incorrect because it omits the bond requirement.

D is incorrect because, although the small business offered to post a bond, the bond must be sufficient to compensate the other party should the TRO be wrongfully entered. In light of the $2 million judgment that is sought, a $5,000 bond would likely be deemed insufficient.

Civil Procedure Outline § III(A)(2): Types of Non-Permanent Injunctions

QUESTION 84
ANSWER & EXPLANATION
Law Applied by Federal Courts

(D) the other creditor, because the fixture filing did not contain an after-acquired property clause.

D is the correct answer. This question tests the *Erie* doctrine. Under the *Erie* doctrine, a federal court hearing a diversity case must apply the statutory and common law of the state in which it sits. Here, the federal court sits in State A. Therefore, it must apply State A's common law, which strictly construes the UCC to require the clause.

A is incorrect. The federal courts are not permitted to exercise their independent judgment to make policy decisions on state law just because they disagree with the state court determinations.

B is incorrect. The federal court must apply the common law of the forum state.

C is incorrect. There is no federal common law of state law matters.

Civil Procedure Outline § II(A)(2)(a): Erie *Doctrine*

QUESTION 85
ANSWER & EXPLANATION
Pre-Trial Procedures

(B)   No, because once a pleading is verified, responsive pleadings must also be verified.

The correct answer is B.   Verification (oath or notarization) of pleadings is generally unnecessary unless required by statute or unless requesting equitable relief.   However, once a pleading is verified, responsive pleadings must also be made under oath.   In this case, because the complaint was verified, the answer needed to be verified as well.

A, C, and D are incorrect because they ignore the Rule stated above.

Civil Procedure Outline § III (B)(2)(c) Nature and Style of Pleadings: Verification not Required

QUESTION 86
ANSWER & EXPLANATION
Jury Trials

(C) Yes, because a court may allow additional peremptory challenges.

The correct answer is C. A peremptory challenge is the right to challenge a potential juror without stating a reason. A party could use a peremptory challenge to remove a prospective juror that is believed to have some social or occupational opinion that is not favorable to the party. Each party may make three peremptory challenges. Fed. R. Civ. P. 47(b). A court may allow additional peremptory challenges. Multiple defendants or plaintiffs may be considered a single party for the purposes of making challenges.

Civil Procedure Outline § IV B(1)(b)(1)(c)(ii)(A) Selection and Composition of Juries: Jury Selection: Jury Selection Process: Voir Dire: Challenge to Prospective Juror: Peremptory Challenge: Number of Challenges

QUESTION 87
ANSWER & EXPLANATION
Motions

(D)   The driver may not file a revised complaint against the trucker.

The correct answer is D. Often, a Rule 12(b) motion dismissal is made *without prejudice*, which means that a plaintiff may re-file its complaint within a limited time period after modification in order to avoid another dismissal on the same grounds. Under certain circumstances, a dismissal may be made *with prejudice*, meaning that the plaintiff is entirely precluded from re-filing a revised complaint against the defendant.

A, B, and C are incorrect because the dismissal of the case was with prejudice. Therefore, the driver is precluded from re-filing a revised complaint. C is also incorrect because it misuses the word "cross-claim," which is (generally speaking) a claim against a co-party.

Civil Procedure Outline § V (A)(1)(a) Pretrial Motions: Motion to Dismiss: Effect of Dismissal without Prejudice, or with Prejudice

QUESTION 88
ANSWER & EXPLANATION
Pre-Trial Procedures

(C)   No, because notice and an opportunity to be heard were not provided to the real estate company.

The correct answer is C. A court can only issue a preliminary injunction after the party seeking the injunction has provided reasonable notice to the non-moving party, and the non-moving party has had an opportunity to be heard. Although the young broker set the matter for a hearing, the facts do not state that he provided notice to the real estate company. Therefore, the young broker did not satisfy the requirement that he provide notice and an opportunity for the real estate company to be heard.

A is incorrect because there is not a set amount of time that a preliminary injunction can be issued. Rather, a preliminary injunction maintains the *status quo* until the parties' claims can be adjudicated.

B is incorrect because it does not address all four factors that a court considers when deciding whether to grant a preliminary injunction. When determining whether to issue a preliminary injunction, a court examines the likelihood that the moving party will succeed on the merits of the lawsuit, whether the moving party has shown that without the injunction they will suffer irreparable injury, whether the injunction would substantially harm other interested parties, and whether there is any public interest concern under the circumstances. Although the young broker has established that he will likely succeed on the merits of his lawsuit because there was a contract for the sale of the mansion, this answer does not address the other three factors the court must consider.

D is incorrect because it also does not address all four factors that the court must consider before granting a preliminary injunction.

Civil Procedure Outline § III(A)(2): Types of Non-Permanent Injunctions

QUESTION 89
ANSWER & EXPLANATION
Verdicts and Judgments

(C)   Yes, because inactivity by the plaintiff alone may justify dismissal.

The correct answer is C. A court may dismiss an action for lack of prosecution. Lack of prosecution refers to a lack of record activity for an extended period of time. Inactivity by the plaintiff alone may, under the circumstances of the case, justify dismissal. For example, a plaintiff who fails to file any documents or conduct any activity in a case for over two years may have the case dismissed for lack of prosecution.

Civil Procedure Outline § VI A(2)(a) Defaults and Involuntary Dismissals: Involuntary Dismissal of Claim: Lack of Prosecution

QUESTION 90
ANSWER & EXPLANATION
Appealability and Review

(D)   de novo

The correct answer is D. An appellate court review of a trial court's determination of a pure issue of law is reviewed using a *de novo* standard. A court reviewing an issue of law under a *de novo* standard provides no deference to the trial court's determination.

Civil Procedure Outline § VII C(2)(a) Scope of Review for Judge and Jury: Standards of Review: De Novo

QUESTION 91
ANSWER & EXPLANATION
Jurisdiction and Venue

(B)   No, because only defendants may remove cases to federal court.

The correct choice is B. Removal is the process of moving a case filed in a state court to a federal court. However, only a defendant may remove a case to federal court. A case that is originally filed in a state court may be removed to a federal court if: (1) the case could have been filed in a federal court (federal subject-matter jurisdiction exists); (2) all defendants agree to remove the case; and (3) the grounds for removal are included in at least one claim of a plaintiff (i.e., the grounds cannot be based on an affirmative defense or a counterclaim).

A, C, and D are incorrect because a plaintiff may not remove a case to federal court.

Civil Procedure Outline § I (A)(4): Removal from State Court to Federal Court

QUESTION 92
ANSWER & EXPLANATION
Pre-Trial Procedures

(C)   Yes, because Driver A's wife filed a motion seeking to supplement the complaint and provided notice to Driver B.

The correct answer is C. A supplemental pleading is used to set forth events that have occurred after the filing of a prior pleading. A party seeking to supplement a pleading must obtain leave of court before filing the supplemental pleading by making a motion to supplement the pleading. Notice of the motion must also be provided to the opposing party. Here, Driver A's wife appropriately filed a motion and served Driver B with a copy of the motion.

A is incorrect because although Driver A's wife appropriately filed a motion to supplement the complaint, this answer fails to address the other requirement that notice be provided to the other party.

B is incorrect because there is no specific time requirement within which a motion to supplement the pleadings must be filed.

D is incorrect because there is no requirement that a motion to supplement the pleading be filed within a specific time after the event. There also is not a requirement that good cause be shown in order to supplement the pleadings. Although leave of court must be obtained before serving the supplemental pleading, the courts' practice is usually liberal in allowing the filing of supplemental pleadings.

Civil Procedure Outline § III(B)(6): Supplemental Pleadings

QUESTION 93
ANSWER & EXPLANATION
Pre-Trial Procedures

(D)   Yes, because the trucker did not address the allegation.

The correct answer is D. An answer is a pleading that challenges a plaintiff's right to the relief that is requested in a complaint. The answer must admit or deny the allegations that are set forth in a complaint.   Alternatively, the answer may assert a defendant's lack of sufficient knowledge to admit or deny an allegation. If a defendant fails to deny, or address, an allegation in the complaint, the court may deem the allegation admitted. In this case, because the trucker failed to address the allegation regarding speed, the court may deem the allegation admitted.

A is incorrect because the trucker need not affirmatively admit the allegation in order for the court to deem the allegation admitted, as explained above. B and C are incorrect because the Rule does not support them.

Civil Procedure Outline § III (B)(3)(b) Nature and Style of Pleadings: Answer

QUESTION 94
ANSWER & EXPLANATION
Jury Trials

(C)   Yes, because multiple defendants or plaintiffs may be considered a single party for the purposes of making challenges.

The correct answer is C. Multiple defendants or plaintiffs may be considered a single party for the purposes of making challenges.

A and B are incorrect because they are erroneous statements of law.

D is incorrect because each party may make three peremptory challenges.

Civil Procedure Outline § IV B(1)(b)(1)(c)(ii)(B) Selection and Composition of Juries: Jury Selection: Jury Selection Process: Voir Dire: Challenge to Prospective Juror: Peremptory Challenge: Multiple Parties Treated as One

QUESTION 95
ANSWER & EXPLANATION
Motions

(C)   File a motion for a more definite statement.

The correct answer is C. A party may file a motion for a more definite statement if served with a pleading that is vague, ambiguous, or unclear, that the party cannot understand or respond to it. A motion for a more definite statement requests that the court require the filing of a revised pleading that is sufficiently clear and definitive.

A is incorrect because a motion to strike is appropriate when a pleading contains redundant, immaterial, impertinent, or scandalous matters. In this case, the facts do not suggest such matters are in the driver's complaint.

B is incorrect because the facts state that the mechanic cannot reasonably frame an answer.

D is incorrect because no judgment has yet been entered.
Civil Procedure Outline § V (A)(2)(a) Pretrial Motions: Motions Addressed to Face of Pleadings: Motion for a More Definite Statement

QUESTION 96
ANSWER & EXPLANATION
Pre-Trial Procedures

(B)   No, because the court did not allow the lawyer a reasonable opportunity to respond.

The correct answer is B. A lawyer must sign all pleadings. Fed. R. Civ. P. 11. Sanctions can be imposed if, after notice and a reasonable opportunity to respond, the court finds that Rule 11 has been violated. Here, although the judge set the matter for a hearing and provided notice of that hearing, he did not allow the lawyer an opportunity to respond to the allegation that he willfully failed to sign the pleadings. The court should not have imposed sanctions without allowing the lawyer an opportunity to respond.

A is incorrect because the court can impose sanctions on its own initiative.

C is incorrect because, although notice must be provided, a reasonable opportunity to respond must also be provided to the responding party. Here, the court provided notice by sending a notice of hearing to all the parties, but the court failed to allow the lawyer an opportunity to respond to the allegations. Therefore, this answer choice is incomplete.

D is incorrect because, although failure to sign pleadings is a violation of Rule 11, sanctions cannot be imposed immediately upon violation of the Rule. Before imposing sanctions, the court must provide notice and an opportunity to respond.

Civil Procedure Outline § III(C)(3): Process for Sanctions

QUESTION 97
ANSWER & EXPLANATION
Verdicts and Judgments

(C) Yes, because the order did not state that the dismissal was an adjudication on the merits.

The correct answer is C. Unless it states otherwise, an involuntary dismissal order acts as an adjudication on the merits.

Civil Procedure Outline § VI A(2)(c) Defaults and Involuntary Dismissals: Involuntary Dismissal of Claim: Adjudication on Merits

QUESTION 98
ANSWER & EXPLANATION
Appealability and Review

(B) abuse of discretion

The correct answer is B. Determinations of the admissibility of evidence are reviewed using an abuse-of-discretion standard. A court reviewing an issue under an abuse-of-discretion standard provides more deference to the trial court's decision.

Civil Procedure Outline § VII C(2)(b) Scope of Review for Judge and Jury: Standards of Review: Abuse of Discretion

QUESTION 99
ANSWER & EXPLANATION
Jurisdiction and Venue

(D) Yes, because the driver was served with process within the forum state.

D is the correct answer. A court has jurisdiction over a party when the party is served with process within the forum state (the state where the court is located). A state is presumed to possess limited legal authority over all of the people who are found within its borders. If a person is served with legal process while present in a state, any length of stay therein, no matter how brief, is sufficient to establish transient jurisdiction in the state.

A is incorrect because the driver was personally served with process while in the forum state.

B is incorrect because the fact that the driver did not make a purchase while in State B is not enough to defeat the court's personal jurisdiction in this case.

C is incorrect because the vacationer's citizenship in State B does not establish the court's personal jurisdiction over the driver in this case.

Civil Procedure Outline § I (B)(1)(a)(1): Personal Jurisdiction

QUESTION 100
ANSWER & EXPLANATION
Pre-Trial Procedures

(D)   No, because the first businessman will not suffer irreparable injury.

The correct answer is D. A temporary restraining order ("TRO") will only be issued on an *ex parte* basis when it is necessary to prevent irreparable injury. Fed. R. Civ. P. 65(b). Here, the first businessman will not suffer irreparable injury if the second businessman is not prevented from selling the airplane to someone else. There are no allegations that this airplane is particularly special or one-of-a-kind, or that his business would somehow suffer irreparable harm if he did not obtain this particular airplane. The first businessman can purchase another five-passenger airplane, and if he is ultimately successful in his lawsuit, monetary damages would be sufficient to cure any wrongdoing. Therefore, the *ex parte* TRO should not be issued.

A is incorrect because it does not address all of the conditions necessary for the court to issue an *ex parte* TRO. Although the moving party must post a bond in an amount that the court deems sufficient to compensate the non-moving party in the event the TRO is wrongfully entered, this is not the only condition that must be satisfied, so this answer choice is incomplete.

B is incorrect because the Rule does not require that notice be provided to the non-moving party before an *ex parte* TRO is issued. Rather, one of the conditions to issuing an *ex parte* TRO is that the moving party certifies the efforts made to give notice or the reasons supporting the claim that notice should not be required. Here, the first businessman certified that notice could not be given because the second businessman planned to sell the airplane to a third businessman in less than 24 hours. Thus, the first businessman has satisfied that condition.

C is incorrect because it does not address any of the conditions the court must consider before issuing an *ex parte* TRO. Rather, C addresses the merits of the underlying lawsuit, which is not one of the conditions to obtaining an *ex parte* TRO.

Civil Procedure Outline § III(A)(2): Types of Non-Permanent Injunctions

QUESTION 101
ANSWER & EXPLANATION
Pre-Trial Procedures

(B)   No, because the trucker served the answer 30 days after service of the complaint.

The correct answer is B.   An answer must be served within 21 days after the service of the complaint.

A is incorrect because a defendant may deny all of the allegations in an answer.   C and D are incorrect because they state an incorrect time limit for serving the answer.

Civil Procedure Outline § III (B)(3)(b)(1) Nature and Style of Pleadings: Answer: Time for Service

QUESTION 102
ANSWER & EXPLANATION
Jury Trials

(B)   No, because a jury must consist of a minimum of 6 and a maximum of 12 jurors.

The correct answer is B.   A jury must consist of a minimum of 6 and a maximum of 12 jurors. Fed. R. Civ. P. 48(a).   Each juror must participate in the verdict unless the court excuses a juror for good cause.   *Id.* citing Fed. R. Civ. P. 47(c).

Civil Procedure Outline § IV B(2)(a) Selection and Composition of Juries: Jury: Jury Composition: Number of Jurors

QUESTION 103
ANSWER & EXPLANATION
Motions

(B)   File a motion to strike.

The correct answer is B.   A party may move to strike redundant, immaterial, impertinent, or scandalous matters in a pleading.   Fed. R. Civ. P. 12(f).   If a court grants the motion, any such matter will be excluded from the record.   In this case, the inclusion of the name-calling in the complaint is likely immaterial and impertinent, and therefore, the mechanic should file a motion to strike the language.

A is incorrect because it is not the best choice of the four available choices in this question.   The mechanic should file a motion to strike the impertinent and immaterial language in the complaint.

C is incorrect because a motion for judgment on the pleadings may be filed *after* the pleadings are closed. In this case, the mechanic has not yet answered, so a motion for judgment on the pleadings would be premature.

D is incorrect because the facts in the question do not indicate that there is no genuine issue as to any material fact, which is the standard for granting a motion for summary judgment.

Civil Procedure Outline § V (A)(2)(b) Pretrial Motions: Motions Addressed to Face of Pleadings: Motion to Strike

QUESTION 104
ANSWER & EXPLANATION
Pre-Trial Procedures

B.   No, because the art enthusiast failed to certify the efforts made to provide notice to the art dealer, or the reasons why notice should not be provided.

The correct answer is B. One of the conditions that must be satisfied before the court can issue an *ex parte* temporary restraining order ("TRO") is that the moving party must certify in writing the efforts made to give notice to the non-moving party or the reasons supporting the claim that notice should not be provided. The art enthusiast failed to do this, so the *ex parte* TRO should not be issued.

A is incorrect because it fails to address all of the conditions necessary for the court to issue an *ex parte* TRO. Although the art enthusiast has satisfied one of the conditions by establishing that he will suffer irreparable harm if the art dealer sells the one-of-a-kind painting to another buyer, the art enthusiast has not satisfied all of the conditions to obtaining an *ex parte* TRO. Therefore, this answer choice is incomplete.

C is incorrect because it also fails to address all of the conditions necessary for the court to issue an *ex parte* TRO. Because the art enthusiast has posted a bond in the amount that the art dealer would receive if he sold the painting to the other buyer, he has posted a bond that would properly compensate the art dealer if the TRO were later determined to have been wrongfully entered. However, this not the only requirement that must be met before an *ex parte* TRO can be issued, so this answer is also incomplete.

D is incorrect because there are no such limitations regarding what types of cases in which an *ex parte* TRO can be issued.

Civil Procedure Outline § III(A)(2): Types of Non-Permanent Injunctions

QUESTION 105
ANSWER & EXPLANATION
Verdicts and Judgments

(D)   Yes, because the parties may stipulate to a non-unanimous verdict.

The correct answer is D. A minimum of 6 and a maximum of 12 jurors must participate in a verdict.   Unless the parties otherwise stipulate, 1) a verdict must be unanimous, and 2) no verdict will be taken from a jury that is reduced in size to fewer than 6 members. Fed. R. Civ. P. 48(b).

A and B are incorrect because they ignore the rule above, which states that parties may stipulate to a less than unanimous verdict.

C is an incorrect statement of law.

Civil Procedure Outline § VI B(1) Jury Verdicts—Types and Challenges: Number of Jurors and Verdict

QUESTION 106
ANSWER & EXPLANATION
Appealability and Review

(B)   No, because an appellate court reviewing a trial court's finding of fact in a bench trial uses the clearly erroneous standard.

The correct answer is B. An appellate court reviewing a trial court's finding of fact in a bench trial uses the clearly erroneous standard. An appellate court reviewing a trial court's finding of fact must be significantly deferential to the lower court. The determination should only be reversed if there is a definite and firm conviction that a mistake has been committed. In other words, if the trial court's finding is plausible, the appellate court will not reverse it.

Civil Procedure Outline § VII C(2)(c) Scope of Review for Judge and Jury: Standards of Review: Clearly Erroneous

QUESTION 107
ANSWER & EXPLANATION
Jurisdiction and Venue

(B)   No, because the driver waived his objection.

The correct answer is B. Today, in almost all jurisdictions, a party may object to, and directly attack, the jurisdiction of a court at the beginning of a case without submitting to the court's jurisdiction. However, if the objecting party also seeks *affirmative* relief from the court, the objection to jurisdiction is waived, and the attack fails. In this case, the driver filed a counterclaim in which he seeks $50,000. Consequently, by seeking such affirmative relief from the court, the driver waived his objection to the court's jurisdiction over him.

A is incorrect because the fact that the driver traveled to State B would not necessarily defeat his objection to personal jurisdiction.

C is incorrect because the driver waived the objection to personal jurisdiction by filing his counterclaim seeking affirmative relief in the court.

D is incorrect because the fact that the accident occurred in State A would not necessarily divest the court in State B of personal jurisdiction.

Civil Procedure Outline § I (B)(1)(a)(4): Personal Jurisdiction

QUESTION 108
ANSWER & EXPLANATION
Pre-Trial Procedures

(D) No, because the car collector did not post a bond that would properly compensate the car dealer if the temporary restraining order were later determined to be wrongfully entered.

The correct answer is D. A party seeking an *ex parte* temporary restraining order ("TRO") must post a bond in an amount sufficient to compensate the non-moving party in the event the TRO is wrongfully entered. Here, the car collector alleged under oath that the car is worth $250,000, so it is very unlikely that a $1,000 bond would be deemed sufficient to compensate the car dealer if the TRO were wrongfully entered. Therefore, the car collector has not posted a sufficient bond, so an *ex parte* TRO should not be issued.

A is incorrect because, although it is true that the car collector provided specific facts under oath establishing the irreparable injury he would suffer if the TRO were not issued, this is not the only requirement that must be satisfied before the court can issue an *ex parte* TRO. Therefore, this answer is incomplete.

B is incorrect because it does not accurately reflect the requirement that the bond must be sufficient to compensate the adverse party if the TRO is wrongfully entered. The requirement is not simply that the car collector post any bond, but rather he must post a bond that the court deems proper to compensate the car dealer in the event the TRO is wrongfully entered.

C is incorrect because it is not required that notice of the request for an *ex parte* TRO be provided to the adverse party. Rather, the requirement is that the moving party certify under oath the efforts made to give notice and the reasons supporting the claim that notice should not be required.

Civil Procedure Outline § III(A)(2): Types of Non-Permanent Injunctions

QUESTION 109
ANSWER & EXPLANATION
Pre-Trial Procedures

(C) Yes, because the opportunist amended the answer within 21 days after serving the initial answer.

The correct answer is C. A party may amend a pleading once as a matter of right within 21 days after serving it.

A, B, and D are incorrect because they ignore the Rule stated above.

Civil Procedure Outline § III (B)(5) Nature and Style of Pleadings: Amendment of Pleadings

QUESTION 110
ANSWER & EXPLANATION
Jury Trials

(A) No, because the lawyer did not object with particularity regarding the court's failure to provide the requested instruction.

The correct answer is A. No party may assign as error the court's giving or failure to give a written instruction to the jury unless:

-   the party objects with particularity for providing, or failing to provide, the written instruction;

-   before the jury retires to consider its verdict.

Civil Procedure Outline § IV C(2) Requests for and Objections to Jury Instructions: Objections—Preservation of Error in Jury Charge

QUESTION 111
ANSWER & EXPLANATION
Motions

(D)   determine whether, on the face of all pleadings, the bicyclist is entitled to judgment.

The correct answer is D. A motion for judgment on the pleadings under Rule 12(c) is similar to a motion to dismiss under Rule 12(b). What distinguishes a Rule 12(c) motion from a Rule 12(b) motion is that a motion for judgment on the pleadings must be filed *after* the pleadings are closed. When deciding a motion for judgment on the pleadings, a court will determine whether, on the face of all pleadings, the movant is entitled to judgment.

A, B, and C are incorrect because they each ignore the rules stated in the above paragraph.

Civil Procedure Outline § V (A)(2)(c) Pretrial Motions: Motions Addressed to Face of Pleadings: Motion for Judgment on the Pleadings

QUESTION 112
ANSWER & EXPLANATION
Pre-Trial Procedures

(A)   No, because the jewelry dealer failed to allege specific facts showing he would suffer irreparable injury if the temporary restraining order was not issued.

The correct answer is A. The party requesting an *ex parte* temporary restraining order ("TRO") must set out in a verified complaint or in an affidavit under oath specific facts that show immediate and irreparable harm will result if the TRO is not issued. Here, the jewelry owner simply alleged that he would suffer irreparable injury, but he failed to set out specific facts that support this conclusion. Therefore, the court should not issue the *ex parte* TRO.

B is incorrect because this is not a consideration for the court when deciding whether to issue an *ex parte* TRO.

C is incorrect because it does not address all the requirements for issuing an *ex parte* TRO. The fact that the diamond owner might sell the diamond if he found out about the request for a TRO supports the jewelry owner's claim that notice should not be required. However, the answer does not address the other two requirements—that specific facts establishing irreparable injury be provided and the posting of a sufficient bond.

D is incorrect because although the jewelry dealer has posted a sufficient bond, this answer fails to address the other conditions to obtaining an *ex parte* TRO. Namely, this answer does not address the requirement that specific facts establish irreparable injury, and the requirement of certification of the efforts to give notice and the reasons why notice should not be required.

Civil Procedure Outline § III(A)(2): Types of Non-Permanent Injunctions

QUESTION 113
ANSWER & EXPLANATION
Verdicts and Judgments

(A) general verdict

The correct answer is A. Generally, jury determinations are made by general verdict (e.g., liable or not liable). In particularly complex cases, the court may require a jury to return a "special verdict" in the form of a special written finding upon each issue of fact. Fed. R. Civ. P. 49(a)(1). Special verdicts are generally disfavored in simple cases.

Civil Procedure Outline § VI B(2)(a) Jury Verdicts—Types and Challenges: Types of Jury Verdicts: General Verdict

QUESTION 114
Appealability and Review

(B) Yes. The factory may appeal the order because the order denies an injunction.

B is the correct answer. A party may appeal, as a matter of right, an interlocutory order or decree that grants, continues, modifies, refuses, or dissolves an injunction

A is incorrect because a party may not appeal all court orders. As a general rule, an interlocutory order is not appealable. An interlocutory order is an order in a case that does not dispose of the case.

C is incorrect because a party may appeal, as a matter of right, an interlocutory order or decree that grants an injunction.

D is incorrect because it provides an incorrect statement of law. The final judgment rule provides that, as a general rule, only final judgments are appealable. The determination on the injunction is not a final judgment.

Civil Procedure Outline § VII (A)(1): Appeal in Specified Types of Cases

QUESTION 115
ANSWER & EXPLANATION
Pre-Trial Procedures

(C)   No, because the judge failed to consider whether the college would suffer irreparable injury without the preliminary injunction, whether the preliminary injunction would substantially harm any other parties, and whether it was in the best public interest.

The correct answer is C. When determining whether to grant a preliminary injunction, courts consider several factors, including the likelihood that the moving party will prevail on the merits of the lawsuit, whether the moving party will suffer irreparable injury without the preliminary injunction, whether the injunction would substantially harm any other interested party, and whether there are any public interest implications under the circumstances. Here, the judge considered only the fact that the college would likely prevail on the lawsuit, and incorrectly stated that this was the only factor that he needed to consider.

A is incorrect because preliminary injunctions are not always entered to prevent the sale of property pending the outcome of litigation regarding that property. The court should consider whether the sale of the property would irreparably harm the moving party, but preliminary injunctions are not automatically entered where a lawsuit involves the sale of property.

B is incorrect because it fails to address all the factors that should be considered by the court before issuing a preliminary injunction. Although the likelihood of success on the merits of the lawsuit is a factor the court considers, it is not the only factor which should weigh in favor of issuing a preliminary injunction.

D is incorrect because unlike a temporary restraining order, a preliminary injunction maintains the *status quo* until the parties' claims can be investigated and adjudicated. While temporary restraining orders are limited to 14 days, no such limitation exists with preliminary injunctions.

Civil Procedure Outline § III(A)(2): Types of Non-Permanent Injunctions

QUESTION 116
Jurisdiction and Venue

(D)   Yes, because the dealer merely placed the car into the stream of commerce.
The correct answer is D. A forum state will possess personal jurisdiction over a defendant if the defendant possesses minimum contacts with the forum state. A person who has never been present in a state still may be subject to personal jurisdiction in the state if the person possesses sufficient minimum contacts with that forum state, such that requiring the person to appear and defend in a court there would not offend traditional notions of fair play and substantial justice. If a defendant places a product into the *stream of commerce*, giving rise to a claim against the defendant in a forum state's court, then when determining whether personal jurisdiction exists, the court may examine the *foreseeability* of the product's presence in the forum state. However,

as the Supreme Court held in *World-Wide Volkswagen Corporation v. Woodson*, merely placing a car into the stream of commerce does not alone warrant personal jurisdiction. In this question, the potential for the car the dealer sold in State A to be driven in State B is not enough to give the court personal jurisdiction over the dealer.

A is incorrect for the reasons explained above. Further, the fact that the dealer financially benefitted from the sale, without more, does not warrant personal jurisdiction in this case.

B is incorrect because, as explained above, merely placing the car into the stream of commerce is not sufficient to establish personal jurisdiction.

C is incorrect because it ignores the relevant facts in the question (i.e., the dealer merely sold the car) that lead to the correct conclusion represented in choice D.

Civil Procedure Outline § I (B)(1)(a)(5): Personal Jurisdiction

QUESTION 117
ANSWER & EXPLANATION
Pre-Trial Procedures

(D)   Yes, because it was served within 21 days after being served with the answer.

The correct answer is D. A party may amend a pleading once as a matter of right within 21 days after serving it. If the pleading is one to which a responsive pleading is required, the party may amend it the earlier of either:

-   21 days after service of a responsive pleading; or

-   21 days after service of a Rule 12(b), (e), or (f) motion.

In this case, the bicyclist had 21 days after service of the responsive pleading (i.e., the answer) to file the amended complaint. Because the bicyclist filed the amended complaint within 21 days of the answer, it was timely and permitted under the Rules.

A, B, and C are incorrect because they ignore the Rule stated above.

Civil Procedure Outline § III (B)(5) Nature and Style of Pleadings: Amendment of Pleadings

QUESTION 118
ANSWER & EXPLANATION
Jury Trails

(B)   No, because the court must afford objecting counsel an opportunity to object outside of the jury's presence.

The correct answer is B.   The court must afford objecting counsel an opportunity to object outside of the jury's presence.

Civil Procedure Outline § IV C(2) Requests for and Objections to Jury Instructions: Objections—Preservation of Error in Jury Charge

QUESTION 119
ANSWER & EXPLANATION
Motions

(A)   A genuine dispute existed as to a material fact in the case.

The correct answer is A.   A motion for summary judgment may be granted if the movant shows that *no genuine dispute exists as to any material fact in the case,* and the movant is entitled to a judgment as a matter of law.   In this case, the facts indicate that a genuine dispute exists as to whether the driver was exceeding the speed limit at the time of the accident and crossed into the wrong lane, which would be relevant to a negligence analysis.   Consequently, the court should not have granted the motion.

B is incorrect because a defendant or plaintiff may move for summary judgment.

C is incorrect because a party may move for summary judgment to obtain a judicial judgment and avoid a trial.

D is incorrect because the facts state that a genuine dispute exists as to material facts in the case.

Civil Procedure Outline § V (A)(3)(a) Pretrial Motions: Motion for Summary Judgment: Legal Standard

QUESTION 120
ANSWER & EXPLANATION
Pre-Trial Procedures

(D)   No, because the answer was filed more than 21 days after service of the complaint.

The correct answer is D. An answer must be served within 21 days after the service of the complaint. Here, the complaint was served on January 1, 2014, but the answer was not served until February 1, 2014, which is more than 21 days later. Therefore, the answer was untimely and improper.

A is incorrect because an answer must be served within 21 days, not 1 month, of service of the complaint.

B is incorrect because a party is not required to only admit or deny every allegation in the complaint. A party can also assert that they lack sufficient knowledge to specifically admit or deny an allegation.

C is incorrect because, although the answer did properly address every allegation in the complaint, it was untimely filed and thus, was not a proper answer.

Civil Procedure Outline § III(B)(3): Types of Pleadings

QUESTION 121
ANSWER & EXPLANATION
Verdicts and Judgments

(C)   special verdict

The correct answer is C. Generally, jury determinations are made by general verdict (e.g., liable or not liable). In particularly complex cases, the court may require a jury to return a "special verdict" in the form of a special written finding upon each issue of fact. Fed. R. Civ. P. 49(a)(1). Special verdicts are generally disfavored in simple cases.

Civil Procedure Outline § VI B(2)(b) Jury Verdicts—Types and Challenges: Types of Jury Verdicts: Special Verdict

QUESTION 122
ANSWER & EXPLANATAION
Appealability and Review

(A)   No, because the objection was not made contemporaneously to the ruling.

A is the correct answer. Generally, a party must object to a ruling of a court that the objecting party considers erroneous in order to preserve the matter for appeal. The objection must be made contemporaneously to the ruling and with particularity regarding the grounds for the objection.

If an objection to the admissibility of evidence is sustained, the non-objecting party is prevented from introducing that evidence at trial. Consequently, in order to challenge the ruling on appeal, the non-objecting party must make an offer of proof that demonstrates what the purported evidence was intended to prove. That party may present appellate arguments in support of the admissibility of the purported evidence.

B is incorrect because it provides an unrelated rule of law. The final judgment rule does not apply to the scope of appeal.

C is incorrect. In order to be preserved for appeal, an objection must be made contemporaneously to the ruling and with particularity regarding the grounds for the objection. In this case, the objection was made with particularity, but not contemporaneously to the ruling.

D is incorrect because it is an incorrect rule of law. Appealability of an evidence determination does not depend upon whether the potential error could have changed the outcome of the case.

Civil Procedure Outline § VII (C)(1)(a): Contemporaneous Objection and Offer of Proof

QUESTION 123
ANSWER & EXPLANATION
Pre-Trial Procedures

B.   Yes, because she violated Rule 11 by presenting a request for punitive damages that was not warranted by existing law.

The correct answer is B. By presenting a filing to the court, an attorney or party represents that the claims, defenses, and other legal contentions therein are warranted by existing law or by a non-frivolous argument for the extension, modification, or reversal of existing law or the establishment of new law. Here, the lawyer knew that binding case law did not allow for punitive damages under the facts, but she requested the punitive damages anyway. Therefore, the attorney has violated Rule 11, and should be sanctioned.

A is incorrect because the lawyer knew there was binding case law that did not allow for punitive damages, and she did not present a non-frivolous argument to change the existing law. The fact that her client was sympathetic would not constitute a non-frivolous argument to change the binding case law prohibiting punitive damages.

C is incorrect because an attorney cannot present a claim, defense, or any other legal contention when existing law prohibits it, or there is not a valid argument to extend, modify, or reverse the existing law.

D is incorrect because Rule 11 is not violated by seeking two types of damages. Rather, Rule 11 is violated when the request for damages is not supported by the facts and not allowed by existing law.

QUESTION 124
ANSWER & EXPLANATION
Jurisdiction and Venue

(C) Yes, because the peg manufacturer was aware that its pegs would be sold in State B, and the peg manufacturer directed acts toward State B showing intent to serve State B's marketplace.

The correct answer is C. The exercise of personal jurisdiction is more likely if a party *purposefully avails* itself of the benefits of the forum state. For example, if a party advertises to a market in the state, then the court would be more likely to exercise jurisdiction over the person. The overall question when conducting any minimum contacts analysis is whether the assertion of jurisdiction is *reasonable under the circumstances*. A court will examine whether the defendant should have reasonably anticipated being brought into court in the jurisdiction. In this case, because the peg manufacturer knew that most of the pegs it sold to the toy manufacturer would be used in toys sold in State B, and because the peg manufacturer solicits business in State B, it is reasonable under the circumstances that the peg manufacturer will be subject to the court's jurisdiction in State B.

A, B, and D are incorrect because each of those incorrect choices ignore the relevant facts in the question which lead to the analysis explained above regarding the correct answer, choice C.

Civil Procedure Outline § I (B)(1)(a)(5): Personal Jurisdiction

QUESTION 125
ANSWER & EXPLANATION
Pre-Trial Procedures

(A) No, because amending the complaint would likely cause undue prejudice to the vacationer.

The correct answer is A. A party may amend a pleading once as a matter of right within 21 days after serving it. If the pleading is one to which a responsive pleading is required, the party may amend it the earlier of either:

-   21 days after service of a responsive pleading; or

-   21 days after service of a Rule 12(b), (e), or (f) motion.

Otherwise, a party may amend the party's pleading only by leave of court or by written consent of the adverse party; and leave must be freely given when justice so requires. Fed. R. Civ. P. 15(a). The Supreme Court has held that amendments should be permitted unless such amendment results in a form of injustice. Categories of injustice include:

- undue delay;

- bad faith or dilatory motive;

- repeated failure to cure defects by amendment;

- undue prejudice to the party opposing the amendment; or

- futility of the amendment.

In this case, the bicyclist seeks to amend the complaint one week prior to trial, and after the parties have engaged in months of discovery. Further, the facts state that nearly two months have passed since discovery was completed. The vacationer has likely conducted depositions and discovery based on the original complaint, and prepared for trial on that information; therefore, a late amendment would likely cause the vacationer undue prejudice, since trial is only one week away. Consequently, of the potential answer choices presented, A is the best choice.

B, C, and D are incorrect because they misconstrue or omit aspects of the Rule stated above.

Civil Procedure Outline § III (B)(5) Nature and Style of Pleadings: Amendment of Pleadings

QUESTION 126
ANSWER & EXPLANATION
Jury Trials

(B)   No, because the judge may not express an opinion regarding the evidence when charging the jury.

The correct answer is B. In charging the jury, the court may not express its opinion regarding the evidence. In this case, the judge improperly expressed an opinion indicating that the judge believed the employee had been negligent and caused the injuries.

Civil Procedure Outline § IV C(3) Requests for and Objections to Jury Instructions: Judge Cannot Express Opinion

QUESTION 127
ANSWER & EXPLANATION
Motions

(B)   No, because the fact in dispute was not material.

The correct answer is B. A fact is "material" if it is relevant to an element of a claim or defense, and its existence would affect the outcome of the case. In this case, the facts state that there is no doubt that the driver was the driver involved in the collision, so the issue of whether the driver was wearing a polo or a button-down shirt is not a material fact as to whether the driver was negligent. (If the identity of the driver was in question, perhaps the issue of what type of shirt worn would be a material fact—but that is not the case in this question.) Consequently, the court's reasoning was flawed. In order for a motion for summary judgment to be granted, the court must find that no genuine dispute exists as to any material fact in the case, and the movant is entitled to a judgment as a matter of law. However, because the type of shirt the driver was wearing is not a material fact, the court should not have denied the motion on that basis.

A is incorrect because it states an incorrect legal standard.

C is incorrect because any party may file a motion for summary judgment.

D is incorrect because the court's reasoning was flawed, as explained above.

Civil Procedure Outline § V (A)(3)(a)(2) Pretrial Motions: Motion for Summary Judgment: Material Fact

QUESTION 128
ANSWER & EXPLANATION
Pre-Trial Procedures

(C)   Yes, because the plaintiff's lawyer failed to serve the motion on the defendant's lawyer.

The correct answer is C. A motion for sanctions should not even be filed with the court unless, 21 days after serving the motion on the other party, the challenged filing is not withdrawn or appropriately corrected. Here, the plaintiff's lawyer failed to serve the defendant's lawyer with their motion and wait the required 21 days before filing the motion with the court.

A is incorrect because the party did violate Rule 11 by failing to sign every pleading, motion, or paper.

B is incorrect because it does not address all of the requirements for a motion for sanctions. Although the motion must describe the specific conduct alleged to have violated Rule 11, it must also be served on the other party; and the other party must fail to withdraw or correct the challenged filing within 21 days. Therefore, this answer choice is incomplete.

D is incorrect because it fails to recognize that the defendant's lawyer was not served with the motion, and as such, was not given an opportunity to withdraw or correct the challenged filing.

Civil Procedure Outline § III(C)(3): Process for Sanctions

QUESTION 129
ANSWER & EXPLANATION
Verdicts and Judgments

(B)   No, because the court may submit general verdict forms to the jury, along with written questions on fact issues.

The correct answer is B. The use of written questions or interrogatories in conjunction with a general verdict affords the court a midpoint between the traditionally favored general verdict and the disfavored special verdict. It is intended to be an improvement on the general verdict, by directing the attention of the jury to the important fact issues, and exposing errors in the deliberative process. Fed. R. Civ. P. 49(b)(1). The jury provides written answers to the written questions.

A is an overbroad, incorrect statement of law.

C and D are incorrect statements of law because they ignore the above rules.

Civil Procedure Outline § VI B(2)(c) Jury Verdicts—Types and Challenges: Types of Jury Verdicts: Written Questions (Interrogatories)

QUESTION 130
ANSWER & EXPLANATION
Appealability and Review

(C) No, because the error would not have affected the trial's result.

C is the correct answer. The harmless error rule provides that any error which does not affect the substantive rights of the parties cannot be the grounds for an appeal. Generally, the standard in a civil case is whether an erroneous charge of the jury or ruling of the court would likely have affected a trial's result.

A is incorrect because this error does not affect the substantive rights of the parties. The harmless error rule provides that any error which does not affect the substantive rights of the parties cannot be the grounds for an appeal.

B is incorrect because an error that does affect a trial's result is sufficient grounds for appeal.

D is incorrect. The appellate court does not have to hear an appeal of the trial court's decision even when errors have been made, if those errors are deemed harmless.

Civil Procedure Outline § VII (C)(1)(b): Harmless Error Rule

QUESTION 131
ANSWER & EXPLANATION
Jurisdiction and Venue

(B)   No, because the businessman was sophisticated, and he engaged in a substantial and continuous business relationship with the corporation, and he received fair notice that he could be subject to personal jurisdiction in State B.

The correct answer is B. This question is based on the Supreme Court's ruling in *Burger King v. Rudzewicz*. The Court held that a Florida court possessed personal jurisdiction over a Michigan franchisee based on a contract that indicated the parties' relationship was established in Florida, and that Florida Law governed their contractual relationship. The Supreme Court ruled, however, that the existence of such a contract cannot, of itself, give rise to a non-forum state party's sufficient minimum contacts with the forum state. Rather, the Supreme Court sustained the personal jurisdiction on the following grounds:

-   The parties engaged in a substantial and continuous business relationship;

-   The non-forum state party received fair notice that it could be subject to personal jurisdiction in the forum state. That notice resulted from the contract's terms and the parties' course of dealings; and

-   The non-forum state party was sophisticated and experienced in business and did not enter into the contract due to duress or economic disadvantage.

A is incorrect because, as stated above, the existence of the contract, cannot, of itself, give rise to a non-forum state party's sufficient minimum contacts with the forum state.

C is incorrect because it ignores the other facts in the question that establish personal jurisdiction.

D is incorrect because the unexpected decline in the economy is not relevant to deciding whether the court has personal jurisdiction over the businessman in this case.

Civil Procedure Outline § I (B)(2): Limits on Exercise of Personal Jurisdiction

QUESTION 132
ANSWER & EXPLANATION
Pre-Trial Procedures

(C)   Yes, even though the statute of limitations has expired, the claim will be treated as if it had been filed on the date of the original complaint.

The correct answer is C. When the claim or defense asserted in an amended pleading arises out of the conduct, transaction, or occurrence set forth or attempted to be set forth in the original pleading, the amendment will be treated as if it was filed on the date of the original pleading.

A and B are incorrect because they ignore the law stated above. D is incorrect because it is an erroneous statement of law.

Civil Procedure Outline § III (B)(5)(1) Nature and Style of Pleadings: Amendment of Pleadings: New Claim

QUESTION 133
ANSWER & EXPLANATION
Motions

(B)   No, because it drew inferences in favor of the trucker.

The correct answer is B. When considering the evidence, a court must draw all inferences in favor of the party opposing the motion for summary judgment. Consequently, it was improper for the court to draw all inferences in favor of the trucker, the movant.

A is incorrect because the court may consider depositions when considering a motion for summary judgment.

C is incorrect because the court must draw all inferences in favor of the party opposing the motion for summary judgment, which in this case, would have been the driver.

D is incorrect because, although the court may consider depositions when making a determination regarding a motion for summary judgment, it must draw inferences in favor of the party opposing the motion.

Civil Procedure Outline § V (A)(3)(a)(3) Pretrial Motions: Motion for Summary Judgment: All Inferences in Favor of Motion Opponent

QUESTION 134
ANSWER & EXPLANATION
Pre-Trial Procedures

(B) Yes, because a court can impose sanctions for violations of Rule 11 on its own initiative.

The correct answer is B. A court can impose sanctions for violations of Rule 11 on its own initiative. Here, the court properly imposed sanctions on its own initiative after providing the plaintiff's lawyer with notice and an opportunity to respond.

A is incorrect because the opposing party does not have to file a motion for sanctions before the court can impose them. A court can impose sanctions on its own initiative.

C is incorrect because it fails to address the requirements that must be met before sanctions can be imposed for violations of Rule 11. Although the plaintiff's lawyer did violate Rule 11 by filing motions without signing them, the answer fails to address the fact that the court must provide notice and an opportunity to respond before imposing sanctions for the violation.

D is incorrect because a hearing is not required before the court imposes sanctions for a violation of Rule 11. Rather, notice and an opportunity to be heard are required. Here, the court provided the plaintiff's lawyer notice and an opportunity to be heard by directing the lawyer to show cause why he had not violated Rule 11. This gave the lawyer 21 days to file a response explaining to the court why he had not violated Rule 11, or why sanctions should not be imposed.

Civil Procedure Outline § III(C)(3): Process for Sanctions

QUESTION 135
ANSWER & EXPLANATION
Verdicts and Judgments

(A) No, because the general verdict and written answers were consistent.

The correct answer is A. If the general verdict and the written answers are consistent, then the court must approve a judgment based on them. Fed. R. Civ. P. 49(b)(2).

B and D are incorrect statements of law.

C is incorrect because it ignores the above rule.

Civil Procedure Outline § VI B(2)(c)(1) Jury Verdicts—Types and Challenges: Types of Jury Verdicts: Written Questions (Interrogatories): Answers Consistent with Verdict

QUESTION 136
Appealability and Review

(A) Abuse of Discretion

A is the correct answer. **Determinations of the admissibility of evidence are reviewed using an abuse-of-discretion standard.** A determination as to whether evidence is irrelevant or highly prejudicial and should be excluded is within the trial court's discretion and is reviewed on appeal using an abuse-of-discretion standard.

B is incorrect because *de novo* standard of review is used by a**n appellate court to review a trial court's determination of a pure issue of law.** Testimony about previous accidents is an issue of evidence, not an issue of law.

C is incorrect. **An appellate court reviewing a trial court's finding of fact in a bench trial uses the clearly erroneous standard. The company's argument on appeal is in regard to admissibility of evidence, not a finding of fact.**

D is incorrect because preservation of error is not a standard of review used by appellate courts. Preservation of error applies to a party's objection during trial.

Civil Procedure Outline § VII (C)(2)(b): Abuse of Discretion Standard of Review

QUESTION 137
ANSWER & EXPLANATION
Jurisdiction and Venue

(B) *In rem* jurisdiction

The correct answer is B. *In rem* jurisdiction is a court's jurisdiction over property that is located within the forum state. In a usual dispute that gives rise to *in personam* (i.e., personal) jurisdiction, two or more people attempt to adjudicate their rights *in relation to each other.* When *in rem* jurisdiction is invoked, a court adjudicates the *entire world's rights in relation to a piece of property.* The property can be either real property (e.g., building or land) or personal property (e.g., decedent's estate). In an *in rem* proceeding, the court may exercise its power to determine the ownership of the property. An *in rem* judicial determination is binding with respect to all possible interest holders if reasonable notice of the proceeding was given.

A is incorrect because a *quasi in rem* action is initiated when a plaintiff seizes property within a forum state by means of attachment or garnishment, which did not occur in this case.

C is incorrect because the term *"in properteris"* is a nonsense word that does not have any legal significance or meaning.

D is incorrect because the facts indicate that the court was called upon to exercise *in rem* jurisdiction over a piece of land within the forum state to determine the ownership of the property.

Civil Procedure Outline § I (B)(3)-(4): In Rem Jurisdiction and Quasi In Rem Jurisdiction

**QUESTION 138
ANSWER & EXPLANATION
Pre-Trial Procedures**

(A)   No, because the amended complaint is based on the same conduct that gave rise to the original complaint, Dave received notice, and Dave knew that but for Pat's misidentification of the driver in the complaint, the action would have been served earlier.

The correct answer is A. The amended pleading in this case will be treated as if it had been filed on the date of the original pleading before the statute of limitations expired. This question is based on the case of *Leonard v. Parry*, 219 F.3d 25 (1st Cir. 2000).

When a plaintiff adds a different defendant after the statute of limitations has expired, the action against the new defendant will satisfy the statute of limitations only if both the notice and mistake requirements are satisfied.

(a)   Notice: Under the notice requirement, an amended pleading adding a new party will relate back to the original pleading with regards to the statute of limitations if the new party had notice of the suit, such that it would not be prejudiced in being required to respond.

(b)   Mistake: Under the mistake requirement, an amended pleading adding a new party will relate back to the original pleading with regards to the statute of limitations if the new party knew or should have known that, but for a mistake in the identification of the proper party, it would have been served earlier.

B is incorrect because it is an erroneous statement of law.

C and D are incorrect because they ignore the law stated above.

Civil Procedure Outline § III (B)(5)(2) Nature and Style of Pleadings: Amendment of Pleadings: New Party

QUESTION 139
ANSWER & EXPLANATION
Motions

(D)   Yes, because a party who asserts that a material fact cannot be genuinely disputed must support its assertion by citing to specific portions of materials in the record.

The correct answer is D.   A party may assert that a material fact can or cannot be genuinely disputed.   Fed. R. Civ. P. 56(c)(1).   A party must support its assertion by citing to specific portions of materials in the record.   Fed. R. Civ. P. 56(c)(1)(A).   These materials may include documents, declarations or affidavits, depositions, stipulations, interrogatory answers, admissions, or electronically stored information.   *Id.*

A, B, and C are erroneous statements.

Civil Procedure Outline § V (A)(3)(b)(1) Pretrial Motions: Motion for Summary Judgment: Procedure: Supporting Factual Positions

QUESTION 140
ANSWER & EXPLANATION
Verdicts and Judgments

(B)   No, because the court believed it had no discretion in the matter.

The correct answer is B.   If the written answers are consistent but at least one of them is inconsistent with the general verdict, then the court may:

-   approve a judgment based on the answers;

-   require the jury to further consider the answers and verdict; or

-   order a new trial.

Fed. R. Civ. P. 49(b)(3).

A is incorrect because, although it is a true statement, it ignores the court's erroneous conclusion that it had no discretion in this case.

C is incorrect because the court had discretion in this case, as provided by the Rule.

D is an incorrect statement of law.

Civil Procedure Outline § VI B(2)(c)(2) Jury Verdicts—Types and Challenges: Types of Jury

Verdicts: Written Questions (Interrogatories): Answers Inconsistent with Verdict

QUESTION 141
ANSWER & EXPLANATION
Pre-Trial Procedures

(C)   Yes, because the court can impose sanctions against both the attorney and the firm.

The correct answer is C. A court can impose sanctions against a lawyer, law firm, or a party for violating Rule 11.

A is incorrect because it fails to address all the requirements that must be satisfied before the court imposes sanctions for violating Rule 11. Before imposing sanctions for violating Rule 11, notice and an opportunity to respond must be provided. This answer fails to address both requirements.

B is incorrect because the court can impose sanctions against a lawyer, law firm, or a party for violating Rule 11.

D is incorrect because the court could properly find that the opposing party violated Rule 11 under the circumstances. By presenting the motions, the attorney represents that the request is not presented for any improper purpose such as to harass or needlessly increase the costs of litigation. Here, the court could properly find an improper purpose behind the filing of fifty motions seeking thousands of documents in a simple contract dispute.

Civil Procedure Outline § III(C)(3): Process for Sanctions

QUESTION 142
ANSWER & EXPLANATION
Appealability and Review

(B)   Clearly Erroneous

B is the correct answer. An appellate court reviewing a trial court's finding of fact in a bench trial uses the clearly erroneous standard. The court's determination that the student was on the tour is a finding of fact.

A is incorrect because the *de novo* standard of review is used by an appellate court to review a trial court's determination of a pure issue of law.

C is incorrect. The harmless error rule provides that any error which does not affect the substantive rights of the parties cannot be the grounds for an appeal. Generally, the standard in a civil case is whether an erroneous charge of the jury or ruling of the court would likely have affected a trial's result. The harmless error rule does not apply to this question.

D is incorrect because the abuse-of-discretion standard is applied when reviewing determinations regarding the admissibility of evidence.

Civil Procedure Outline § VII (C)(2)(c): Clearly Erroneous Standard of Review

QUESTION 143
ANSWER & EXPLANATION
Jurisdiction and Venue

(B)   No, because the defendant has not been given reasonable notice of the lawsuit.

The correct answer is B. The plaintiff is responsible for service of the summons and a copy of the complaint on the defendant. On the facts given in this question, if the plaintiff takes the clerk's advice and does nothing more, the defendant will not receive service of the summons and a copy of the complaint, which would run afoul of the constitutional requirement of due process concerning the defendant's right to receive notice of the action.

A, C, and D are incorrect because if the plaintiff does nothing more, the defendant will not receive proper service of the summons and a copy of the complaint.

Civil Procedure Outline § I (C)(1): Service of Process and Notice: Issuance

QUESTION 144
ANSWER & EXPLANATION
Pre-Trial Procedures

(A)   No, because the employee did not obtain leave of court to file the supplemental pleading.

The correct answer is A. A supplemental pleading is used to set forth events that have happened since the filing date of a prior pleading that is sought to be supplemented. Leave of court, after giving notice to all other parties and making a motion to file a supplemental pleading, must be obtained to serve such a supplemental pleading. The courts' practice is usually liberal in allowing the filing of a supplemental pleading.

B, C, and D are incorrect because they ignore or violate the Rule stated above.

Civil Procedure Outline § III (B)(6) Nature and Style of Pleadings: Supplemental Pleadings

QUESTION 145
ANSWER & EXPLANATION
Verdicts and Judgments

(B)   The court must not enter a judgment.

The correct answer is B. If the written answers are inconsistent and at least one of them is inconsistent with the general verdict, then the court must:

- not enter a judgment; and

- require the jury to further consider the answers and verdict; or

- order a new trial.

Fed. R. Civ. P. 49(b)(4).

Civil Procedure Outline § VI B(2)(c)(3) Jury Verdicts—Types and Challenges: Types of Jury Verdicts: Inconsistent Answers that Are Inconsistent with Verdict

QUESTION 146
Pre-Trial Procedures

(C)   Yes, because the court can impose non-monetary directives and order the party to pay a penalty for violating Rule 11.

The correct answer is C. A sanction imposed for violation of Rule 11 is limited to that which is sufficient to deter repetition of the conduct or comparable conduct by others similarly situated. Sanctions for violation of Rule 11 may include non-monetary directives, an order to pay a penalty into court, or an order directing payment to the moving party of some or all reasonable attorney's fees and other expenses incurred as a result of the violation. Here, the court properly directed the party to withdraw the frivolous claim and ordered the payment of a fine.

A is incorrect because the court may properly direct a lawyer or party to pay a penalty to the court as a sanction for violating Rule 11.

B is incorrect because there is no such limitation on the sanctions the court can impose for violating Rule 11. Rather, sanctions for violations of Rule 11 are limited to that which is sufficient to deter repetition of the conduct or comparable conduct by others similarly situated.

D is incorrect because the court cannot impose any sanction it desires. Rather, sanctions for violation of Rule 11 may include non-monetary directives, an order to pay a penalty into court, or an order directing payment to the moving party of some or all reasonable attorney's fees and other expenses incurred as a result of the violation.

Civil Procedure Outline § III(C)(4): Nature of Sanctions

QUESTION 147
ANSWER & EXPLANATION
Jurisdiction and Venue

(B) No, because the defendant was served before the 120-day time limit expired.

The correct answer is B. The summons and complaint must be served on the defendant within 120 days after the filing of the complaint. If a summons and complaint are not served on a defendant within 120 days after filing the complaint, and the party seeking service cannot show good cause, the action should be dismissed as to that defendant, without prejudice.

Civil Procedure Outline § I (C)(5): Service of Process and Notice: Time for Service

QUESTION 148
ANSWER & EXPLANATION
Pre-Trial Procedures

(A) No, because the employee did not obtain leave of court to file the supplemental pleading.

The correct answer is A. A supplemental pleading is used to set forth events that have happened since the filing date of a prior pleading that is sought to be supplemented. Leave of court, after giving notice to all other parties and making a motion to file a supplemental pleading, must be obtained to serve such a supplemental pleading. The courts' practice is usually liberal in allowing the filing of a supplemental pleading.

B, C, and D are incorrect because they ignore or violate the Rule stated above.

Civil Procedure Outline § III (B)(6) Nature and Style of Pleadings: Supplemental Pleadings

QUESTION 149
ANSWER & EXPLANATION
Motions

(C) Yes, because a party can object that the potential evidence cited as support for a motion for summary judgment would not be admissible at trial.

The correct answer is C. A party can object that the potential evidence cited as support would not be admissible at trial. Fed. R. Civ. P. 56(c)(2).

A, B, and D are all erroneous statements.

Civil Procedure Outline § V (A)(3)(b)(2) Pretrial Motions: Motion for Summary Judgment: Procedure: Objection—Fact is Not Supported by Admissible Evidence

QUESTION 150
ANSWER & EXPLANATION
Verdicts and Judgments

(C) Yes, because a party making a motion to alter or amend a judgment must file the motion within 28 days after entry of the judgment.

The correct answer is C. A party making a motion to alter or amend a judgment must file the motion within 28 days after entry of the judgment. Fed. R. Civ. P. 59(e).

Civil Procedure Outline § VI B(3)(a)(1) Jury Verdicts—Types and Challenges: Challenge to Jury Verdict: Post-trial Motion Challenging Jury Verdict: Motion to Alter or Amend Judgment

QUESTION 151
ANSWER & EXPLANATION
Pre-Trial Procedures

(C) Yes, because the court can award reasonable expenses and attorney's fees to the prevailing party.

The correct answer is C. If warranted, the court may award to the party prevailing on the motion reasonable expenses and attorney's fees incurred in bringing or opposing the motion. Thus, the court has discretion to award expenses and attorney's fees to whichever party prevails on the motion. Here, because the opposing party prevailed on the motion, the court could award reasonable expenses and attorney's fees that were incurred in defending against the motion.

A is incorrect because the court can award reasonable expenses and attorney's fees to the prevailing party, regardless of whether it was the party who brought the motion or defended against it.

B is incorrect because there is no such requirement that the court find the motion for sanctions was frivolous before awarding expenses and attorney's fees. Rather, reasonable expenses and attorney's fees can be awarded in the court's discretion to the prevailing party.

D is incorrect because it implies that the court can only award expenses and attorney's fees if the opposing party fails to correct the complained of action. The court may award expenses and attorney's fees regardless of whether the opposing party corrects the complained of action. The 21 day provision requires that the party bringing the motion serve the opposing party with the motion and then wait 21 days before filing the motion with the court. If the opposing party does not correct the complained of action within those 21 days, then the party may file the motion with the court.

Civil Procedure Outline § III(C)(3): Process for Sanctions

QUESTION 152
ANSWER & EXPLANATION
Jurisdiction and Venue

(D) Yes, because the defendant's request was proper, and the defendant does not have good cause for the failure to comply with the request.

The correct answer is D. A person or entity subject to service that receives proper notice of an action has a duty to avoid unnecessary costs of serving the summons. Therefore, in order to avoid costs, a plaintiff may notify a defendant of the commencement of an action and request that the defendant waive the service of the summons. The notice and request *must be in writing* and addressed to the defendant. It must be dispatched by first class mail or other reliable means. A waiver of service of process must:

-   contain a copy of the complaint;

-   inform the defendant of the consequences of compliance (waiver of defenses relating to service of process); and

-   inform the defendant of the consequences of non-compliance with the request (e.g., additional costs).

A defendant must be given a reasonable time to return the waiver, which must be at least 30 days from the date on which the request is sent.

If a defendant located within the United States fails to comply with a proper request for waiver, a court will impose the costs subsequently incurred in effecting service on the defendant *unless good cause* for the failure to comply is shown.

A is incorrect because 30 days is a reasonable time to return the waiver.

B is incorrect because a plaintiff may request that the defendant waive the service of summons.

C is incorrect because first class mail is a reliable means for sending the notice.

Civil Procedure Outline § I (C)(7): Service of Process and Notice: Waiver of Service

QUESTION 153
ANSWER & EXPLANATION
Pre-Trial Procedures

(B)   No, the attorney violated Rule 11.

The correct answer is B. Every pleading, motion, or other paper of a party represented by an attorney must be signed by at least one attorney of record. If an attorney willfully violates Rule 11, the attorney may be subjected to disciplinary action.

A is incorrect because Rule 11 is the relevant rule implicated by the facts in this question.

C and D are incorrect because the attorney must sign the complaint regardless of the identifying information in the caption of the complaint and the attorney's familiarity with the judge.

Civil Procedure Outline § III (C)(1) Nature and Style of Pleadings: Signature Requirement

QUESTION 154
ANSWER & EXPLANATION
Motions

(C)   Yes, because when considering a motion for summary judgment, the court may consider materials in the record that were not cited by a party.

The correct answer is C. The court must consider the materials cited by the parties, but may also consider other materials in the record. Fed. R. Civ. P. 56(c)(3).

A, B, and D are incorrect because they are erroneous statements.

Civil Procedure Outline § V (A)(3)(b)(3) Pretrial Motions: Motion for Summary Judgment: Procedure: Materials Not Cited

QUESTION 155
ANSWER & EXPLANATION
Verdicts and Judgments

(A) *Remittitur*, which is the reduction of an award for damages.

The correct answer is A. If a court believes that a verdict is so excessive that a new trial should be granted for that reason only, the court may recommend to the parties that they accept a *remittitur*. *Remittitur* is the reduction of an award for damages. *Remittitur* can be entered only with the consent of the party awarded damages. It is to be entered only if the amount of the excess can be separately and fairly ascertained.

B is incorrect because *additur* is the converse to *remittitur*. *Additur* is the increase of an award for damages that are inadequate. *Additur* may undercut the right to a trial by jury. Further, it is not permitted in the federal court system.

C and D are essentially nonsense answers.

Civil Procedure Outline § VI B(3)(b) Jury Verdicts—Types and Challenges: Challenge to Jury Verdict: Remittitur (Alternative to Granting New Trial)

QUESTION 156
ANSWER & EXPLANATION
Pre-Trial Procedures

(A) Yes, because the attorney willfully failed to sign every pleading, motion, and other paper.

The correct answer is A. Every pleading, motion, or other paper of a party represented by an attorney must be signed by at least one attorney of record. Fed. R. Civ. P. 11. If an attorney willfully violates Rule 11, he may be subjected to disciplinary action.

B is incorrect because the attorney must sign *every* pleading, motion, or other paper filed with the court.

C is incorrect because there is no requirement that the attorney intend to annoy or harass opposing counsel in order to impose disciplinary action for violations of Rule 11. Rather, a willful violation of Rule 11, regardless of motive, can result in imposition of disciplinary action.

D is incorrect because if a party is represented by an attorney, that attorney must sign every pleading, motion, or other paper regardless of whether the client also signs the document.

Civil Procedure Outline § III(C)(3): Process for Sanctions

QUESTION 157
ANSWER & EXPLANATION
Jurisdiction and Venue

(A) No, because the opportunist lives in the northern district of State C.

The correct answer is A. Venue rules concern the propriety of the location of the court in which proceedings are conducted. Venue rules are based on the location of the parties and legal questions at issue. Venue is proper in a judicial district where any defendant resides (i.e., is domiciled), if all defendants reside in the same state of the judicial district. In this case, there is only one defendant, and the defendant lives in the northern district of State C. Therefore, venue is proper in the northern district in State C.

B is incorrect because it is an erroneous statement of law.

C and D are incorrect because venue is proper in the district where the opportunist lives, as explained above.

Civil Procedure Outline § I (D)(1)(a)(1)(a): Venue Generally: Residence

QUESTION 158
ANSWER & EXPLANATION
Pre-Trial Procedures

(C)   Yes, because the motions were filed for an improper purpose.

The correct answer is C.

By presenting a filing to the court, an attorney or party represents that the claim, defense, request, demand, objection, contention, or argument is not presented or maintained for any improper purpose, such as to harass or to cause unnecessary delay or needless increase in the cost of litigation. In this case, the purpose of the filings was to harass the painter and cause unnecessary delay. Consequently, sanctions may be imposed.

A and B are incorrect because they ignore the Rule barring filings for improper purposes. D is incorrect because evaluating whether the fee was excessive is not relevant to the filing of the repetitive motions in this case.

Civil Procedure Outline § III (C)(2)(a) Nature and Style of Pleadings: Representations: No Improper Purpose

QUESTION 159
ANSWER & EXPLANATION
Motions

(A) No, because the affidavit is not based on personal knowledge.

The correct answer is A. A declaration or affidavit used to oppose or support a motion for summary judgment must:

- be based on personal knowledge of the person (i.e., declarant or affiant);

- state facts that would be admissible in evidence; and

- show that the person is competent to testify on the matters stated.

In this case, the facts state that the affidavit is not based on the personal knowledge of the affiant (i.e., the friend). Therefore, the court should not consider the facts alleged in the affidavit.

B and D are incorrect statements of law. C is incorrect because, although the affidavit is properly sworn, it is faulty for the reasons stated above.

Civil Procedure Outline § V (A)(3)(b)(4) Pretrial Motions: Motion for Summary Judgment: Procedure: Declarations or Affidavits

QUESTION 160
ANSWER & EXPLANATION
Verdicts and Judgments

(D) Yes, because the court must set forth the findings of fact separately from conclusions of law.

The correct answer is D. A judge makes findings of fact and conclusions of law when exercising judicial duties. In a jury trial, the jury is the finder of fact and the judge decides the questions of law. In a bench trial, the judge is both the finder of fact and decides the questions of law. In a bench trial, a judge must set forth the findings of fact separately from conclusions of law. They must be made on the record in order to preserve issues for appeal. The judge may either present them in a written decision or state them on the record after the close of the evidence. Fed. R. Civ. P. 52(a)(1).

A is incorrect because this question concerns a bench trial, in which the judge must set forth the findings of fact.

B is incorrect because it ignores the rule that the judge may set forth the findings of fact by stating them on the record.

C is incorrect because it is an erroneous statement of law.

Civil Procedure Outline § VI C(1)(a)(1) Judicial Findings and Conclusions: Findings of Fact and Conclusions of Law: Judicial Determinations: Bench Trial

QUESTION 161
ANSWER & EXPLANATION
Pre-Trial Procedures

(C)   No, because a pleading may be inconsistent or alternative.

The correct answer is C. A pleading may be inconsistent or alternative. Although a plaintiff could not recover for both breach of contract and unjust enrichment, he may plead both claims as alternative forms of relief and recover for one or the other.

A is incorrect because there is no such limitation on the number of causes of action that can be brought in a complaint.

B is incorrect because the common law "Election of Remedies" doctrine was rejected by the Rules. Under the Election of Remedies doctrine, a plaintiff was required to choose a method of recovery for harm. Once a method of recovery was selected, the plaintiff could not assert an alternative or inconsistent method of recovery. Thus, because a party cannot recover on both a breach of contract and an unjust enrichment claim, he would not be able to plead both causes of action under the common law. However, this doctrine has been rejected and under the Rules, inconsistent and alternative causes of action can be pled.

D is incorrect because breach of contract and unjust enrichment are mutually exclusive causes of action, therefore, a plaintiff could not recover for both. Unjust enrichment operates only when there is not a contract that provides a remedy when the other party is unjustly enriched. If a contract provides for a remedy, then a party cannot recover under an unjust enrichment cause of action.

Civil Procedure Outline § III(B)(2): Nature and Style of Pleadings

QUESTION 162
ANSWER & EXPLANATION
Jurisdiction and Venue

(C)   Yes, because the accident occurred in the northern district of State A.

The correct answer is C. Venue is proper in a judicial district in which a substantial part of the events or omissions giving rise to the claim occurred; or in which most of the property that is subject to the action is located.

A, B, and D are incorrect because, as explained above, venue is proper in the northern district of State A because it is the district in which a substantial part of the events or omissions giving rise to the claim occurred (i.e., the accident).

Civil Procedure Outline § I (D)(1)(a)(1)(b): Venue Generally: Residence

QUESTION 163
ANSWER & EXPLANATION
Pre-Trial Procedures

(C)   Yes, because the pleading presented a baseless claim.

The correct answer is C. By presenting a filing to the court, an attorney or party represents that the claims, defenses, and other legal contentions therein are warranted by existing law or by a non-frivolous argument for the extension, modification, or reversal of existing law or the establishment of new law. In this case, the homeowner's claim appears baseless and without merit. Consequently, sanctions would be appropriate.

A and B are incorrect because they ignore the Rule stated above. D is incorrect because a lawyer may use facts relayed by a client, as long as the lawyer complies with the Rules when using those facts.

Civil Procedure Outline § III (C)(2)(b) Nature and Style of Pleadings: Representations: Legal Grounding

QUESTION 164
ANSWER & EXPLANATION
Motions

(B)   No, because the court did not provide reasons for the denial.

The correct answer is B. When granting or denying a motion for summary judgment, the court should provide the reasons for the granting or denial.

A is incorrect because the court must consider the materials cited by the parties, but may also consider other materials in the record when deciding a motion for summary judgment.

C and D are incorrect because the court did not provide the reasons for its decision.

Civil Procedure Outline § V A(3)(d)(1) Pretrial Motions: Motion for Summary Judgment: Judgment: Reasons Should be on Record

QUESTION 165
ANSWER & EXPLANATION
Verdicts and Judgments

(A) No, because the judge is not required to set forth conclusions of law in an order granting a motion for summary judgment.

The correct answer is A. A judge is not required to set forth findings of fact or conclusions of law when ruling on any motion unless they are specifically required by the Rule for the motion. Fed. R. Civ. P. 52(a)(3). For example, an order granting a motion to dismiss, or a motion for summary judgment, does not need to contain conclusions of law.

B, C, and D are incorrect statements of law.

Civil Procedure Outline § VI C(1)(a)(3) Judicial Findings and Conclusions: Findings of Fact and Conclusions of Law: Judicial Determinations: Motions

QUESTION 166
ANSWER & EXPLANATION
Pre-Trial Procedures

(C) No, because the complaint was verified, all responsive pleadings also had to be verified.

The correct answer is C. Verification of pleadings, which means that they are either notarized or under oath, is generally not necessary unless required by statute or unless equitable relief is being requested. However, once a pleading is verified, all responsive pleadings must also be made under oath. Here, because the complaint was verified with the plaintiff's affidavit, the defendant's answer also had to be verified.

A is incorrect because responsive pleadings must only be verified when the pleading to which it is responding was verified.

B is incorrect because responsive pleadings must be under oath if the pleading to which it is responding was verified.

D is incorrect because an attorney filing a responsive pleading must file the document under oath when responding to a pleading that was verified. Thus, while it was within the plaintiff's attorney's discretion to file a verified complaint, it was not within the defendant's attorney's discretion whether to file a verified answer.

Civil Procedure Outline § III(B)(2): Nature and Style of Pleadings

QUESTION 167
ANSWER & EXPLANATION
Jurisdiction and Venue

(A)   No, because venue would be proper in either the southern or northern district of State B.

The correct answer is A. Venue is proper in a judicial district where any defendant resides if all defendants reside in the same state of the judicial district. Here, although the trucker and the motorcyclist reside in different districts, they both reside in the same state. Because the motorcyclist lives in the northern district of State B, venue is proper in that district.

B is incorrect because, although venue would be proper in the northern or southern districts of State B, no defendant lives in the eastern or western district of State B. Therefore, venue would not be proper in the eastern or western districts on the facts of this case.

C is incorrect because it is not necessary for all of the defendants to live in the same district; as long as all of the defendants live in the same state, and the court in which the claim is filed is in a district in which one of the defendants lives, then venue is proper.

D is incorrect because venue is proper as explained above. Note that venue could be proper in the northern district of State A because the accident occurred there, but that does not negate the fact that venue is also proper in the northern district of State B in this case.

Civil Procedure Outline § I (D)(1)(a)(1): Individual Parties

QUESTION 168
ANSWER & EXPLANATION
Pre-Trial Procedures

(B)   No, because the court may impose sanctions on its own initiative.

The correct answer is B. If after giving notice and a reasonable opportunity to respond a court finds that Rule 11 has been violated, the court may impose an appropriate sanction upon the lawyers, law firms, or parties that have committed, or are responsible for the violation. Sanctions may be imposed either by motion or on the court's own initiative.

A and C are incorrect because they are erroneous statements of law.

D is incorrect because the defendant, the defendant's attorney, and the attorney's law firm may be sanctioned for violations of Rule 11.

Civil Procedure Outline § III (C)(3)(b) Rule 11: Process for Sanctions: On Court's Initiative

QUESTION 169
ANSWER & EXPLANATION
Motions

(A)   No, because a court may partially grant a motion for summary judgment as to certain claims or defenses.

The correct answer is A. A court may grant or deny the motion for summary judgment. If a court grants a motion for summary judgment, the order may be only partial, with respect to certain claims or defenses, or complete.

B and C are incorrect because they are erroneous statements of law.

D is incorrect because the trucker's status as plaintiff is irrelevant as to whether the court can partially grant the motion for summary judgment.

Civil Procedure Outline § V (A)(3)(d)(1) Pretrial Motions: Motion for Summary Judgment: Judgment

QUESTION 170
ANSWER & EXPLANATION
Verdicts and Judgments

(A)   No, because an appeals court will only set aside a judicial finding of fact if it is clearly erroneous.

The correct answer is A. An appeals court will only set aside a judicial finding of fact if it is clearly erroneous.

Civil Procedure Outline § VI C(1)(d) Judicial Findings and Conclusions: Findings of Fact and Conclusions of Law: Clearly Erroneous Standard on Appeal

QUESTION 171
ANSWER & EXPLANATION
Pre-Trial Procedures

(C)   Yes, because the defendant addressed the allegations in paragraphs 1, 2, and 5 through 20, and the allegations in paragraphs 3 and 4 will be deemed admitted.

The correct answer is C. An answer must admit or deny the allegations set forth in the complaint. The answer may also assert a defendant's lack of sufficient knowledge to admit or deny an allegation. If a defendant fails to address an allegation in the complaint, that allegation will be deemed admitted. Here, the defendant properly addressed the allegations in paragraphs 1, 2, and 5 through 20. The fact that the defendant failed to specifically address the allegations in paragraphs 3 and 4 does not mean that the answer is improper; it simply means that those allegations will be deemed admitted.

A is incorrect because a defendant is not required to admit or deny every allegation in the complaint. The defendant may also assert lack of sufficient knowledge to respond, or simply not respond to an allegation, in which case the allegation will be deemed admitted.

B is incorrect because a defendant is not required to admit, deny, or allege lack of sufficient knowledge to respond in order to present a proper answer. However, if a defendant fails to address an allegation in the complaint, that allegation will be deemed admitted.

D is incorrect because it implies that the only requirement for presenting a proper answer is that the defendant denies the causes of action. A proper answer can admit, deny, or allege lack of sufficient knowledge to respond to the allegations. Any allegations that are not specifically addressed are deemed admitted.

Civil Procedure Outline § III(B)(3): Types of Pleadings

QUESTION 172
ANSWER & EXPLANATION
Jurisdiction and Venue

(D) Yes, because the motorcyclist lives in the northern district of State B and the trucker lives in the southern district of State B.

The correct answer is D. A federal district court may transfer a civil action to any other federal district or division where the action might have been brought, or to any district or division to which all parties have consented. More than one venue may be a proper venue to hear a dispute. A defendant may seek to change the initial venue that the plaintiff selected to a venue that the defendant prefers. A defendant may be entitled to a change or transfer of venue if the initial venue is improper, or if a subsequent venue would be more convenient to the parties and witnesses. In this case, the plaintiff could have originally brought the case in State B, in either the northern or southern district; therefore, venue would be proper in the northern district of State B. Further, the facts indicate that it will be more convenient for the parties and for one of the two witnesses, which further lends support to the conclusion that the court may grant the motion.

A is incorrect for the reasons explained above.

B and C are incorrect because, although venue would be proper in the northern district of State A because the accident occurred there, the action could also have been brought in the northern district of State B, where the motorcyclist lives.

Civil Procedure Outline § I (D)(3)(a): Venue Transfer: General Grounds for Change of Venue

QUESTION 173
ANSWER & EXPLANATION
Pre-Trial Procedures

(C) Yes, because the defendant did not serve the defendant with the motion and wait 21 days before filing the motion with the court.

The correct answer is C. A motion for sanctions must describe the specific conduct alleged to have violated Rule 11. The motion should not be filed with the court unless, within 21 days after service of the motion, the challenged filing is not withdrawn or appropriately corrected. In this case, the defendant did not serve the motion on the defendant and wait 21 days before filing it with the court.

Accordingly, D is incorrect because it states the incorrect number of days provided by Rule 11.

A is incorrect because it states a fact that would stem from the defendant's failure to serve the motion on the defendant as required by Rule 11.

B is incorrect because it states an allegation that would support granting the motion.

Civil Procedure Outline § III (C)(3)(a) Rule 11: Process for Sanctions: By Motion

QUESTION 174
ANSWER & EXPLANATION
Motions

(D) Yes, because the plaintiff needed further discovery to avoid judgment for the defendant.

The correct answer is D. If a nonmovant cannot present facts essential to justify its opposition to a motion for summary judgment, the nonmovant may submit an affidavit or declaration specifying the reasons the facts are not available. In response to such a submission, a court may:

- defer considering the motion or deny it;

- allow time to obtain affidavits or declarations or to take discovery; or

- issue any other appropriate order.

Therefore, for example, if a defendant moves for summary judgment before the plaintiff has had an adequate opportunity for discovery, the plaintiff may submit an affidavit detailing the need for further discovery to avoid judgment for the defendant. The court may defer considering the motion for summary judgment until later in the case.

A and B are incorrect because, as explained above, the court may defer ruling on the motion.

C is incorrect because the fact that the damages allegedly exceed one million dollars is not relevant as to whether the court may defer ruling on the motion until later in the case.

Civil Procedure Outline § V (A)(3)(d)(3) Pretrial Motions: Motion for Summary Judgment: Judgment: When Facts not Available to Nonmovant

QUESTION 175
ANSWER & EXPLANATION
Verdicts and Judgments

(A)   No, because the cases do not involve the same cause of action.

The correct answer is A. The doctrine of claim preclusion forbids re-litigating entire claims, which were, or could have been, litigated in prior actions. The modern view regarding the scope of a "claim" is that it includes all of the party's rights to remedies against the other party with respect to the same transaction from which the action arose.
For claim preclusion to apply, the following requirements must be met:

- Same parties must exist in both lawsuits;

- The prior judgment must have been rendered by a court of competent jurisdiction;

- A final judgment on the merits must exist; and

- The same cause of action must be involved in both cases.

B is incorrect because there is no indication that the prior judgment was not rendered by a court of competent jurisdiction.

C and D are incorrect because they ignore the fact that the cases do not involve the same cause of action.

Civil Procedure Outline § VI D(1)(a) Effect; Claim and Issue Preclusion: Res Judicata: Claim Preclusion

QUESTION 176
ANSWER & EXPLANATION
Pre-Trial Procedures

(B)   Yes, because an answer can be amended once within 21 days after serving it.

The correct answer is B. If a pleading is one that does not require a responsive pleading, a party may amend it once as a matter of right within 21 days after serving it. Here, the defendant filed his answer. Fifteen days later, the defendant filed an amended answer. Because answers do not require responsive pleadings and the amendment was filed within 21 days after service of the answer, it was a proper amendment.

A is incorrect because an answer cannot be amended at any time. It can be amended once as a matter of right within 21 days after serving it. Otherwise, amendments are only permitted by leave of court or by written consent of the adverse party.

C is incorrect because an answer can be amended within 21 after service of the answer, not the complaint.

D is incorrect because answers can be amended once as a matter of right within 21 days after serving it. After this time, amendments can be filed with leave of court or with written consent of the adverse party.

Civil Procedure Outline § III(B)(5): Amendment of Pleadings

QUESTION 177
ANSWER & EXPLANATION
Jurisdiction and Venue

(B)   Yes, because the plaintiff brought the case in the wrong venue.

The correct answer is B. For venue purposes, a defendant corporation is deemed to reside in any judicial district in which it is subject to personal jurisdiction at the time the action is commenced. For the purpose of determining a court's personal jurisdiction, a defendant-corporation that resides in a state with more than one judicial district is considered to reside in any district within that state where the corporation has contacts sufficient to establish personal jurisdiction if that district were a separate state. In this case, the corporation does not have any contact with the southern district of State A; therefore, if the southern district of State A were viewed as a separate "state," the court in the southern district would not have personal jurisdiction over the corporation. Consequently, venue would not be proper there. Therefore, the case was brought in the wrong venue.

A is incorrect because venue would also be appropriate in the northern district of State A where the corporation's principal place of business is located.

C and D are incorrect because, as stated previously, the corporation does not have any contact with the southern district of State A; consequently, venue is not proper in the southern district.

Civil Procedure Outline § I (D)(1)(a)(2): Venue Generally: Corporate Parties

QUESTION 178
ANSWER & EXPLANATION
Pre-Trial Procedures

(A)   No, because the painter prevailed on the motion.

The correct answer is A. The court may award to the party prevailing on a motion for sanctions the reasonable expenses and attorney fees incurred in presenting or opposing the motion.

B is incorrect because the fact that the painter completed the work on the house does not necessarily entitle the painter to an award of attorney fees.

C and D are incorrect because they ignore the law stated above regarding the award of fees to the prevailing party.

Civil Procedure Outline § III (C)(3)(a) Rule 11: Process for Sanctions: By Motion

QUESTION 179
ANSWER & EXPLANATION
Motions

(A)   No, because it was filed more than 30 days after the end of discovery.

The correct answer is A. Generally, a party may file a motion for summary judgment until 30 days after the end of discovery, unless:

-   the court orders otherwise; or

-   a local rule sets a different time to file a motion for summary judgment.

In this case, there are no facts indicating the court ordered that the motion could be filed more than 30 days after the end of discovery, and there is no indication that a local rule set a different time. Consequently, the motion is untimely.

B, C, and D are incorrect because they are erroneous statements.

Civil Procedure Outline § V (A)(3)(e) Pretrial Motions: Motion for Summary Judgment: Judgment: Timing of Motion

QUESTION 180
ANSWER & EXPLANATION
Pre-Trial Procedures

(D) Yes, because the complaint was amended within 21 days after service of the answer.

The correct answer is D. If a pleading is one to which a responsive pleading is required, the party may amend it once as a matter of right the earlier of either 21 days after service of a responsive pleading, or 21 days after service of a Rule 12(b), (e), or (f) motion. A complaint is a pleading that requires a responsive pleading. Thus, it can be amended within 21 days after service of the answer. Here, the plaintiff amended his complaint 14 days after the answer was served, so the amendment was proper.

A is incorrect because complaints are pleadings that require a responsive pleading. As such, an amendment can be made within 21 days after the responsive pleading is filed, not 21 days after service of the complaint.

B is incorrect because a complaint cannot be amended at any time. Rather, because a complaint requires a responsive pleading, it can be amended once as a matter of right within 21 days after service of the answer, or 21 after service of a Rule 12(b), (e), or (f) motion. Otherwise, an amendment can be made only with leave of court or with written consent of the adverse party.

C is incorrect because a complaint can be amended once as a matter of right within 21 days after service of a responsive pleading, or 21 days after service of a Rule 12(b), (e), or (f) motion. After this time, amendments can be made only with leave of court or written consent of the adverse party.

Civil Procedure Outline § III(B)(5): Amendment of Pleadings

QUESTION 181
ANSWER & EXPLANATION
Verdicts and Judgments

(C) Yes, because the consumer had a full and fair opportunity to litigate the same issue in the prior action.

The correct answer is C. The traditional requirements for asserting collateral estoppel are:

- a valid and final judgment was rendered in a prior action;

- an issue of fact was actually litigated, determined, and essential to the judgment in the prior action;

- the same issue arises in a subsequent action; and

- mutuality, meaning the same parties are litigants in both actions.

However, the modern approach to issue preclusion *eliminates the fourth element of mutuality.* Pursuant to the modern approach, a party who is precluded from re-litigating an issue with an opposing party, is also precluded from doing so with another person *unless* he lacked a full and fair opportunity to litigate the issue in the first action, or other circumstances justify affording him an opportunity to re-litigate the issue.

A is incorrect because the modern approach to issue preclusion does not require that the parties in both lawsuits be mutual.

B is incorrect because issue preclusion prevents a party from re-litigating issues (as opposed to entire claims) that have been previously litigated and determined in a prior action. Choice B misstates the law.

D is incorrect because it ignores the rule stated above regarding the modern approach, which does not require mutuality.

Civil Procedure Outline § VI D(1)(b)(2) Effect; Claim and Issue Preclusion: Res Judicata: Issue Preclusion

**QUESTION 182
ANSWER & EXPLANATION
Jurisdiction and Venue**

(C)   Yes, because the case is based on state law that could also support a federal claim.

The correct answer is C. Federal question analysis is governed by the Well-Pleaded Complaint Rule. Under this rule, federal jurisdiction exists when a federal question is presented on the face of a plaintiff's properly pleaded complaint. A federal question is "presented" when the complaint invokes any type of federal law as the primary basis for relief. For a court to have federal subject-matter jurisdiction over a case, the plaintiff must affirmatively invoke federal subject-matter jurisdiction by pleading a federal-law claim within the complaint. A federal court does not have federal question subject-matter jurisdiction over a case based on state law that could also support a federal claim. (Therefore, a plaintiff can avoid federal question jurisdiction by relying exclusively on state law to present a claim.) Because the plaintiff's claim in this case is based on state law that could also support a federal claim, the court does not have federal question jurisdiction over this case. Note that diversity jurisdiction would not be appropriate because the parties are not diverse.

A, B, and D are incorrect because the fact that the claim is based on state law that could also support a federal claim is the reason the court does not have jurisdiction over this case. Note that answer D conflates the requirements for federal question jurisdiction and diversity jurisdiction: There is no amount in controversy requirement for federal question jurisdiction.

Civil Procedure Outline § I (A)(1)(a): Federal Question Jurisdiction: Well-Pleaded Complaint Rule

QUESTION 183
ANSWER & EXPLANATION
Pre-Trial Procedures

(C)   Yes, because a court may sanction the lawyer and the lawyer's law firm.

The correct answer is C. If, after notice and a reasonable opportunity to respond, a court finds that Rule 11 has been violated, the court may impose an appropriate sanction upon the lawyers, law firms, or parties that have committed, or are responsible for the violation. A court may direct a lawyer, law firm, or party to withdraw or correct the questioned filing, or to show cause why it has not violated the Rule.

A and B are incorrect because the ignore the above Rule. D is incorrect because a court may sanction a party on the court's own initiative.

Civil Procedure Outline § III (C)(3) Rule 11: Process for Sanctions

QUESTION 184
ANSWER & EXPLANATION
Motions

(B)   No, because in reaching its decision, the court weighed the evidence and determined the credibility of witnesses.

The correct answer is B. When deciding a motion for judgment as a matter of law, a trial court may not:

-   determine the credibility of witnesses;

-   weigh the evidence; or

- otherwise replace the jury's view of the evidence with that of its own.

Consequently, it was not proper for the court to weigh the evidence and determine the credibility of witnesses.

A is incorrect because, although a motion for judgment as a matter of law may be made at any time after the close of the opponent's evidence, it must be made *before* the case is submitted to the jury.

C is incorrect for the reasons articulated in the explanation for the correct answer, B.

D is incorrect because it ignores the fact that the court improperly weighed the evidence and determined the credibility of witnesses.

Civil Procedure Outline § V (B)(1)(b) Pretrial Motions: Motion for Judgment as a Matter of Law: Ruling on Motion: Court Cannot Substitute Judgment for Jury

QUESTION 185
ANSWER & EXPLANATION
Jurisdiction and Venue

(A) No, because the complaint asserts that a federal defense that the defendant may raise is insufficient to defeat the claim.

The correct answer is A. Under the Well-Pleaded Complaint Rule, a federal court lacks original jurisdiction over a case in which a plaintiff's complaint presents a state-law cause of action, but also asserts that: 1) federal law deprives a defendant of a defense that the defendant might raise (e.g., federal immunity); or 2) a federal defense that a defendant may raise is not sufficient to defeat a claim of the complaint. Consequently, because the complaint asserts that a federal defense the defendant may raise is insufficient to defeat the claim, the federal court lacks original jurisdiction over the case, and therefore, removal would be improper.

B is incorrect because it is an erroneous statement of law.

C is incorrect because the fact that the complaint asserts a federal defense the defendant may raise is insufficient to defeat the claim.

D is incorrect because the plaintiff is "master of the claim," and may avoid federal jurisdiction by relying on a state-law cause of action and asserting that a federal defense the defendant may raise is insufficient to defeat the plaintiff's claim.

Civil Procedure Outline § I (A)(1)(a)(2): Federal Question Jurisdiction: Federal Defense Insufficient

QUESTION 186
ANSWER & EXPLANATION
Pre-Trial Procedures

(B) **No, because he failed to obtain either leave of court or written consent of the adverse party.**

The correct answer is B. If a party wishes to amend its pleadings after expiration of the 21 days after service of the pleading or responsive pleading, the party must obtain leave of court or written consent of the adverse party. Fed. R. Civ. P. 15(a). Leave must be freely given when justice so requires. The Supreme Court has held that amendments should be permitted unless such amendment results in a form of injustice. Here, the plaintiff obtained only oral consent of the adverse party, but the Rule requires *written* consent of the adverse party.

A is incorrect because oral consent by the adverse party is insufficient. To amend a pleading after the allowable time frame, a party must obtain leave of court or written consent of the adverse party.

C is incorrect because if a pleading is one that requires a responsive pleading, an amendment can be filed once as a matter of right within 21 days after service of the responsive pleading. Here, because a complaint is a pleading that requires a responsive pleading, the plaintiff had 21 days after service of the answer to file an amended complaint as a matter of right. The plaintiff did not file his amendment within 21 days of service of the answer; therefore, he had to seek leave of court or written consent of the adverse party in order to amend his complaint.

D is incorrect because, although an amendment could have been filed once as a matter of right within 21 days after service of the answer, an amendment can be filed after that time with leave of court or with written consent of the adverse party.

Civil Procedure Outline § III(B)(5): Amendment of Pleadings

QUESTION 187
ANSWER & EXPLANATION
Pre-Trial Procedures

(D) **Yes, because a court may impose a sanction requiring a party to pay a penalty into court.**

The correct answer is D. A sanction imposed for violation of Rule 11 is limited to that which is sufficient to deter repetition of the conduct or comparable conduct by others similarly situated.

The sanction may include:

- non-monetary directives,

- an order to pay a penalty into court, or,

- if imposed on motion and warranted for effective deterrence, an order directing payment to the movant of some or all of the reasonable attorney's fees and other expenses incurred as a direct result of the violation.

A, B, and C are incorrect because they are erroneous statements of law.

Civil Procedure Outline § III (C)(4) Rule 11: Nature of Sanctions

QUESTION 188
ANSWER & EXPLANATION
Motions

(C) Yes, because the court found that there was no way the jury could find for the trucker.

The correct answer is C. A motion for judgment as a matter of law should be granted if there is no legally sufficient evidentiary basis for the jury to find in favor of the non-moving party. In other words, the court should only grant this motion if it finds that, based on the evidence presented, there is no way that the jury could find for the opposing party. Accordingly, in this case, the court applied the proper standard in granting the motion.

A, B, and D are all incorrect because when deciding a motion for judgment as a matter of law the court should not determine the credibility of witnesses, weigh the evidence, or otherwise replace the jury's view of the evidence with that of its own.

Civil Procedure Outline § V (B)(1)(a)-(b) Pretrial Motions: Motion for Judgment as a Matter of Law: Ruling on Motion

QUESTION 189
ANSWER & EXPLANATION
Jurisdiction and Venue

(A) No, because the amount in controversy requirement was satisfied in the driver's complaint.

The correct answer is A. A party can invoke diversity jurisdiction only if the amount in controversy exceeds $75,000, exclusive of interest and costs. If the amount in controversy is $75,000 or less, diversity jurisdiction does not exist. It does not matter if the party actually recovers $75,000 or more. So long as the sum that is demanded by a plaintiff in the complaint satisfies the jurisdictional amount, it will be accepted, unless it appears to a legal certainty that the claim is really for less than the jurisdictional amount. In this case, there is no indication to a legal certainty that the driver's claim was "really for less" than the jurisdictional amount. Consequently, the motorcyclist will be unsuccessful in challenging the court's jurisdiction.

B is incorrect because it is an erroneous statement of law. A party can challenge the existence of subject-matter jurisdiction at any time in the case, even on appeal.

C is incorrect because the fact that a party recovers less than the amount sought in the complaint does not necessarily defeat the court's jurisdiction. The facts in this question do not suggest that the driver's claim was worth less than the $75,500 sought in the complaint.

D is incorrect because it is an erroneous conflation of the amount in controversy concept and the diversity of citizenship concept necessary for diversity jurisdiction.

Civil Procedure Outline § I (A)(2)(b): Diversity Jurisdiction: Amount in Controversy

QUESTION 190
ANSWER & EXPLANATION
Pre-Trial Procedures

(A)   No, because the court did not order the driver to reply.

The correct answer is A. A party may file a reply to an answer only if the court orders it.

B, C, and D are incorrect because they include erroneous statements of law.

Civil Procedure Outline § III (B)(3)(e) Nature and Style of Pleadings: Reply to an Answer

QUESTION 191
ANSWER & EXPLANATION
Motions

(D)   The motion is untimely.

The correct answer is D. A party may move for judgment as a matter of law at any time after the close of the opponent's evidence, and before the case is submitted to the jury.

A and C are erroneous statements of law.

B is incorrect because the fact that a witness has been convicted of a crime involving dishonesty would not prohibit the court from granting a motion for judgment as a matter of law.

Civil Procedure Outline § V (B)(2) Pretrial Motions: Motion for Judgment as a Matter of Law: Timing of Motion

QUESTION 192
ANSWER & EXPLANATION
Jurisdiction and Venue

(B)   No, because the taxi driver's claim is a permissive counterclaim.

The correct answer is B.   If a counterclaim is permissive (i.e., not arising from the same transaction or occurrence), then it must possess an independent jurisdictional basis for federal jurisdiction.   A permissive counterclaim must independently fulfill the jurisdictional amount requirement.   In order to assert a counterclaim that is unrelated to the same transaction or occurrence, the amount of the defendant's claim must exceed $75,000.   In this case, the parties are diverse and the amount in controversy is satisfied. Consequently, the taxi driver's claim is a permissive counterclaim and it will survive the contractor's motion to dismiss.

A is incorrect because the taxi driver's claim is not a compulsory counterclaim (i.e., the taxi driver's claim did not arise from the contract claim filed by the contractor).

C is incorrect because "*de-minimis* counterclaim" is an erroneous characterization of the claim in this case.

D is incorrect because, although it is true that the facts indicate that federal law is not the basis of the taxi driver's claim, the court has an independent basis for jurisdiction over the claim (i.e., diversity jurisdiction): the parties are diverse and the damages sought by the taxi driver satisfy the amount in controversy requirement.

Civil Procedure Outline § I (A)(2)(b)(3)(b): Diversity Jurisdiction: Counterclaims, Permissive

QUESTION 193
ANSWER & EXPLANATION
Pre-Trial Procedures

(D)   Yes, because the claim arose out of the same occurrence that was the subject matter of the opposing party's claim.

The correct answer is D.   This question concerns joinder of claims.   Due to the claim preclusion doctrine of *res judicata*, a party should present a complete claim to the court.   Although a party is not required to present the entire claim, if the party fails to do so, the party will be barred from bringing any other related claim in a later suit.   A court conducts a transaction test to determine whether two separate requests for relief arise from the same claim for *res judicata* purposes. A defending party must put forward any claim that the defending party possesses:

> against an opposing party if the claim . . . arises out of the transaction or occurrence that is the subject matter of the opposing party's claim.

The failure to assert such a counterclaim precludes its assertion in a subsequent action. Fed. R. Civ. P. 13(a)(1)(A). In this case, the motorcyclist's claim arose out of the same occurrence that was the subject matter of the driver's original claim. Therefore, the motorcyclist's failure to assert the counterclaim precluded its assertion in a subsequent action.

A, B, and C are incorrect because they ignore the rules stated above.

Civil Procedure Outline § III (D)(1)(a) Joinder of Claims: Compulsory Joinder of Claims

QUESTION 194
ANSWER & EXPLANATION
Motions

(C)   The defendant filed the renewed motion 30 days after the judgment.

The correct answer is C. A renewed motion for judgment as a matter of law must be filed within 28 days of the judgment.

A is incorrect because, in order to preserve a subsequent renewed motion for judgment as a matter of law, it is necessary for the moving party to first timely move for a judgment as a matter of law. Obviously, a party will only file a renewed motion when the initial motion has been denied.

B is incorrect because a renewed motion for judgment as a matter of law is made after a judgment is entered.

D is incorrect because the renewed motion must be made within 28 days of the judgment.

Civil Procedure Outline § V (B)(2)(b)(1) Pretrial Motions: Motion for Judgment as a Matter of Law: Timing of Motion: Reserve Renewed Motion: Timing of Renewed Motion

QUESTION 195
ANSWER & EXPLANAATION
Jurisdiction and Venue

(D)   Yes, because removal was improper.

The correct answer is D. Removal is the process of moving a case filed in a state court to a federal court. Only a defendant may remove a case to federal court. However, the defendant cannot be a resident of the forum state when the federal court's jurisdiction would be based on diversity. Once a case is removed to a federal court, a party may move to remand the case back to state court. The case may be remanded to the state court if the removal was improper. In this case, the doctor is a citizen of State B, the forum state; consequently, removal to the federal court in State B was improper, and the case should be remanded to the state court.

A is incorrect because, as stated above, removal was improper in this case.

B is incorrect because it is an erroneous statement of law.

C is incorrect because the fact that the patient did not raise a federal claim is not dispositive as to the question of whether the case will be remanded to the state court in this case.

Civil Procedure Outline § I (A)(4)(a)-(c): Removal from State Court to Federal Court: Removal Requirements; Motion to Remand

QUESTION 196
ANSWER & EXPLANATION
Pre-Trial Procedures

(C) cross-claim

The correct answer is C. A defendant may assert a claim arising out of the same transaction against a party that is already involved in the litigation (i.e., co-defendant).

A and D are incorrect because, although factually accurate, they fail to identify the proper designation of the motorcyclist's claim.

B is incorrect because it is an erroneous statement.

Civil Procedure Outline § III (D)(1)(b)(3) Joinder of Claims: Permissive Joinder of Claims: Cross-Claims

QUESTION 197
ANSWER & EXPLANATION
Motions

(A) Weigh the evidence.

The correct answer is A. Unlike a motion for judgment as a matter of law, a trial judge considering a motion for a new trial is free to weigh the evidence, and need not view it in the light most favorable to the verdict winner. 11 Charles Alan Wright and Arthur R. Miller, Federal Practice and Procedure § 2806 (3d ed. 2007). But the judge must honor the jury's wisdom. *Id.* The judge should not grant a new trial on the basis that the jury's verdict is contrary to the weight of the evidence unless the verdict causes a miscarriage of justice. *United States v. Landau,* 155 F.3d 93 (2d Cir. 1998).

B is incorrect because no pre-verdict motion needs to be made as a prerequisite to making a motion for new trial after a verdict.

C is incorrect because a party may file a motion for a new trial within 28 days of the judgment.

D is incorrect because a court may not ignore the jury's wisdom.

Civil Procedure Outline § V (C)(2)(b) Post-Trial Motions: Motion for a New Trial: Grounds for a New Trial

QUESTION 198
ANSWER & EXPLANATION
Jurisdiction and Venue

(C)   Yes, because the doctor properly filed the notice of removal.

The correct answer is C. A case that is originally filed in a state court may be removed to a federal court if:

- the case could have been filed in a federal court (federal subject-matter jurisdiction exists);

- all defendants agree to remove the case; and

- the grounds for removal are included in at least one claim of a plaintiff (i.e., the grounds cannot be based on an affirmative defense or a counterclaim).

In order to remove a case, a defendant files a notice of removal containing a short and plain statement of the grounds for removal, together with a copy of all process, pleadings, and orders served upon the defendant(s) in the action. In this case, the facts indicate that the federal court would have diversity jurisdiction over the case. Further, the doctor properly filed the notice of removal, and there are no facts indicating that removal would otherwise be improper. Consequently, the doctor should be able to remove the case to federal court.

A is incorrect because a defendant is not required to file a motion to remove a case. Removal is automatic.

B is incorrect because the doctor had 30 days from the date the patient served the complaint in which to seek removal. Consequently, the doctor's notice of removal was timely.

D is incorrect because it is an erroneous statement of law.

Civil Procedure Outline § I (A)(4)(a)-(b): Removal from State Court to Federal Court: Removal Requirements; Removal Procedure

QUESTION 199
ANSWER & EXPLANATION
Pre-Trial Procedures

(C)   Yes, because the management company was an indispensable party.

The correct answer is C. An indispensable party is a party without which a case cannot proceed if that party cannot be joined. When determining whether a party is indispensable, a court will generally examine the following factors:

- the extent to which a judgment rendered without the party might prejudice an absentee or existing parties;

- whether the prejudice can be lessened or avoided by appropriately shaping the relief granted;

- whether adequate relief can be granted without the absentee; and

- whether the plaintiff has an adequate remedy if the action is dismissed for non-joinder.

Several decided cases have held that causes of action seeking the rescission of a contract must be dismissed unless all parties to the contract, and any others having a substantial interest in it, can be joined. In this case, the facts indicate that the management company is a party to the contract and has a substantial interest in it. Consequently, the best answer choice is C.

A is incorrect because it ignores the above rules.

B is incorrect because it is an erroneous statement.

D is incorrect because it ignores the issue raised in this question (i.e., whether the management company is an indispensable party).

Civil Procedure Outline § III (D)(2)(a)(2) Joinder of Parties: Indispensable Parties

QUESTION 200
ANSWER & EXPLANATION
Motions

(D)   The court found that the award of damages was excessive.

The correct answer is D. In order for a motion for a new trial to be granted, there must be a fundamental error affecting the trial outcome or its fairness such as irregularity, misconduct, new evidence, legal error, inadmissible evidence, instruction error, or excessive damages, etc. 11 Charles Alan Wright and Arthur R. Miller, *Federal Practice and Procedure* § 2805-2806 (3d ed. 2007).

A is incorrect because the judge should not grant a new trial on the basis that the jury's verdict is contrary to the weight of the evidence unless the verdict causes a miscarriage of justice. *United States v. Landau,* 155 F.3d 93 (2d Cir. 1998).

B is incorrect for this reason: determining the credibility of witnesses is peculiarly for the jury, and it is an invasion of the jury's province to grant a new trial merely because the evidence was sharply in conflict. *Latino v. Kaizer,* 58 F.3d 310 (7th Cir. 1995).

C is incorrect because it incorporates an erroneous standard for granting the motion. The correct standard for granting a motion for a new trial is that there must be a *fundamental* error affecting the trial outcome.

Civil Procedure Outline § V (C)(2)(b) Post-Trial Motions: Motion for a New Trial: Grounds for a New Trial

QUESTION 201
ANSWER & EXPLANATION
Jurisdiction and Venue

(C)   Yes, because the driver improperly added a non-diverse party in order to defeat diversity jurisdiction.

The correct answer is C. If the plaintiff fraudulently joins a party to destroy diversity in order to prevent removal, a defendant may remove the case if he would have been able to remove the case absent the fraudulent joinder. In order to determine whether joinder is fraudulent for removal purposes, a federal court will inquire whether there is absolutely no chance that the cause of action against the purported defendant will succeed. If the plaintiff has no chance to succeed, then the court may find fraudulent joinder. In this case, the facts clearly state that the passenger was not injured and suffered no damages in the accident. Consequently, the joinder of the passenger was fraudulent for removal purposes because there is no chance that the passenger could succeed in the case. Further, there is no indication in the facts suggesting that the trucker could not have removed the case absent the fraudulent joinder. Therefore, the trucker may remove the case to the federal court.

A is incorrect because it contains an erroneous statement of law.

B is incorrect because the defendant *cannot* be a resident of the forum state for purposes of removal. Consequently, had the trucker been a resident of State B, removal would not be proper. This answer choice contains the erroneous proposition that a defendant must be a resident of the forum state in order to remove a case.

D is incorrect because it is an overbroad assertion that is not the best answer choice on the facts raised in this question.

Civil Procedure Outline § I (A)(4)(a)(1): Removal from State Court to Federal Court: Fraudulent Joinder

QUESTION 202
ANSWER & EXPLANATION
Pre-Trial Procedures

(C) Yes, because the rancher and farmer asserted a right to relief that arose out of the same event, with a common question of law or fact.

The correct answer is C. Multiple plaintiffs may join claims against a defendant in a single action when those claims arise out of a single event and share at least one common issue of law or fact. Rule 20(a)(1) states that:

> Persons may join in one action as plaintiffs if: (A) they assert any right to relief jointly, severally, or in the alternative with respect to or arising out of the same transaction, occurrence, or series of transactions or occurrences; and (B) any question of law or fact common to all plaintiffs will arise in the action.

In this case, the rancher and farmer's claim arose out of a single event (the several-day period in which the factory polluted the stream), and the claim shares at least one common issue of law or fact (e.g., whether the factory was negligent). Consequently, choice C is the best answer.

A is incorrect because it incorrectly implies that a party must be indispensable in order for joinder to occur.

B and D are incorrect because they are erroneous statements of law.

Civil Procedure Outline § III (D)(2)(b)(1) Joinder of Parties: Permissive Joinder of Plaintiffs

QUESTION 203
ANSWER & EXPLANATION
Motions

(C)   Move for a new trial.

The correct answer is C. At *voir dire*, prospective jurors are questioned in part to determine their potential bias. A motion for a new trial can be made alleging non-disclosure by a prospective juror during *voir dire*. Even though such a motion usually does not succeed, this motion needs to be granted if disqualification of a juror for cause would have been justified. Wright and Miller, *Federal Practice and Procedure* § 2810; *McCoy v. Goldston,* 652 F.2d 654 (6th Cir. 1981).   A trial court can conduct a hearing to ascertain if a prospective juror actually is biased before granting a motion for a new trial. *Olson v. Bradrick,* 645 F. Supp. 645 (D. Conn. 1986). In this question, because facts have arisen that show the juror failed to disclose the juror's romantic relationship with the trucker, the driver should move for a new trial on that ground.

A is incorrect because raising a claim of improper venue is not related to whether the juror was biased. Further, an objection to venue after the trial is complete would be untimely, as such an objection must be asserted in the first responsive motion or pleading.

B is incorrect because a party must move for a judgment as a matter of law before the case is submitted to the jury.

D is incorrect because it would not be appropriate to schedule an *ex parte* (one side only) hearing with the court.

Civil Procedure Outline § V (C)(2)(b)(1) Post-Trial Motions: Motion for a New Trial: Grounds for a New Trial: Juror Bias

QUESTION 204
ANSWER & EXPLANATION
Jurisdiction and Venue

(D)   Yes, because a plaintiff may prevent removal by not pleading damages sufficient to allow removal and not joining a diverse party.

The correct answer is D. A plaintiff may prevent a defendant from removing a case by:

-   not raising a federal claim; or

-   not joining a party of diverse citizenship, and

-   not pleading damages sufficient to allow removal (i.e., possibly requesting a lesser amount of damages than the amount in controversy).

In this case, the driver's damages were less than the jurisdictional amount necessary for diversity jurisdiction. By refusing to join the passenger to the claim, the driver may successfully prevent removal.

A is incorrect because it is an incorrect statement of law.

B is incorrect because there is no indication in the facts that the driver made a fraudulent filing.

C is incorrect because although it is true that the accident occurred in State B, that fact alone does not indicate how the driver's actions were proper in preventing removal in this case.

Civil Procedure Outline § I (A)(4)(a)(2): Removal from State Court to Federal Court: Preventing Removal

QUESTION 205
ANSWER & EXPLANATION
Pre-Trial Procedures

(D)   Yes, because the claim arises from a single transaction with a common issue of fact or law.

The correct answer is D. Just as a multiple plaintiffs may join in an action, a plaintiff may join multiple defendants in an action when the claims against each defendant arise from a single transaction and share a common issue of fact or law. The permissive joinder rule allows a plaintiff to choose and name the defendants but does not require that a plaintiff name all defendants who might be joined. Rule 20(a)(2) provides that:

> Persons -- as well as a vessel, cargo, or other property subject to admiralty process in rem -- may be joined in one action as defendants if: (A) any right to relief is asserted against them jointly, severally, or in the alternative with respect to or arising out of the same transaction, occurrence, or series of transactions or occurrences; and (B) any question of law or fact common to all defendants will arise in the action.

In this case, the claim against the contractor and laborer arose from a single transaction and a common issue of law or fact. Consequently, D is the best choice.

A is incorrect because it ignores the contractor's potential negligence in hiring the laborer and it assumes that the laborer was intoxicated.

B and C are incorrect because they are erroneous statements of law.

Civil Procedure Outline § III (D)(2)(b)(2) Joinder of Parties: Permissive Joinder of Defendants

**QUESTION 206
ANSWER & EXPLANATION
Motions**

(A)   No, because the evidence could have been obtained with due diligence.

The correct answer is A. A party may make a motion pursuant to Rule 60 to obtain relief from a judgment. Relief will be available if the judgment is a result of a mistake or even excusable fault. On motion, the court may relieve a party from a final judgment pursuant to Rule 60 for, among other things, the following:

-   mistake, inadvertence, surprise, or excusable neglect;

-   newly discovered evidence which by due diligence could not have been discovered in time to move for a new trial;

-   fraud, misrepresentation, or other misconduct of an adverse party; or

-   any other reason justifying relief from the operation of the judgment.

In this case, the facts indicate that the expert was available before trial, but the mechanic chose not to use the expert's services. Consequently, the facts indicate that the mechanic could have obtained the evidence with due diligence. Therefore, the court should not grant the motion.

B is an erroneous statement of law.

C is incorrect because the facts do not suggest that the mechanic's failure to obtain the expert's report was excusable. Rather, the mechanic chose not to use the expert's services.

D is incorrect because it ignores the fact that the expert's report could have been obtained with the exercise of due diligence.

Civil Procedure Outline § V (C)(4)(b) Post-Trial Motions: Rule 60 Motion: Other Grounds

**QUESTION 207
ANSWER & EXPLANATION
Jurisdiction and Venue**

(C)   Yes, because the doctor planned to answer the complaint 30 days after removing the case to federal court.

The correct answer is C. In a removed action in which the defendant has not answered, the defendant must answer and/or present defenses within (the longer period of):

- 21 days after the receipt of a copy of the complaint or summons; or

- within 7 days after the filing of the notice for removal.

In this case, by failing to answer the complaint within 7 days after filing the notice for removal, the doctor is at risk for the entering of a default judgment.

A is incorrect because filing a timely notice of removal will not insulate a defendant from the risks associated with failing to file a timely answer.

B is incorrect because the answer would be untimely if filed 30 days after removing the case to federal court.

D is incorrect because there is no indication in the facts that the notice of removal was fraudulently filed.

Civil Procedure Outline § I (A)(4)(d)(1): Removal from State Court to Federal Court: Effect on Time to Answer

QUESTION 208
ANSWER & EXPLANATION
Pre-Trial Procedures

(B)   The son has a right to intervene in the action in order to protect his inheritance interest that may be affected by the litigation.

The correct answer is B. Intervention is a procedure that permits a non-party to participate in ongoing litigation in order to protect an interest that may be affected. A non-party has a right to intervene in an action when, under certain circumstances, the applicant asserts an interest which relates to the property or transaction that is the subject of the litigation. In this case, the son's inheritance may be affected by the litigation. Consequently, B is the best choice.

A, C, and D are essentially nonsensical answers that ignore the rules stated above.

Civil Procedure Outline § III (D)(3)(a)(1) Miscellaneous Joinder Concepts: Intervention: Intervention of Right

QUESTION 209
ANSWER & EXPLANATION
Motions

(C) Yes, because the court may correct a mistake in a judgment on its own initiative.

The correct answer is C. Clerical mistakes in judgments arising from oversight or omission may be corrected by the court at any time of its own initiative or on motion of any party.

A, B, and D are incorrect for the reason stated above.

Civil Procedure Outline § V (C)(3)(a) Post-Trial Motions: Rule 60 Motion: Clerical Mistakes

QUESTION 210
ANSWER & EXPLANATION
Jurisdiction and Venue

(B) No, because the vacationer lured the driver into the forum state.

The correct answer is B. Service of process that is procured by fraudulently luring a defendant into the forum state will not be upheld as valid to provide personal jurisdiction.

A is incorrect because service of process in the driver's state of domicile (State A) would not vest the court in State B with personal jurisdiction over the driver in this case.

C is incorrect because the vacationer's citizenship in State B does not establish the court's personal jurisdiction over the driver.

D is incorrect for the reasons stated above. Although in most instances service of process in the forum state will vest that forum's court with personal jurisdiction, in this case, the vacationer lured the driver into the forum state. Service of process that is procured by luring a defendant into the forum state is not valid to provide personal jurisdiction.

Civil Procedure Outline § I (B)(1)(a)(1): Bases of Personal Jurisdiction: Transient

QUESTION 211
ANSWER & EXPLANATION
Pre-Trial Procedures

(A) Impleader

The correct answer is A. A defending party may bring a third-party complaint against a third party. The defending party becomes a third-party plaintiff and the non-party becomes a third-party defendant. The process of bringing a third-party complaint is called impleader. Impleader is appropriate only when a defending party, as a third-party plaintiff, makes a claim for some kind of derivative or secondary liability against a third-party defendant. In other words, the third-party plaintiff must assert that the third-party defendant is responsible for all or part of damages stemming from the claim against the third-party plaintiff. A third-party complaint would be appropriate when alleging liability due to indemnity, suretyship, subrogation, or contribution and warranty from parties other than joint tortfeasors.

B is incorrect because intervention is a procedure that permits a non-party to participate in ongoing litigation in order to protect an interest that may be affected.

C is incorrect because interpleader permits a party (as a "stakeholder") to avoid the risk of potential multiple liability by requiring two or more other claimants with actual or potential claims against the stakeholder to assert their respective claims in one suit.

D is incorrect because it is not a term associated with joinder concepts.

Civil Procedure Outline § III (D)(3)(b)(1) Miscellaneous Joinder Concepts: Third-Party Practice: Impleader

QUESTION 212
ANSWER & EXPLANATION
Motions

(D)   Yes, because it was filed less than four months after the entry of the judgment.

The correct answer is D. A Rule 60 Motion must be made within a reasonable time from judgment. Although no firm rule exists, four months has been considered a reasonable time.

Civil Procedure Outline § V (C)(3)(c) Post-Trial Motions: Rule 60 Motion: Timing

QUESTION 213
ANSWER & EXPLANATION
Jurisdiction and Venue

(B)   No, because the patient filed the motion for remand more than 30 days from being served with the removal notice.

The correct answer is B. Once a case is removed to a federal court, a party may move to remand the case back to state court. A party must move for remand with the federal court within 30 days from being served with a removal notice. In this case, the patient's motion for remand was untimely. Consequently, the court should not grant the motion.

A is incorrect because a defendant may not be a resident of the forum state when subject-matter jurisdiction in that forum is based on diversity of the parties, as it would be in this case. Consequently, the doctor would not be able to remove the case to the federal court in State C, where he is domiciled.

C is incorrect because a motion for remand must be filed within 30 days from the date of service of the removal notice.

D is incorrect because there is no indication that removal was improper in this case.

Civil Procedure Outline § I (A)(4)(c)(1): Removal from State Court to Federal Court: Motion to Remand: Timing

QUESTION 214
ANSWER & EXPLANATION
Pre-Trial Procedures

(C) Yes, because 14 days had not yet elapsed since the company served its answer.

The correct answer is C. A potential third-party plaintiff does not need leave of court to serve a third-party complaint if no more than 14 days have passed since the party served its original answer. If more than 14 days have passed since filing its answer, then the third-party plaintiff must file a motion for leave to file the third-party complaint. The motion should state the defending party's reasons for joining the non-party in a case.

A, B, and D are incorrect because of their erroneous statements of law in relation to the facts.

Civil Procedure Outline § III (D)(3)(b)(2) Miscellaneous Joinder Concepts: Third-Party Practice: When Motion Required

QUESTION 215
ANSWER & EXPLANATION
Motions

(C) Yes, because if a court does not grant a motion for summary judgment, the court may issue an order establishing a material fact that is not genuinely in dispute.

The correct answer is C. If a court does not grant a motion for summary judgment, then the court can issue an order establishing a material fact that is not genuinely in dispute. Fed. R. Civ.

P. 56(g). The fact will be established in the case. The fact can include an item of damages or other relief. *Id.*

A and B are incorrect for the above reasons. D is incorrect because the fact that the replacement value in this case exceeded the amount in controversy requirement is not relevant as to whether the court can issue an order establishing an item of damages.

Civil Procedure Outline § V (A)(3)(d)(2) Pretrial Motions: Motion for Summary Judgment: Judgment: Judgment: Court May Establish Fact as Established

QUESTION 216
ANSWER & EXPLANATION
Jurisdiction and Venue

(D)   Yes, because the website is passive.

The correct answer is D. Generally, the owner of a website on the internet is not subject to personal jurisdiction everywhere, solely on the basis that the owner maintains a website that can be accessed everywhere. As a general proposition, the likelihood that the owner would be subject to personal jurisdiction may be proportionate to the extent to which the website is interactive. *Zippo Mfg. Co. v. Zippo Dot Com, Inc.,* 952 F. Supp. 1119 (W.D. Pa. 1997). Thus, such jurisdiction probably would not be supported merely on the basis of an entirely passive website. In this case, the guitar teacher's website merely provides information to the public and viewers of the website cannot upload or download content. Further, the guitar teacher doesn't use the website to advertise the teaching studio, but rather, the purpose of the website is to facilitate public interest in music in general. Consequently, because the website merely presents information to the public, the guitar teacher will likely be successful in challenging the court's personal jurisdiction.

A is incorrect because the fact that a website can be accessed anywhere would not, alone, vest a court with personal jurisdiction.

B and C are incorrect because whether the guitar teacher was negligent does not dictate the outcome of the question of whether the court has personal jurisdiction over the guitar teacher.

Civil Procedure Outline § I (B)(5)(a)(1): Personal Jurisdiction: General and Specific Instruction: Continuous and Systematic

QUESTION 217
ANSWER & EXPLANATION
Pre-Trial Procedure

(A) No, because the third-party claim falls within the federal court's supplemental jurisdiction.

The correct answer is A.   A third-party claim falls within a federal court's supplemental jurisdiction. Therefore, no independent ground for subject-matter jurisdiction is required.

B is incorrect because lack of subject-matter jurisdiction may never be waived as a defense; it may be asserted at any time. However, in this case, no independent ground for subject-matter jurisdiction is required, and therefore the trucker's motion is meritless.

C is incorrect because it assumes that the lack of diversity between the parties defeats the court's subject-matter jurisdiction. Because the court has supplemental jurisdiction over the third-party complaint, no independent ground for subject-matter jurisdiction is necessary.

D is incorrect because it ignores the court's supplemental jurisdiction over the claim.

Civil Procedure Outline § III (D)(3)(b)(5) Miscellaneous Joinder Concepts: Third-Party Practice: When Qualifies under Supplemental Jurisdiction

QUESTION 218
ANSWER & EXPLANATION
Jurisdiction and Venue

(B)   No, because the patient personally handed the summons and complaint to the doctor.

The correct answer is B. The summons and complaint may be served by:

-   any citizen of the United States;

-   who is over 18 years of age; and

-   not a party.

In this case, the patient is a party to the lawsuit; therefore, it was improper for the patient to personally hand the summons and complaint to the defendant.

A is incorrect because the patient had 120 days after filing the complaint to effectuate service of process. Therefore, the service was timely; however, the service was improper as explained above.

C is incorrect because although the service was timely, it was improper.

D is incorrect because the service was improper.

Civil Procedure Outline § I (C)(6): Service of Process and Notice: Who May Serve

QUESTION 219
ANSWER & EXPLANATION
Pre-Trial Procedure

(A)   No, because joinder is not impractical.

The correct answer is A. In order to bring an action as a class action, plaintiffs must demonstrate that the numerous members of a class render joinder of them all impractical. In this case, there are only two plaintiffs. Consequently, joinder is not impractical.

B is incorrect because a class action may be based on a claim of negligence.

C and D are incorrect because they ignore the fact that the rancher and dairy farmer will be unable to show that joinder is impractical.

Civil Procedure Outline § III (D)(4)(a)(1) Miscellaneous Joinder Concepts: Class Actions: Certification Prerequisites: Numerosity

QUESTION 220
ANSWER & EXPLANATION
Jurisdiction and Venue

(C)   Yes, even though the opportunist was served with the summons and complaint in State C, which is outside the personal jurisdiction of the forum court.

The correct answer is C. Notice may be given by serving (i.e., delivering) the requisite legal papers upon a party in person, *even if* the service occurs outside of the court's scope of personal jurisdiction.

A is incorrect because notice may be given outside of the court's scope of personal jurisdiction.

B is incorrect because the inventor's cousin is 18 years of age, is a U.S. citizen, and is not a party to the case; therefore, the cousin may serve the opportunist.

D is incorrect because the service was not untimely. The inventor had 120 days after filing the complaint to effectuate service of process.

Civil Procedure Outline § I (C)(8)(a)(1): Service of Process and Notice: Notice

QUESTION 221
ANSWER & EXPLANATION
Pre-Trial Procedure

(B)   The insurance company is a stakeholder in an interpleader action.

The correct answer is B. Interpleader permits a party (as a "stakeholder") to avoid the risk of potential multiple liability by requiring two or more other claimants with actual or potential claims against the stakeholder to assert their respective claims in one suit. Interpleader can be brought either as a separate action, a cross-claim, or a counterclaim. Interpleader is a somewhat infrequently used, but significant, joinder device whose core function is to save stakeholders, such as bailees and insurance companies, from logically inconsistent liability to claimants with respect to a single thing or asset.

A is incorrect because the insurance company did not file a severance action.

C and D are incorrect because of their erroneous statements about the law in relation to the facts.

Civil Procedure Outline § III (D)(3)(c) Miscellaneous Joinder Concepts: Interpleader

QUESTION 222
ANSWER & EXPLANATION
Jurisdiction and Venue

(D) The court applied the doctrine of *forum non conveniens*.

The correct answer is D. The doctrine of *forum non conveniens* allows for the dismissal of a case despite the existence of proper venue, personal jurisdiction, and subject-matter jurisdiction if:

-   another forum is more convenient; and

-   the interests of justice would be served by litigating the case elsewhere.

In this case, the accident occurred in State B where the witnesses and evidence are more readily available. For example, the paramedics, doctors, emergency room personnel, police, and the witness to the accident are residents of State B. Consequently, the interests of justice would be best served by litigating the case in State B.

Answers A, B, and C are incorrect because they are merely inapplicable Latin phrases conflated with the word "forum."

Civil Procedure Outline § I (D)(2): Forum Non Conveniens

QUESTION 223
ANSWER & EXPLANATION
Pre-Trial Procedures

(C)   Yes, because the court must ensure that the counsel for the class is experienced and qualified to carry out the litigation.

The correct answer is C. In order to bring an action as a class action, plaintiffs must satisfy the adequacy of representation requirement. The requirement involves a two-part inquiry. First, a court must ask whether the representative's interests are aligned closely enough with the other class members to ensure fair representation of the absentee class members. Second, the court must ensure that the counsel for the class are experienced and qualified to carry out the litigation in order to fairly and adequately protect the interests of the class.

A and B are incorrect because they ignore the above rule.

D is incorrect because "strict scrutiny" has no application to the facts of this question.

Civil Procedure Outline § III (D)(4)(a)(4) Miscellaneous Joinder Concepts: Class Actions: Certification Prerequisites: Adequacy of Representation.

QUESTION 224
ANSWER & EXPLANATION
Jurisdiction and Venue

(A) No, because the complaint states a claim based on federal law.

The correct answer is A.

Congress has conferred upon federal courts, the jurisdiction to decide federal questions. 28 U.S.C. § 1331. A federal district court possesses limited original jurisdiction over a case arising under the United States Constitution, federal statutory or common law, and federal treaties. Article III requires that an actual "case or controversy" exist between the parties. A "case or controversy" involves a federal question only when a plaintiff's complaint states a claim or cause of action that involves federal law.

B and D contain erroneous statements of law.

C is incorrect because diversity of citizenship is not a requirement for a federal court to exercise federal question jurisdiction.

Civil Procedure Outline § I (A)(1) Federal Subject-Matter Jurisdiction: Federal Question Jurisdiction

QUESTION 225
Pre-Trial Procedures

(A)   No, because the driver did not give reasonable notice to the trucker.

The correct answer is A. A deposition is a legal proceeding in which a party or attorney questions a witness under oath. The testifying witness is called the deponent. A deposition usually occurs before a trial and takes place outside of court. A party desiring to take an oral deposition must give reasonable notice to every other party, stating the time, place, names, and addresses of all persons to be deposed. Fed. R. Civ. P. 30.

B is incorrect because it is not improper to take a deposition outside of court.

C and D are incorrect because they ignore the Rule regarding notice.

Civil Procedure Outline § III (E)(1)(a)(1) Discovery, Disclosure, and Sanctions: Discovery Methods and Concepts: Depositions: Oral Examination

QUESTION 226
ANSWER & EXPLANATION
Jurisdiction and Venue

(B)   No, because the plaintiff relied exclusively on state law to present the claim.

The correct answer is B. The Well-Pleaded Complaint Rule makes a plaintiff the master of the claim. The plaintiff must affirmatively invoke federal subject-matter jurisdiction by pleading a federal-law claim within the complaint. A federal court does not have federal question subject-matter jurisdiction over a case based on state law that could also support a federal claim. Therefore, a plaintiff can avoid federal question jurisdiction by relying exclusively on state law to present a claim.

A is incorrect because it states an erroneous legal concept—there is no "Well-Pleaded Diversity Rule."

C is incorrect because it ignores the fact that the plaintiff relied exclusively on state law.

D is incorrect because the amount in controversy concept is relevant to diversity jurisdiction, not federal question jurisdiction.

Civil Procedure Outline § I (A)(1)(a)(1) Federal Subject-Matter Jurisdiction: Federal Question Jurisdiction: Well-Pleaded Complaint Rule: Plaintiff is Master of Claim

QUESTION 227
ANSWER & EXPLANATION
Pre-Trial Procedures

(D) Serve a subpoena *duces tecum* on the corporation.

The correct answer is D. A subpoena *duces tecum* is a subpoena that includes a request that the person produce certain documents. A party may serve a subpoena *duces tecum* on someone requiring the production of documents relevant to a dispute. The party that issues the subpoena may review the materials in advance of the deposition, and question the witness about them during the deposition.

A, B, and C are incorrect because they refer to erroneous terms in relation to subpeonas.

Civil Procedure Outline § III (E)(1)(a)(4) Discovery, Disclosure, and Sanctions: Discovery Methods and Concepts: Depositions: Subpoena Duces Tecum

QUESTION 228
ANSWER & EXPLANATION
Jurisdiction and Venue

(A)   No, because a federal defense is insufficient to confer federal question jurisdiction.

The correct answer is A. Under the Well-Pleaded Complaint Rule, a federal court lacks original jurisdiction over a case in which a plaintiff's complaint presents a state-law cause of action, but also asserts that: 1) federal law deprives a defendant of a defense that the defendant might raise (e.g., federal immunity); or 2) a federal defense that a defendant may raise is not sufficient to defeat a claim of the complaint.

B is incorrect because jurisdiction is not determined by whether the defendant has had an opportunity to defend the claim.

C and D are erroneous statements of law.

Civil Procedure Outline § I (A)(1)(a)(2) Federal Subject-Matter Jurisdiction: Federal Question Jurisdiction: Well-Pleaded Complaint Rule: Federal Defense Insufficient

QUESTION 229
ANSWER & EXPLANATION
Pre-Trial Procedures

(C) Yes, because the driver may file a verified petition for a pre-filing deposition in the federal court in the trucker's county of residence.

The correct answer is C. A petitioner may attempt to have a deposition before an actual case is filed in court. Fed. R. Civ. P. 27(a). A person or entity seeking to have a pre-filing deposition may file a verified petition in the federal district court in the county of the residence of any expected adverse party.

A and B are incorrect because they ignore the above Rule.

D is incorrect because it ignores the above Rule and notice of deposition requirement.

Civil Procedure Outline § III (E)(1)(a)(5) Discovery, Disclosure, and Sanctions: Discovery Methods and Concepts: Depositions: Deposition Before Action is Filed.

QUESTION 230
ANSWER & EXPLANATION
Jurisdiction and Venue

(A) No, because the volunteer and the theater manager have complete diversity of citizenship.

The correct answer is A. Diversity subject-matter jurisdiction exists if: 1) the opposing parties are citizens of different states; and 2) the amount in controversy exceeds $75,000, exclusive of interests and costs. Complete diversity of citizenship must exist between the parties on each side of a case. All of the plaintiffs must be citizens from different states than all of the defendants. Complete diversity means that there is no diversity jurisdiction when any party on one side of a dispute is a citizen of the same state as any party on the opposing side of the dispute. In this case, the facts state that the volunteer and the theater manager are from different states; consequently, diversity of citizenship exists between all of the parties. The magician is *not* a party to the lawsuit. Therefore, the magician's citizenship is not a controlling factor regarding the court's subject-matter jurisdiction.

B is incorrect because there is no indication in the facts that this case is based on federal law.

C is incorrect because it ignores the above rule.

D is incorrect because (1) the amount in controversy is satisfied (i.e., it exceeds $75,000) and (2) the magician's citizenship is not a controlling factor regarding the court's diversity jurisdiction.

Civil Procedure Outline § I (A)(2)(a) Federal Subject-Matter Jurisdiction: Diversity of Citizenship Jurisdiction: Complete Diversity of Citizenship

QUESTION 231
ANSWREW & EXPLANATION
Pre-Trial Procedures

(A)   No, because interrogatories may only be served on a party.

The correct answer is A. Interrogatories are written questions asked by one party of an opposing party, who must answer them in writing under oath. Interrogatories may only be served on a party. Fed. R. Civ. P. 33. The answers to interrogatories can be used as evidence in the trial.

B, C, and D are incorrect because they misconstrue the above law.

Civil Procedure Outline § III (E)(1)(b) Discovery, Disclosure, and Sanctions: Discovery Methods and Concepts: Interrogatories

QUESTION 232
ANSWER & EXPLANATION
Jurisdiction and Venue

(C)   Yes, because the amount in controversy requirement is not satisfied.

The correct answer is C. Diversity subject-matter jurisdiction exists if: 1) the opposing parties are citizens of different states; and 2) the amount in controversy exceeds $75,000, exclusive of interests and costs. A party can invoke diversity jurisdiction only if the amount in controversy *exceeds* $75,000, *exclusive* of interest and costs. If the amount in controversy is $75,000 or less, diversity jurisdiction does not exist. It does not matter if the party actually recovers $75,000 or more. So long as the sum that is demanded by a plaintiff in the complaint satisfies the jurisdictional amount, it will be accepted, unless it appears to a legal certainty that the claim is really for less than the jurisdictional amount.

In this case, the amount in controversy amount is not satisfied because it does not exceed $75,000, exclusive of interest and costs.

A and B are incorrect because they ignore or misapply the above rules.

D is incorrect because the location of the court is not a factor in regard to citizenship of the parties.

Civil Procedure Outline § I (A)(2)(b)(1) Federal Subject-Matter Jurisdiction: Diversity of Citizenship Jurisdiction: Amount in Controversy

QUESTION 233
ANSWER & EXPLANATION
Pre-Trial Procedures

(C) Yes, because the answers were served within 30 days of being served with the interrogatories.

The correct answer is C. A party must serve answers to interrogatories within 30 days of being served. Fed. R. Civ. P. 33(b)(3).

Civil Procedure Outline § III (E)(1)(b)(3) Discovery, Disclosure, and Sanctions: Discovery Methods and Concepts: Interrogatories: Time to Respond

QUESTION 234
ANSWER & EXPLANATION
Jurisdiction and Venue

(A) No, the carpenter and the plumber may not aggregate their individual claims against the company, regardless of how similar the claims are.

The correct answer is A. If a plaintiff possesses two unrelated claims, which total over $75,000, against a single defendant, a plaintiff may sue in federal court because the aggregate exceeds $75,000. However, if two different plaintiffs each possess a claim that does not exceed $75,000, against one defendant, they cannot aggregate the claims, regardless of how similar the claims are. A plaintiff may aggregate claims against multiple defendants if they are joint tortfeasors under one claim.

B, C, and D are incorrect because they are erroneous legal statements or ignore the above rules.

Civil Procedure Outline § I (A)(2)(b)(2) Federal Subject-Matter Jurisdiction: Diversity of Citizenship Jurisdiction: Amount in Controversy

QUESTION 235
ANSWER & EXPLANATION
Pre-Trial Procedures

(C)   Yes, because failure to serve a response to a request for an admission within 30 days may be construed as an admission.

The correct answer is C.

A request for admission is a written statement served by one party, on another party, requesting that the responding party admit or deny the truth of a statement. Fed. R. Civ. P. 36. A party may serve a request for admission on any other party regarding any issue of fact. A party cannot request an admission regarding an issue of law. A party must serve a response to a request for admission within 30 days of being served. A failure to respond may be construed as an admission.

A, B, and D are incorrect because they ignore the rules stated above.

Civil Procedure Outline § III (E)(1)(c)(1) Discovery, Disclosure, and Sanctions: Discovery Methods and Concepts: Requests for Admission: Time to Respond

QUESTION 236
ANSWER & EXPLANATION
Jurisdiction and Venue

(B)   No, because the contractor's permissive counterclaim does not independently fulfill the jurisdictional amount requirement.

The correct answer is B. If a counterclaim is permissive (i.e., not arising from the same transaction or occurrence), then it must possess an independent jurisdictional basis for federal subject-matter jurisdiction. A permissive counterclaim must independently fulfill the jurisdictional amount requirement. In order to assert a counterclaim that is unrelated to the same transaction or occurrence, the amount of the defendant's claim must exceed $75,000.

A is incorrect because whether the contractor had filed the initial lawsuit has no bearing in this matter. The contractor's claim does not satisfy the jurisdictional amount, so even if it had been filed prior to the homeowner's lawsuit, the court would not have subject matter-jurisdiction over the claim.

C and D are incorrect statements of law.

Civil Procedure Outline § I (A)(2)(b)(3)(b) Federal Subject-Matter Jurisdiction: Diversity of Citizenship Jurisdiction: Amount in Controversy: Counterclaims: Permissive

QUESTION 237
ANSWER & EXPLANATION
Pre-Trial Procedures

(A) No, because the parties did not agree to the multiple formats, nor did the court order multiple formats for production.

The correct answer is A. A party may request any other party to produce and/or permit inspection or copying of designated documents, electronically stored information, or other tangible things. Fed. R. Civ. P. 34(a). Unless the parties agree or the court orders otherwise, the following procedures apply:

- a party need not produce the same electronically stored information in more than one form;

- if a request does not specify a form, then a party must produce the electronically stored information in the form that is ordinarily maintained or in a reasonably usable form; and

- a party must produce documents as they are maintained in the usual course of business or must label and organize the documents to fit the request's categories.

B, C, and D are incorrect because they ignore the rules stated above.

Civil Procedure Outline § III (E)(1)(d)(3) Discovery, Disclosure, and Sanctions: Discovery Methods and Concepts: Request for Production: Electronically Stored Information

QUESTION 238
ANSWER & EXPLANATION
Jurisdiction and Venue

(C) No, because the demand was not served within 14 days of the service of the notice of removal.

The correct answer is C. A party entitled to trial by jury must serve a demand within 14 days after the notice of removal is filed if the party is the removing party, or if not the moving party, within 14 days after service on the party of the notice of removal. A party who, prior to removal, made an express demand for trial by jury in accordance with state law, need not make a demand for a jury trial after removal.

Civil Procedure Outline § I (A)(4)(d)(2) Federal Subject-Matter Jurisdiction: Removal from State Court to Federal Court: Effect on Timing: Jury Demand

QUESTION 239
ANSWER & EXPLANATION
Pre-Trial Procedures

(C) Yes, because even without a request, a party must produce the names and contact information of all persons likely to have discoverable information.

The correct answer is C. In a federal action, the parties are required to produce certain evidence without a discovery request. The parties in a federal case must make initial disclosures to an opponent early during the case. Fed. R. Civ. P. 26(a)(1). A party must provide the initial disclosures to each opposing party's counsel. Initial disclosures include:

-   names and contact information of all persons likely to have discoverable information;

-   a copy or description of relevant "documents, electronically stored information, and tangible things" within the parties' possession;

-   a computation of each category of damages that are sought and the documents upon which the computations are based, such as documents showing injury; and

-   any insurance agreement under which an insurance company might be liable to satisfy a judgment.

Initial disclosures must be made based on the information reasonably available to the party. The party cannot fail to make initial disclosures simply because it has not fully investigated, or because another party has not made disclosures or has not made adequate disclosures.

A, B, and D are incorrect because they ignore the rules stated above.

Civil Procedure Outline § III (E)(2)(a) Discovery, Disclosure, and Sanctions: Required Disclosures: Initial Disclosures

QUESTION 240
ANSWER & EXPLANATION
Jurisdiction and Venue

(D) Yes, because a court examines property and tax records, registrations, and other relevant documents to determine if a state is a person's domicile.

The correct answer is D. A court uses an objective test to determine domicile. A court examines property and tax records, registrations, and other relevant documents, to determine if a state is a person's domicile.

A and B contain erroneous statements of law.

C is incorrect because it includes only one part of the test for domicile—i.e., physical presence. A state is a person's domicile if the person possesses: 1) a physical presence in the state (i.e., residency); and 2) the person possesses an intent to reside there indefinitely (*First Restatement*), or to make it his home for the time at least (*Second Restatement*).

Civil Procedure Outline § I (B)(1)(a)(2)(a) Personal Jurisdiction: Bases of Personal Jurisdiction: Grounds for Personal Jurisdiction: Domicile: Objective Test

QUESTION 241
ANSWER & EXPLANATION
Pre-Trial Procedures

(A) No, because it was not made at least 90 days prior to trial.

The correct answer is A. A party must disclose the identity of any expert who may be used at trial. Fed. R. Civ. P. 26(a)(2)(A). Unless otherwise directed by the court, a party must make the disclosure at least 90 days before the date trial is set to begin. If the expert testimony will be used solely to rebut evidence identified by another party, then the disclosure must be made 30 days after the other party's disclosure.

B, C, and D are incorrect because they ignore the rules stated above.

Civil Procedure Outline § III (E)(2)(b) Discovery, Disclosure, and Sanctions: Required Disclosures: Disclosure of Expert Testimony

QUESTION 242
ANSWER & EXPLANATION
Jurisdiction and Venue

(A) No, because in almost all jurisdictions, a party may directly attack the jurisdiction of the court at the beginning of the case without submitting to the court's jurisdiction.

The correct answer is A. Today, in almost all jurisdictions, a party may object to, and directly attack, the jurisdiction of a court at the beginning of a case without submitting to the court's jurisdiction. However, if the objecting party also seeks *affirmative* relief from the court, the objection to jurisdiction is waived, and the attack fails.

B and C are incorrect statements of law.

D is incorrect because if the songwriter had sought affirmative relief, the songwriter would have waived the objection to jurisdiction.

Civil Procedure Outline § I (B)(1)(a)(4) Personal Jurisdiction: Bases of Personal Jurisdiction: Grounds for Personal Jurisdiction: Appearance:

QUESTION 243
ANSWER & EXPLANATION
Pre-Trial Procedures

(B)   No, because they were not made at least 30 days before trial.

The correct answer is B. Pretrial disclosures must be made 30 days before trial. In addition to initial and expert witness disclosures, a party must provide the following information that may be presented at trial for purposes other than the impeachment of a witness:

- the identity of and contact information for each witness who may be called to testify;

- a designation of those witnesses whose testimony is to be presented by deposition, along with a transcript of relevant portions of each deposition; and

- an identification of each document or exhibit that may be offered as evidence at the trial.

In this case, the trucker failed to timely make the required pretrial disclosures 30 days before trial.

A, C, and D are incorrect because they ignore the rule stated above.

Civil Procedure Outline § III (E)(2)(c) Discovery, Disclosure, and Sanctions: Required Disclosures: Pretrial Disclosures

QUESTION 244
ANSWER & EXPLANATION
Jurisdiction and Venue

(B) No, because the chef did not have sufficient minimum contacts with State B, to reasonably require the chef to appear and defend the lawsuit there.

The correct answer is B. For exam purposes, the most important type of personal jurisdiction determination will be to analyze the extent of a person's minimum contacts with a forum state. In other words, the most commonly tested basis for personal jurisdiction is: if a person's contacts with a forum state are sufficient to reasonably require the person to defend a lawsuit that is filed in the forum state.

Even if no other basis for personal jurisdiction applies, a forum state will possess personal jurisdiction over a defendant if the defendant possesses minimum contacts with the forum state.

International Shoe Company v. Washington provides the general rule that a person who has never been present in a state still may be subject to personal jurisdiction in the state if the person possesses:

- "sufficient minimum contacts" with that forum state,

- such that requiring the person to appear and defend in a court there would not

- "offend traditional notions of fair play and substantial justice."

In this case, the facts indicate that the chef does not advertise the restaurant, nearly all of the business comes from the people who reside in town, and the chef didn't speak with the traveler. It is unlikely that the act of selling food to the traveler subjected the chef to the court's personal jurisdiction. Further, the distance from State A to State B reduces the likelihood that it was foreseeable that the chef would be subject to the jurisdiction of the court in State B.

A is incorrect because even if the chef had spoken with the traveler, that, in and of itself, would not necessarily confer personal jurisdiction over the chef in State B.

C is incorrect because it implies that the chef submitted to the court's jurisdiction by placing the food into the stream of commerce. However, the facts of this case do not suggest that it was foreseeable to the degree necessary for the chef to reasonably anticipate being haled into court in State B.

D is incorrect because it erroneously conflates the requirements for diversity jurisdiction with the requirements for personal jurisdiction.

Civil Procedure Outline § I (B)(1)(a)(5) Personal Jurisdiction: Bases of Personal Jurisdiction: Grounds for Personal Jurisdiction: Minimum Contacts

QUESTION 245
ANSWER & EXPLANATION
Pre-Trial Procedures

(A) No, because the information is relevant and might lead to discovery of admissible evidence.

The correct answer is A. The scope of discovery is broad and construed liberally. A party is entitled to discovery regarding any information that is relevant to any party's claim or defense, provided that the information is neither privileged nor attorney work-product. Fed. R. Civ. P. 26(b)(1). However, a court can order discovery of any relevant matter, even privileged information, upon a showing of good cause. Relevant information does not have to be admissible at trial, so long as the information might lead to discovery of admissible evidence. The relevance of information sought by a party during discovery will be determined on a case-by-case basis, depending on the circumstances and the facts. *Hill v. Motel 6*, 205 F.R.D. 490 (S.D. Ohio 2001).

B and C are incorrect because they ignore the above rules.

D is incorrect because it is an incorrect statement of law. Certain disclosures must be disclosed without a discovery request. *See Civil Procedure Outline § III (E)(2): Required Disclosures.*

Civil Procedure Outline § III (E)(3)(a) Discovery, Disclosure, and Sanctions: Discovery Scope and Limits: Broad Scope of Discovery

QUESTION 246
ANSWER & EXPLANATION
Jurisdiction and Venue

(B)   No, because the website is not passive, and the online retailer seeks business with State B's residents.

The correct answer is B. Generally, the owner of a website on the internet is not subject to personal jurisdiction everywhere, solely on the basis that the owner maintains the website that can be accessed everywhere. As a general proposition, the likelihood that the owner would be subject to personal jurisdiction may be proportionate to the extent to which the website is interactive. *Zippo Mfg. Co. v. Zippo Dot Com, Inc.*, 952 F. Supp. 1119 (W.D. Pa. 1997). Thus, such jurisdiction probably would not be supported merely on the basis of an entirely passive website. *Id.*

A is incorrect because the mere fact that the seller owns and operates the website is insufficient to permit the court to exercise personal jurisdiction.

C and D are incorrect because they ignore the above rules.

Civil Procedure Outline § I (B)(1)(a)(5)(a)(i) Personal Jurisdiction: Bases of Personal Jurisdiction: Grounds for Personal Jurisdiction: Minimum Contacts: General and Specific Jurisdiction: Continuous and Systematic

QUESTION 247
ANSWER & EXPLANATION
Pre-Trial Procedures

(C)   Yes, because the expense of the proposed discovery outweighs its likely benefit.

The correct answer is C. A court *may* limit the scope of discovery, including the number or length of depositions and interrogatories, as well as the number of requests for production. A trial court *must* limit the extent or frequency of discovery if:

- the discovery is unreasonably duplicative or cumulative, or the party can obtain it from another source that is more convenient, less expensive, or less burdensome;

- the party requesting discovery has sufficient opportunity to obtain the information by discovery; or

- the expense or burden of the proposed discovery outweighs its likely benefit.

Fed. R. Civ. P. 26(b)(2)(C).

Civil Procedure Outline § III (E)(3)(b) Discovery, Disclosure, and Sanctions: Discovery Scope and Limits: Limitations on Frequency and Extent

QUESTION 248
ANSWER & EXPLANATION
Jurisdiction and Venue

(B)   No, because a federal court may use the long-arm statute of the forum state in which it is located.

The correct answer is B. Although no general federal long-arm statute exists, Rule 4(k)(1)(A) authorizes a federal court to utilize the long-arm statue of the forum state in which it is located. Consequently, the federal courts possess the same scope of personal jurisdiction as the forum state courts.

A, C, and D are incorrect because they contain erroneous legal assertions.

Civil Procedure Outline § I (B)(2)(a)(3) Personal Jurisdiction: Limits of Exercise of Personal Jurisdiction: Long-Arm Statute: Federal Courts

QUESTION 249
ANSWER & EXPLANATION
Pre-Trial Procedures

(D)   Yes, because the report was prepared to address a threat of imminent litigation.

The correct answer is D. Generally, materials that are prepared in *anticipation of litigation* or for trial (by or for a party or its representative) are protected from discovery. Fed. R. Civ. P. 26(b)(3)(A). A party's representative can include its lawyer, consultant, indemnitor, surety, insurer, or agent. *Id.*

For example, investigative reports or accident reports, which a party routinely completes after an accident, are protected from discovery *only if* they are prepared to address a threat of imminent litigation. *Broadnax v. ABF Freight Sys., Inc.*, 180 F.R.D. 343, 346 (N.D. Ill. 1998); *Wikel v. Wal-Mart Stores, Inc.,* 197 F.R.D. 493 (N.D. Okla. 2000). In the absence of any threat of litigation when the reports are completed, they are discoverable. *Id.*; Fed. R. Civ. P. 26(b)(3) (Advisory Committee's Note).

In this case, because the report was prepared in anticipation of litigation, it is not discoverable.

Civil Procedure Outline § III (E)(3)(c)(1) Discovery, Disclosure, and Sanctions: Discovery Scope and Limits: Attorney Work-Product and Related Concepts: Materials Prepared in Anticipation of Litigation or for Trial

QUESTION 250
ANSWER & EXPLANATION
Jurisdiction and Venue

(D)   Yes, because the existence of the forum-selection clause is not dispositive of the issue.

The correct answer is D. The existence of a forum-selection clause in a contract will be a significant factor in a court's decision of whether to exercise jurisdiction over a party. The court must evaluate the fairness of the proposed exercise of jurisdiction in light of the forum-selection clause. Although that clause must be treated as a significant factor when a court evaluates jurisdiction, the Supreme Court has held that the existence of a forum-selection clause is not dispositive of the issue of jurisdiction.

As mentioned under the Civil Procedure outline's subtopic of "Consent" to personal jurisdiction, an inequality of bargaining power between the parties may warrant giving less effect to their contract's forum-selection clause. Similarly, litigating in its preordained forum may impose significant and unusual hardships on one of the parties. The questions for evaluating a forum-selection clause are: 1) Does the forum selected in the clause have some connection to the contract?; and 2) Has a party overreached by attempting to include the clause in the contract?

In this case, the parties appear to have unequal bargaining power and the forum selected does not appear to have significant connection to the contract. Further, it appears that because the customer lives 1,600 miles away from the forum state, the clause is unfair. Consequently, although the existence of the clause is a significant factor for the court to consider, D is the best choice.

A, B, and C are incorrect statements of law.

Civil Procedure Outline § I (B)(2)(b)(1) Personal Jurisdiction: Limits on Exercise of Personal Jurisdiction: Traditional Limitations: Choice of Forum by Agreement

QUESTION 251
ANSWER & EXPLANATION
Pre-Trial Procedures

(C)   Yes, and the trucker may be awarded expenses incurred in the filing of the motion.

The correct answer is C. Any person may obtain his or her own previous statements about the action or its subject matter simply upon request. If the request is refused, the person may request a court order and be awarded expenses.

Civil Procedure Outline § III (E)(3)(c)(1) Discovery, Disclosure, and Sanctions: Discovery Scope and Limits: Attorney Work-Product and Related Concepts: Materials Prepared in Anticipation of Litigation or for Trial

QUESTION 252
ANSWER & EXPLANATION
Jurisdiction and Venue

(C)   *Quasi in rem*

The correct answer is C. A *quasi in rem* action is different from an *in personam* action that determines the rights of parties to certain property that is at issue. A *quasi in rem* action is initiated when a plaintiff seizes property within a forum state by means of attachment or garnishment. Traditionally, the property seized is used as a pretext for a court to decide a case without possessing personal jurisdiction over a defendant. Although the court may decide issues in a case that are unrelated to the property, the amount of the judgment is limited to the value of the property that is seized. The judgment cannot be sued upon in any other court. The United States Supreme Court has severely limited, if not eliminated, classic *quasi in rem* jurisdiction absent the existence of some other adequate ground for personal jurisdiction.

A and B are incorrect for the reasons stated above.

D is incorrect because "*quasi in personam*" does not exist.

Civil Procedure Outline § I (B)(4) Personal Jurisdiction: Quasi In Rem Jurisdiction

QUESTION 253
ANSWER & EXPLANATION
Pre-Trial Procedures

(D)   Although it was permissible for the court to grant the motion, the court must protect

against disclosure of the mental impressions and conclusions of the plaintiff's lawyer.

The correct answer is D. Generally, materials that are prepared in *anticipation of litigation* or for trial (by or for a party or its representative) are protected from discovery. Fed. R. Civ. P. 26(b)(3)(A). However, a party may discover these protected materials if:

- the materials are otherwise discoverable;

- the party shows its substantial need for the materials to prepare its case; and

- the party is unable, without undue hardship, to obtain the substantial equivalent of the materials by other means. *Id.*

If a court orders discovery of materials prepared in anticipation of litigation or for trial, then the court must protect against disclosure of the *mental impressions*, opinions, conclusions, or legal theories of a party's lawyer or representative about the litigation. Fed. R. Civ. P. 26(b)(3)(B).

Civil Procedure Outline § III (E)(3)(c)(1)(a) Discovery, Disclosure, and Sanctions: Discovery Scope and Limits: Attorney Work-Product and Related Concepts: Materials Prepared in Anticipation of Litigation or for Trial: Substantial Need and Undue Hardship Exception

QUESTION 254
ANSWER & EXPLANATION
Jurisdiction and Venue

(A)   No, because the contractor personally served the complaint and summons.

The correct answer is A. The summons and complaint may be served by:

- any citizen of the United States;

- who is over 18 years of age; and

- *not a party.*

In this case, because the contractor is the plaintiff, and therefore a party to the lawsuit, it was improper for the contractor to personally hand deliver the summons and complaint to the homeowner.

B, C, and D are incorrect because they contain erroneous legal assertions.

Civil Procedure Outline § I (C)(6) Service of Process and Notice: Who May Serve

QUESTION 255
ANSWER & EXPLANATION
Pre-Trial Procedures

(C)   Yes, because the e-mail concerned compensation for the expert's testimony and data provided by the lawyer that the expert considered in forming opinions.

The correct answer is C.   Communications between a party's lawyer and expert witness, "regardless of the form of the communications," are protected from disclosure, unless the communications:

-   concern compensation for the expert's testimony or study;

-   identify data or facts that the lawyer provided and that the expert considered in forming their opinions; or

-   identify assumptions that the lawyer provided and that the expert relied on.

Fed. R. Civ. P. 26(b)(4)(C).

Civil Procedure Outline § III (E)(3)(c)(2)(b) Discovery, Disclosure, and Sanctions: Discovery Scope and Limits: Attorney Work-Product and Related Concepts: Expert Witness Retained in Preparation for Trial: Communications between Lawyer and Expert

QUESTION 256
ANSWER & EXPLANATION
Jurisdiction and Venue

(B)   No, because service of process may occur outside of the court's scope of personal jurisdiction.

The correct answer is B.   Notice may be given by serving (i.e., delivering) the requisite legal papers upon a party in person, *even if* the service occurs outside of the court's scope of personal jurisdiction.   The papers served on a party must be *reasonably calculated* to adequately inform the defending party of the nature of a cause of action that is asserted by the claiming party.   The defending party must be provided with a reasonable time to respond and prepare a defense to the cause of action.

A, C, and D are incorrect because they contain erroneous legal assertions.

Civil Procedure Outline § I (C)(8)(a)(1) Service of Process: Constitutional Requirements: Notice and Opportunity to be Heard: Notice

QUESTION 257
ANSWER & EXPLANATION
Pre-Trial Procedures

(A) No, because the expert was hired solely for trial preparation and is not expected to testify at trial.

The correct answer is A. Generally, a party may not discover facts known or opinions held by an expert who is employed by a party's lawyer solely for trial preparation, and who is not expected to be called as a witness at trial. However, this information may be discoverable upon a showing of exceptional circumstances if it is impracticable for the party to obtain facts or opinions on the same subject, by any other means. In this case, there is no indication that it would be impracticable for the driver to obtain facts or opinions on the same subject by other means. Consequently, the motorcyclist need not disclose the information.

Civil Procedure Outline § III (E)(3)(c)(2)(b)(i) Discovery, Disclosure, and Sanctions: Discovery Scope and Limits: Attorney Work-Product and Related Concepts: Expert Witness Retained in Preparation for Trial: Communications between Lawyer and Expert: Experts Employed only for Trial Preparation

QUESTION 258
ANSWER & EXPLANATION
Jurisdiction and Venue

(D)   Venue would be proper in the southern or western district of State B.

The correct answer is D. There are three factors that must be analyzed in order to determine appropriate venue for actions involving individuals. These factors apply to cases in which the subject-matter jurisdiction is based on either diversity of citizenship or a federal question:

1. Venue is proper in a judicial district where any defendant resides (i.e., is domiciled), if all defendants reside in the same state of the judicial district; or

2. Venue is proper in a judicial district in which a substantial part of the events or omissions giving rise to the claim occurred; or in which most of the property that is subject to the action is located.

3. Venue is proper in a judicial district in which any of the defendants are subject to personal jurisdiction in the action, if there is no district in which the action may otherwise be brought.

Venue would be proper in the southern district of State B because the grocer resides there. Further, venue in the western district of State B is proper because that is where the contract negotiations occurred, and it is where the contract was signed.

Civil Procedure Outline § I (D)(1)(a)(1) Venue, Forum Non Conveniens, and Transfer: Venue Generally: Federal Court: Individual Parties

QUESTION 259
ANSWER & EXPLANATION
Pre-Trial Procedures

(B) No, because the patient did not describe the nature of the materials in a way that would permit the doctor to assess the claim.

The correct answer is B. To withhold otherwise discoverable information based on a claim of privilege or a claim that the information is protected as trial preparation material:

-   The party must expressly make the claim;

-   The party must describe the nature of the documents, communications, or tangible things not disclosed; and

-   The party must make such description in a way that does not reveal the privileged information but allows the other party to assess the claim.

In this case, the patient only satisfied the requirement that the claim be expressly made.

A and D are incorrect because they are false statements of law.

C is incorrect because it ignores the above rules.

Civil Procedure Outline § III (E)(3)(c)(3) Discovery, Disclosure, and Sanctions: Discovery Scope and Limits: Attorney Work-Product and Related Concepts: Claiming Attorney Work-Product Protection

QUESTION 260
ANSWER & EXPLANATION
Jurisdiction and Venue

(C) Yes, because the court may, on its own motion, transfer venue.

The correct answer is C. A federal district court may transfer a civil action to any other federal district or division where the action might have been brought, or to any district or division to which all parties have consented. A defendant may file a motion to transfer venue on the basis that the existing venue is inappropriate and another venue would be more appropriate. A federal court may, *sua sponte* (i.e., of its own will), make its own motion to transfer venue.

A, B, and D are incorrect statements of law.

Civil Procedure Outline § I (D)(3)(b) Venue, Forum Non Conveniens, and Transfer: Venue Transfer: Motion for Change of Venue

QUESTION 261
ANSWER & EXPLANATION
Pre-Trial Procedures

(A) **No, because the corporation did not certify that the corporation, in good faith, conferred or attempted to confer with the geek to try to resolve the dispute over the materials.**

The correct answer is A. In the discovery context, a protective order is an order protecting a party from producing discovery. A party or person from whom discovery is being sought may file a motion for a protective order. Fed. R. Civ. P. 26(c). The motion must certify that the requesting party has in good faith conferred or attempted to confer with the other parties to try to resolve the dispute. The court may make any order that justice requires in order to protect a party or person from annoyance, embarrassment, oppression, undue burden, or expense.

Civil Procedure Outline § III (E)(4) Discovery, Disclosure, and Sanctions: Protective Orders

QUESTION 262
ANSWER & EXPLANATION
Jurisdiction and Venue

(D) **Yes, because a federal district court may transfer a case to any venue to which the parties have consented, if the transfer would increase the convenience of parties and witnesses and promote the interests of justice.**

The correct answer is D. A federal district court may transfer a case to *any* venue to which the parties have consented, *only if* that would increase the convenience of parties and witnesses and promote the interests of justice. In that event, the court may make a consent venue transfer despite the inability to have originally filed the case in the transfer venue. 28 U.S.C. § 1404(a).

Civil Procedure Outline § I (D)(3)(c) Venue, Forum Non Conveniens, and Transfer: Venue Transfer: Consent to Change of Venue

QUESTION 263
ANSWER & EXPLANATION
Pre-Trial Procedures

(C)   Yes, because a court may require that trade secrets not be revealed.

The correct answer is C. A protective order may do any of the following:

-   forbid disclosure or discovery;

-   specify the terms for the disclosure or discovery, including time and place;

-   set a discovery method;

-   forbid inquiry into certain matters or limit the scope of disclosure or discovery of certain matters;

-   designate the persons who may be present while discovery is conducted;

-   require that discovery be sealed;

-   require that trade secrets or confidential information not be revealed, or revealed only in specified ways;

-   require that parties file documents or information in sealed envelopes, only to be opened by court order.

A and D are incorrect because they contain erroneous reasoning suggesting that the status of the party has a bearing on whether the court can enter a protective order preventing disclosure of trade secrets.

B is incorrect because it is an erroneous statement of law.

Civil Procedure Outline § III (E)(4) Discovery, Disclosure, and Sanctions: Protective Orders

QUESTION 264
ANSWER & EXPLANATION
Pre-Trial Procedures

(C)   Yes, because the trucker has a duty to amend its answers to the interrogatories.

The correct answer is C. A party is under a duty to timely supplement or correct its discovery disclosures when the party learns that the disclosure or response is incomplete or incorrect in some material respect, and the additional or corrective information has not already been made known to the party during discovery. Fed. R. Civ. P. 26(e). A party is also under a duty to amend its answers to interrogatories, requests for production, and admissions, if new information comes to light that impacts its previous disclosures that are contained in those types of discovery responses. However, this rule does not apply to depositions. Nonetheless, if a party's expert witness must disclose a report, then the party has a duty to supplement the information contained in the report and information provided during a deposition of the expert. Fed. R. Civ. P. 26(e)(2).

A and B are incorrect because they ignore the above rule.

D is incorrect because the issue of whether the trucker was negligent does not impact the trucker's duty to amend the answers to the interrogatories.

Civil Procedure Outline § III (E)(5) Discovery, Disclosure, and Sanctions: Supplementing Disclosures

Made in the USA
San Bernardino, CA
19 January 2015